Existential Literature
An Introduction

Linda E. Patrik
Union College

Australia • Canada • Mexico • Singapore • Spain • United Kingdom • United States

WADSWORTH
THOMSON LEARNING

Philosophy Editor: *Peter Adams*
Assistant Editor: *Kara Kindstrom*
Editorial Assistant: *Mark Andrews*
Marketing Manager: *Dave Garrison*
Print Buyer: *April Reynolds*
Permissions Editor: *Roberta Broyer*
Production Service: *Ruth Cottrell*

Copy Editor: *Steven Summerlight*
Cover Designer: *Yvo Riezebos*
Cover Image: *PhotoDisc*
Cover Printer: *Webcom Limited*
Compositor: *Ruth Cottrell Books*
Printer/Binder: *Webcom Limited*

Printed in Canada
1 2 3 4 5 6 7 04 03 02 01

Library of Congress Cataloging-in-Publication Data

Existential literature : an introduction / [compiled by] Linda E. Patrik
p. cm.
ISBN 0-534-56705-3
1. Existentialism—Literary collections. 2. Existentialism in literature. 3. Existentialism.
I. Patrik, Linda E.

PN6071.E9 E95 2000
808.8′0384—dc21 00-032467

Wadsworth/Thomson Learning
10 Davis Drive
Belmont, CA 94002-3098
USA

For information about our products, contact us:
Thomson Learning Academic Resource Center
1-800-423-0563
http://www.wadsworth.com

International Headquarters
Thomson Learning
International Division
290 Harbor Drive, 2nd Floor
Stamford, CT 06902-7477
USA

UK/Europe/Middle East/South Africa
Thomson Learning
Berkshire House
168-173 High Holborn
London WC1V 7AA
United Kingdom

Asia
Thomson Learning
60 Albert Street, #15-01
Albert Complex
Singapore 189969

Canada
Nelson/Thomson Learning
1120 Birchmount Road
Toronto, Ontario M1K 5G4
Canada

For My Parents

Contents

Preface xi

PART ONE

Existentialist Views on the Human Condition 1

CHAPTER 1

Fyodor Dostoyevsky's "Notes from Underground" 3

Introduction: The Sickness of Too Much Consciousness 3

DOSTOYEVSKY'S "Notes from Underground: Part I" (Excerpts) 4

Basic Existentialist Concepts 10

- Subjectivity 10
- Individuality 11

Questions for Discussion 11

CHAPTER 2

Jean-Paul Sartre's *Nausea* 12

Introduction: Lived Experience 12

SARTRE'S *Nausea* (Excerpts) 13

Basic Existentialist Concepts 22

- Contingency 22
- For-itself 23
- In-itself 23

Questions for Discussion 23

CHAPTER 3

Jean-Paul Sartre's *The Flies* 24

Introduction: Existence Precedes Essence 24

SARTRE'S *The Flies* (Excerpts) 25

Basic Existentialist Concepts 40

- Freedom 40
- Responsibility 40
- Project 41
- Anguish 42

Questions for Discussion 42

CHAPTER 4
Albert Camus' *The Stranger* 43
Introduction: Existential Estrangement 43
CAMUS' *The Stranger* (Excerpts) 44
Basic Existentialist Concepts 50
Alienation 50
Authenticity 50
Questions for Discussion 51

CHAPTER 5
Albert Camus' "The Myth of Sisyphus" 52
Introduction: The Absurd Hero 52
CAMUS' "The Myth of Sisyphus" (Excerpt) 52
Basic Existentialist Concepts 54
Absurdity 54
Questions for Discussion 55

CHAPTER 6
Simone de Beauvoir's *A Very Easy Death* 56
Introduction: Autobiographical Consciousness 56
BEAUVOIR'S *A Very Easy Death* (Excerpts) 57
Basic Existentialist Concepts 65
Finitude 65
Lived Body 65
Questions for Discussion 66

PART TWO
Existentialist Views on Relations with Others 67

CHAPTER 7
Jean-Paul Sartre's *No Exit* 69
Introduction: Hell Is Other People 69
SARTRE'S *No Exit* (Excerpts) 70
Basic Existentialist Concepts 85

Being-with-Others 85
The Look 86
Bad Faith 86
Questions for Discussion 88

Chapter 8
Simone de Beauvoir's "The Woman Destroyed" 89
Introduction: Critique of Women's Dependency 89
Beauvoir's "The Woman Destroyed" (Excerpts) 90
Basic Existentialist Concepts 101
Woman as Other 101
Questions for Discussion 102

Chapter 9
Richard Wright's "The Man Who Lived Underground" 103
Introduction: Black Activism and Existentialism 103
Wright's "The Man Who Lived Underground" 104
Basic Existentialist Concepts 132
Insider–Outsider 132
Questions for Discussion 133

Part Three
Existentialist Views on Religion 135

Chapter 10
Friedrich Nietzsche's *Thus Spoke Zarathustra* 137
Introduction: Critique of Morality 137
Nietzsche's *Thus Spoke Zarathustra* (Excerpts) 138
Basic Existentialist Concepts 148
The Herd 148
The Superman 148
Will to Power 148
Transvaluation of Values 148
Questions for Discussion 149

CHAPTER 11
Søren Kierkegaard's *Fear and Trembling* 150
Introduction: Critique of Organized Religion 150
KIERKEGAARD'S *Fear and Trembling* (Excerpts) 151
Basic Existentialist Concepts 164
Despair 164
Leap of Faith 164
Teleological Suspension of the Ethical 165
Questions for Discussion 165

CHAPTER 12
Fyodor Dostoyevsky's "The Grand Inquisitor" 166
Introduction: Religious Doubt and Debate 166
DOSTOYEVSKY'S "The Grand Inquisitor" (Excerpts) 167
Basic Existentialist Concepts 179
Burden of Freedom 179
Questions for Discussion 179

CHAPTER 13
Franz Kafka's "Before the Law" 180
Introduction: Inscrutability of God's Law 180
KAFKA'S "Before the Law" 181
Basic Existentialist Concepts 185
Insecurity 185
Questions for Discussion 185

Suggestions for Further Reading 187

Preface

Existentialists wrote novels, plays, short stories, literary essays, and autobiographical works to express the same theories that they developed in their nonfictional, philosophical writings. These literary works captured the attention of readers on both sides of the Atlantic after World War II because these works offered a defense of individual freedom and a critique of authoritarian social norms at a time when the world was recovering from Nazism. With their uncompromising commitment to freedom and their stark descriptions of characters' innermost thoughts, existentialists were able to voice the deepest longings and fears of individuals who value freedom.

This anthology includes selections from existential literature of the nineteenth and twentieth centuries, with supportive material on the philosophical ideas contained in these works. Existential literature provides easier access to existentialism than do the nonfictional, philosophical works of existentialists, especially for readers unfamiliar with the jargon and argument style of twentieth-century European philosophy. But without some background in the philosophical theories of existentialism, readers would see characters instead of philosophical issues, thus missing both the originality of existentialism and the criticisms it makes against its philosophical predecessors. For this reason, short explanations of basic existentialist concepts supplement the literary selections so that readers can enrich their appreciation of existentialist fiction with some understanding of existentialist philosophy.

The French existentialists—Beauvoir, Camus, and Sartre—receive the most attention in this anthology. Not only were they the core members of the twentieth-century existentialist movement, but their literary works popularized existentialism around the world. They forged a connection between philosophy and literature that has not since been duplicated.

Three nineteenth-century thinkers are included in this anthology: Kierkegaard for his emphasis on individuality and freedom; Dostoyevsky for his descriptions of self-consciousness and his investigations into freedom unloosed from religious constraints; and Nietzsche for his advocacy of freedom, his critique of society's moral codes, and his unflinching inquiry into the consequences of atheism. Although these three were never described as existentialists during their lifetimes, many of their ideas became the seeds from which later existentialism grew. These three thinkers were the precursors of existentialism, the ones who asked the questions that made later existentialists think.

Finally, two twentieth-century writers, Franz Kafka and Richard Wright, are included in this anthology even though they are not, strictly speaking, existentialists. Kafka wrote before existentialism was established as a philosophical movement, but because his exploration of absurdity and his questioning of religion raised troubling themes similar to those raised by existentialists, some of his work expressed ideas that became part of the existentialist trend. Wright lived in Paris during the height of the existentialist movement, and he produced works that reverberated with existentialist themes. He became actively engaged with existentialism when he left the United States for Paris. His later works explored such existentialist concerns as the tension between individual freedom and political solutions to injustice.

The purpose of this anthology is to introduce existentialism to readers who have not previously encountered existentialist philosophy. Whether used on its own or used in combination with other, unabridged existentialist texts, it aims to provide clear literary examples of the ideas that are central to existentialism. The anthology's ultimate purpose is to show how important freedom was to a group of earlier thinkers, even though they recognized the potential for conflict between individual freedom and societal peace.

I would like to thank the following reviewers for their ideas and comments: Christa Davis Acampora, University of Maine; Houston A. Craighead, Winthrop University; Timothy Davis, The Essex Campus of the Community College of Baltimore County; Richard Kamber, The College of New Jersey; William Lovitt, California State University, Sacramento; and Fredrick McGlynn, University of Montana.

Although I, too, value freedom, I also value the practical virtues by which an anthology such as this comes to completion. Without the following people, who have generously exerted these practical virtues on behalf of this book, this anthology would be neither visible nor readable: at Wadsworth, Peter Adams for overseeing its various phases, and Mindy Newfarmer for shepherding it through its review stages; Ruth Cottrell for shaping it into proper legibility and form; Marianne Snowden, Elizabeth A. Slowinski, and Michael V. Daly for their secretarial support; the library support of Mary Cahill and Dave Gerhan; the emotional support of my husband, David Kaczynski; the carrel offered by Cornell University's Olin Library; the training in phenomenology and existentialism gained at Northwestern University; and the discussions of students at Union College who have studied with me over the years. I am grateful to all who have helped with this project.

Part One

Existentialist Views on the Human Condition

1 *Fyodor Dostoyevsky's "Notes from Underground"*
2 *Jean-Paul Sartre's* Nausea
3 *Jean-Paul Sartre's* The Flies
4 *Albert Camus'* The Stranger
5 *Albert Camus' "The Myth of Sisyphus"*
6 *Simone de Beauvoir's* A Very Easy Death

Chapter 1

Fyodor Dostoyevsky's "Notes from Underground"

Introduction: The Sickness of Too Much Consciousness

Fyodor Dostoyevsky (1821–1881) wrote troubling, powerful novels and short stories that dared to pose the kinds of moral questions that most of us would rather not face: If there is no God to decide what is right and wrong, then are all actions permitted? Can evil be resisted, or do we have uncontrollable urges to do evil to ourselves and others? Is it possible to commit criminal acts as though they were a test of one's freedom—and never experience guilt about them? As a Christian, Dostoyevsky also raised questions about the freedom that allows us to sin; many of his characters struggle with religious questions while they push the limits of their freedom.

In "Notes from Underground," Dostoyevsky gives us one of his most disturbing characters—an antihero rather than a hero, who reveals his innermost thoughts and feelings without censorship. In his own defense, the underground man makes an argument with an odd twist: He claims that too much consciousness is a sickness and that a symptom of this sickness is an inability to act. Yet the underground man prefers acute, uncensored self-reflection to the more active pursuits of normal, "healthy" people. While criticizing the belief that reason and science can solve the world's problems, the underground man advances a paradox: that individuals are willing to do what is harmful to themselves to prove they have the complete freedom to do so. In fact, he thinks this freedom to contradict one's own interests is actually our "most advantageous advantage."

Later existentialist writers in the twentieth century take up Dostoyevsky's literary technique of exposing negative, embarrassing, and even criminal thoughts of individuals—that is, our underground thoughts. Most of us try to repress such thoughts, but Dostoyevsky and later existentialists describe them with lucidity for the purpose of revealing the fullness of human consciousness. (See the selections from Sartre's *Nausea*, Beauvoir's "The Woman Destroyed," and Wright's "The Man Who Lived Underground" for twentieth-century examples of this narrative technique of unearthing a character's innermost emotions, resentments, and urges.)

Dostoyevsky's "Notes from Underground: Part I" (Excerpts)[1]

I am a sick man. . . . I am a spiteful man. An unattractive man. I think that my liver hurts. But actually, I don't know a damn thing about my illness. I am not even sure what it is that hurts. I am not in treatment and never have been, although I respect both medicine and doctors. Besides, I am superstitious in the extreme; well, at least to the extent of respecting medicine. (I am sufficiently educated not to be superstitious, but I am.) No sir, I refuse to see a doctor simply out of spite. Now, that is something that you probably will fail to understand. Well, I understand it. Naturally, I will not be able to explain to you precisely whom I will injure in this instance by my spite. I know perfectly well that I am certainly not giving the doctors a "dirty deal" by not seeking treatment. I know better than anyone that I will only harm myself by this, and no one else. And yet, if I don't seek a cure, it is out of spite. My liver hurts? Good, let it hurt still more!

I have been living like this for a long time—about twenty years. Now I am forty. I used to be in the civil service; today I am not. I was a mean official. I was rude, and found pleasure in it. After all, I took no bribes, and so I had to recompense myself at least by this. (A poor joke, but I will not cross it out. I wrote it, thinking it would be extremely witty; but now I see that it was only a vile little attempt at showing off, and just for that I'll let it stand!)

When petitioners came to my desk seeking information, I gnashed my teeth at them, and gloated insatiably whenever I succeeded in distressing them. I almost always succeeded. Most of them were timid folk: naturally—petitioners. But there were also some fops, and among these I particularly detested a certain officer. He absolutely refused to submit and clattered revoltingly with his sword. I battled him over that sword for a year and a half. And finally I got the best of him. He stopped clattering. This, however, happened long ago, when I was still a young man. But do you know, gentlemen, what was the main thing about my spite? Why, the whole point, the vilest part of it, was that I was constantly and shamefully aware, even at moments of the most violent spleen, that I was not at all a spiteful, no, not even an embittered, man. That I was merely frightening sparrows to no purpose, diverting myself. I might be foaming at the mouth, but bring me a doll, give me some tea, with a bit of sugar, and I'd most likely calm down. Indeed, I would be deeply touched, my very heart would melt, though later I'd surely gnash my teeth at myself and suffer from insomnia for months. That's how it is with me.

I lied just now when I said that I had been a mean official. I lied out of sheer spite. I was merely fooling around, both with the petitioners and with the officer, but in reality I could never have become malicious. I was aware at every moment of many, many altogether contrary elements. I felt them swarming inside me, those contrary elements. I knew that they had swarmed inside me all my life, begging to be let out, but I never, never allowed them to come out, just for spite. They tormented me to the point of shame, they drove me to convulsions—I was so sick and tired of them in the end. Sick and tired! But perhaps you think, dear sirs, that I am now repenting of something before you, asking your forgiveness for something? . . . Indeed, I am quite certain that you think so. But then, I assure you it doesn't make the slightest difference to me if you do. . . .

I could not become malicious. In fact, I could not become anything: neither bad nor good, neither a scoundrel nor an honest man, neither a hero nor an insect. And now, I am

[1] From *Notes from Underground* by Fyodor Dostoyevsky, translated by Mirra Ginsburg.

eking out my days in my corner, taunting myself with the bitter and entirely useless consolation that an intelligent man cannot seriously become anything; that only a fool can become something. Yes, sir, an intelligent nineteenth-century man must be, is morally bound to be, an essentially characterless creature; and a man of character, a man of action—an essentially limited creature. This is my conviction at the age of forty. I am forty now, and forty years—why, it is all of a lifetime, it is the deepest old age. Living past forty is indecent, vulgar, immoral! Now answer me, sincerely, honestly, who lives past forty? I'll tell you who does: fools and scoundrels. I will say this right to the face of all those venerable old men, all those silver-haired, sweet-smelling old men! I have a right to say it, because I will live to sixty myself. To seventy! To eighty! . . . Wait, let me catch my breath. . . .

I want to tell you, gentlemen, whether you wish to hear it or not, why I was unable to become even so much as an insect. I'll tell you solemnly that I have often wanted to become an insect. But even that was not granted me. I swear to you, sirs, that excessive consciousness is a disease—a genuine, absolute disease. For everyday human existence it would more than suffice to have the ordinary share of human consciousness; that is to say, one half, one quarter of that which falls to the lot of a cultivated man in our wretched nineteenth century, a man who has, moreover, the particular misfortune of living in Petersburg, this most abstract and intentional city on earth. (Cities, you know, may be intentional or unintentional.) It would, for instance, be quite enough to have the amount of consciousness by which all the so-called simple, direct people and men of action live. I'll wager that you think I'm writing all this merely out of bravado, and bravado in bad taste at that, clattering my sword like that officer, just to exercise my wit at the expense of men of action. But, my dear sirs, who would take pride in his own diseases, and brag about them too?

Ah, what am I saying? Everybody does it. It's precisely their diseases that people pride themselves on, and I do—more perhaps than anybody else. Let's not argue; my objection was absurd. But that aside, I am firmly convinced that not only excess of consciousness, but any consciousness at all is a disease. I stand on that. However, let us leave this for a moment, too. Tell me, now: why has it always been, as though in spite, that at the moments when I was most capable of feeling all the refinements of "the lofty and the beautiful," as they used to say among us once upon a time, yes, at those very moments I . . . no, not felt, but perpetrated such unseemly acts, such acts as . . . well, in a word, such acts as are, perhaps, committed by everyone, but which in my case occurred, as if on purpose, just when I was most keenly aware that they should never occur at all? The more aware I was of goodness and of everything "lofty and beautiful," the deeper I sank into my slime, and the more likely I was to get mired down in it altogether. But the main point is that all this seemed to take place within me not by chance, but as though it had to be so. As though this were my most normal condition rather than a disease or a corruption, so that in the end I even lost the will to fight this corruption. In the end I almost came to believe (or perhaps I really did come to believe) that this was indeed my normal condition.

And yet at first, in the beginning, how much torment I endured in this struggle! I did not think that this happened with others as well, and therefore kept it to myself all through my life as a deep secret. I was ashamed (perhaps I am still ashamed, even now.) I reached a point where, trudging back to my corner on some foul Petersburg night, I would feel a certain hidden, morbid, nasty little pleasure in the acute awareness that I had once again committed something vile that day, that what had been done could no longer be undone; and I would gnaw and gnaw at myself in silence, tearing and nagging at myself until the bitterness would finally begin to turn into a kind of shameful, damnable sweetness and, in the end—into a definite, positive pleasure! Yes, a pleasure, a pleasure! I stand by that. The very reason why I brought it up is that I've always wanted to find out: do other people experience such pleasures?

Take people who know how to avenge themselves or, generally, how to stand up for themselves. How do they do it? If, let us say, they are seized with feelings of revenge, nothing exists within them at the moment except those feelings. Such a man will push on straight toward his goal like a raging bull with lowered horns, and only a wall might stop him. . . .

Well, then, in my view such a direct, simple man is the true, normal human being, the kind of human being that tender mother nature herself had hoped to see when she was lovingly creating him on earth. I envy such a man to the point of loathing. He is stupid, I admit, but perhaps a normal man should be stupid, how do we know? Perhaps it's even very beautiful that way. And what particularly confirms me in this—if I may call it so—suspicion, is that if you take, for example, the antithesis of the normal man, that is, a man of heightened consciousness who has, surely, emerged not from the lap of nature but from a retort (this is almost mystical, gentlemen, but I suspect that too), this retort-man often gives up so completely in the face of his antithesis that he honestly feels himself, with all his heightened consciousness, to be a mouse, not a man. He may be an acutely conscious mouse, but a mouse all the same, while the other is a man, and consequently . . . and so on and so forth.

And the main thing, again, is that it's he, he himself, who considers himself a mouse; nobody else asks him to, and that is the important point.

Let's take a look now at this mouse in action. Let's suppose, for example, that it has also been mistreated (and it is almost always mistreated) and also longs to avenge itself. . . . The wretched mouse has, in addition to the first vileness, already managed to hedge itself around with a host of other vilenesses in the form of questions and doubts; it has added to the one initial question so many other unresolved questions that, willy-nilly, it will be caught up in a fatal morass, a stinking mess consisting of its own doubts and agitations, and, finally, of the spittle that rains upon it from the mouths of the direct men of action who solemnly stand around it as judges and arbiters, roaring with laughter at it as loudly as their healthy throats permit. Naturally, the only thing that's left to it is to shrug its little shoulders at the whole business in sheer disgust, and slip back ignominiously into its hole with a smile of feigned contempt in which it doesn't itself believe.

And there, in its loathsome, stinking underground hole, our mouse, insulted, crushed, destroyed by ridicule, immediately settles into cold, venomous, and, worst of all, lifelong malice. For forty years on end it will recall its humiliation, to the last and most shameful detail, each time embellishing the recollection with still more shameful details, spitefully teasing and whipping itself up with its own fantasies. It will be ashamed of its fantasies, and yet it will recall and go over everything again and again, piling all sorts of imaginary wrongs upon itself under the pretext that they also could have happened, and never forgiving anything. It may even begin to avenge itself, but somehow in fits and starts, in trivialities, from behind the stove, as it were, incognito, without faith either in its right to vengeance or in its possible success, and knowing in advance that all of its attempts will make it suffer a hundred times more than the object of its vengeance, who may, for all you know, pay less attention to it than to a fleabite. Why, on its very deathbed the mouse will remember everything again, with all the interest accrued throughout the years, and. . . .

But it's precisely in this cold, loathsome half-despair, half-belief, in this deliberate burying of yourself underground for forty years out of sheer pain, in this assiduously constructed, and yet somewhat dubious hopelessness, in all this poison of unfulfilled desires turned inward, this fever of vacillations, of resolutions adopted for eternity, and of repentances a moment later that you find the very essence of that strange, sharp pleasure that I spoke about. It is so subtle, so elusive, so difficult to grasp that people with the slightest limitations, or even simply those with strong nerves, will not be able to understand an iota of it. . . .

. . . [T]he direct, inevitable, and logical product of consciousness is inertia—a conscious sitting down with folded arms. I have spoken about this before. I repeat, I repeat with emphasis: all direct and active men are active precisely because they are dull and limited. How can this be explained? Well, it's just this way: because of their limitation, they mistake the most immediate and secondary causes for primary ones, and so convince themselves more quickly and more easily than others that they have found a firm, incontestable basis for their activity. This puts their minds at ease, and that, after all, is the main thing. For, naturally, to enter upon any course of action, one must be completely reassured in advance, and free of any trace of doubt. And how am I, for instance, to put my mind at ease? Where are the primary causes I can lean on, where are my basic premises? Where am I to find them? I exercise myself in thought, and hence, within my mind, every primary cause immediately drags after itself another, still more primary, and so on to infinity. Such is the very essence of all consciousness and thought. . . .

. . . Why, gentlemen, perhaps the only reason I regard myself as an intelligent man is that I've never in my whole life been able either to begin or to finish anything. Call me an idle babbler if you wish, a harmless, irritating babbler, like all the rest of us. But what is to be done if the direct, the sole vocation of every intelligent man is babbling—in other words, deliberately pouring water through a sieve? . . .

. . . Oh, tell me who was the first to declare, to proclaim, that man does vile things only because he does not realize his true interests; that if he were enlightened, if his eyes were opened to his true, normal interests, he would immediately cease committing abominations but would immediately become good and noble, because, being enlightened and understanding his true advantage, he would inevitably see that only goodness is to his advantage, and everybody knows that no man will knowingly act against his own interests. Consequently, he would of necessity, as it were, begin to do good. Oh, child! Oh, pure innocent babe! Who has ever, in all these millennia, seen men acting solely for the sake of advantage? What's to be done with the millions of facts that attest to their *knowingly*—that is, with full awareness of their true interests—dismissing these interests as secondary and rushing off in another direction, at risk, at hazard, without anyone or anything compelling them to do so, but as if solely in order to reject the designated road, and stubbornly, willfully carving out another—a difficult, absurd one—seeking it out virtually in the dark?

Evidently, then, this stubbornness and willfulness has really pleased them more than any advantage . . .Advantage! What is advantage? Will you take it upon yourself to define with absolute precision where exactly man's advantage lies? And what if his advantage on a *given* occasion not only may, but must, lie exactly in choosing for himself the harmful rather than the advantageous? And if this is so, if there can be such an occasion, then the entire rule is shattered to smithereens. What do you think, can there be such an occasion? You're laughing. You may laugh, gentlemen, but answer me: have man's advantages been calculated with absolute certainty? Are there, perhaps, advantages which not only don't fit, but cannot be fitted, into any classification? After all, gentlemen, as far as I know, your entire scheme of human advantages is derived from average statistical figures and scientific-economic formulas. Your advantages are prosperity, wealth, freedom, peace of mind, and so on and so forth. So that a man who would, for instance, openly and knowingly choose to act in opposition to this whole scheme would, in your opinion—and of course in mine too—be an obscurantist or a complete madman, wouldn't he? Yet there is something astonishing about this: how is it that, in calculating man's advantages, all these statisticians, sages, and humanitarians invariably omit one of them? In fact, they don't even consider it in the form in which it should be considered, yet the entire reckoning depends on it. It would do no great harm to take this advantage and add it to the roster. But the whole trouble is that this peculiar advantage doesn't fit into any category or any scheme.

I have a friend, for example . . . Ah, gentlemen! But you know him too; everybody knows him! Whenever he is about to do anything, this gentleman will immediately describe to you, clearly and eloquently, precisely how it must be done in accordance with the laws of truth and reason. More than that: he'll talk to you with fervor and passion about genuine, normal human interests. He'll ridicule nearsighted fools who do not understand either their own advantage or the true meaning of virtue. And then, exactly fifteen minutes later, without any sudden external cause, but moved by something within him that is stronger than all his interests, he'll do a turnabout, acting in total contradiction to what he himself has just been saying—against the laws of reason and against his own advantage, in short, against everything. . . . I will warn you that this friend of mine is a collective personage, and therefore it is rather difficult to blame him alone.

And that's just it, gentlemen. Isn't there, indeed, something that is dearer to almost every man than his very best interests, or (not to violate logic) isn't there a certain most advantageous advantage (it's precisely the one that is omitted, the one we've mentioned just before), which is more important and more advantageous than all other advantages, and for the sake of which a man is prepared, if need be, to go against all laws, against reason, honor, peace, prosperity—in short, against all those fine and useful things—just so as to achieve this primary, this most advantageous of advantages which is more precious to him than all else?

"Well, then it's still for the sake of advantage," you'll interrupt me. Wait, we shall yet get to the point of this. Besides, it's not a matter of word play; for this advantage is remarkable precisely because it destroys all our classifications and constantly breaks down all the schemes devised by the lovers of humanity for the happiness of mankind. In short, it interferes with everything.

But before I name this advantage, I want to compromise myself personally, and will therefore impertinently declare that all these excellent schemes, all these theories about teaching mankind to understand its true, normal interests, so that, inevitably seeking to achieve these interests, it would immediately become good and noble, are for the time being—in my view—nothing but idle exercises in logic! Yes, gentlemen, exercises in logic! Why, merely to assert, say that this theory of the regeneration of mankind through the pursuit of its own advantage is, to my mind, almost like . . . well, like asserting . . . that civilization makes man more gentle, and consequently less bloodthirsty and less capable of war. Logically, it might seem to follow. But man is so addicted to systems and to abstract conclusions that he is prepared deliberately to distort the truth, to close his eyes and ears, but justify his logic at all cost. . . .

In any case, if man has not become more bloodthirsty as a result of civilization, he has certainly become bloodthirsty in a nastier, uglier way than before. Before, he used to regard bloodshed as a matter of justice, and he exterminated those who had to be destroyed with a clear conscience. But today, though we regard the spilling of blood as an abomination, we still engage in this abomination, and to a far greater extent than before.

. . . even today, though man has learned to see more clearly on occasion than he did in barbarian ages, he is still far from having *habituated himself* to behave according to the dictates of reason and science. Nevertheless, you are entirely confident that he is sure to learn, when he rids himself completely of certain of his old bad habits and when good sense and science fully reeducate human nature and direct it into normal channels. You are confident that man himself will then cease to err *voluntarily* and will, so to speak, perforce never want to set his will at variance with his normal interests. More than that: you say that then science itself will teach man (though this, to my mind, is already a luxury) that he really does not possess, and never did possess, either a will or a whim of his own; that he is, in fact, no more than a kind of piano key or organ stop; and that, besides, there is such a thing in the world as the laws of nature; so that everything that is done by man isn't in the least a matter of his own will, but happens of itself, according to these laws.

Consequently, all that is needed is to discover the laws of nature; then man will no longer be answerable for his actions, and life will become exceedingly easy. All human actions will, of course, be classified according to these laws—mathematically, like a logarithm table, up to 108,000—and entered in a special almanac. Or, still better, certain edifying volumes will be published, similar to our encyclopedic dictionaries, in which everything will be calculated and designated with such precision that there will no longer be any actions or adventures in the world.

. . . I would not be in the least surprised to see a certain gentleman get up, out of the blue, in the midst of the general future reign of reason, with an ignoble—or, better, with a retrograde and mocking—physiognomy, and say to us, with his arms akimbo: "What, my dear sirs, if we should smash all this good sense to smithereens with one hard kick, to the sole end of sending all these logarithms to the devil and living a while again according to our own stupid will!" And even this wouldn't be so bad. What really hurts is that he would unquestionably win followers: that's how man is constituted. And all for the most trifling reason, which hardly seems worth mentioning: namely, that man, whoever he might be, has always and everywhere preferred to act according to his own wishes rather than according to the dictates of reason and advantage. And his wishes may well be contrary to his advantage; indeed, sometimes they *positively should be* (this, now, is my idea).

One's own free, untrammeled desires, one's own whim, no matter how extravagant, one's own fancy, be it wrought up at times to the point of madness—all of this is precisely that most advantageous of advantages which is omitted, which fits into no classification, and which is constantly knocking all systems and theories to hell. And where did our sages get the idea that man must have normal, virtuous desires? What made them imagine that man must necessarily wish what is sensible and advantageous? What man needs is only his own *independent* wishing, whatever that independence may cost and wherever it may lead. And the devil knows what this wishing. . . .

. . . Forgive me, gentlemen, for all my philosophizing—it's my forty years underground! Allow me to indulge my fancy. You see, gentlemen, reason is unquestionably a fine thing, but reason is no more than reason, and it gives fulfillment only to man's reasoning capacity, while desires are a manifestation of the whole of life—I mean the whole of human life, both with its reason and with all its itches and scratches. And though our life in these manifestations will often turn out a pretty sorry mess, it is still life and not a mere extraction of square roots. After all, I quite naturally want to live in order to fulfill my whole capacity for living, and not in order to fulfill my reasoning capacity alone, which is no more than some one-twentieth of my capacity for living. What does reason know? It knows only what it has managed to learn (and it may never learn anything else; that isn't very reassuring, but why not admit it?), while human nature acts as a complete entity, with all that is in it, consciously or unconsciously; and though it may be wrong, it's nevertheless alive.

I suspect, gentlemen, that you look upon me with pity. You repeat to me that an educated and enlightened man—in short, man as he will be in the future—cannot knowingly desire something disadvantageous to himself; that this is mathematics. I entirely agree—it is indeed mathematics. But I repeat to you for the hundredth time: there is only one occasion, one only, when man may purposely, consciously choose for himself even the harmful and the stupid, even the stupidest thing—just so that he will *have the right* to wish the stupidest thing, and not be bound by the duty to have only intelligent wishes. For this most stupid thing, this whim of ours, gentlemen, may really be more advantageous to us than anything on earth, especially in certain cases. In fact, it may be the most advantageous of all advantages even when it brings us obvious harm and contradicts the most sensible conclusions of our reason concerning our advantage. Because, at any rate, it preserves for us the most important and most precious thing—our personality, our individuality.

There are people who assert that this is indeed the most precious thing to man. Of course, wishing may, if it chooses, coincide with reason, especially if this isn't overdone but used in moderation; that is both beneficial and, at times, even praiseworthy. But desires will often—indeed, in most cases—stubbornly and directly contradict reason, and . . . and . . . and do you know, gentlemen, that too is beneficial and even highly praiseworthy at times. . . .

And in conclusion, gentlemen, the best thing is to do nothing! The best thing is conscious inertia! And so, hurrah for the underground! Though I have said that I envy the normal man to the point of the bitterest gall, yet, under the conditions in which I see him, I do not want to be one. (Though, all the same, I shall not cease to envy him.) No, no, the underground is, at any rate, more advantageous! There, at least, one can. . . . Ah, but I'm lying again! Lying, because I know, as clearly as two times two, that it's not at all the underground which is best, but something different, altogether different, something I long for and can never find! To the devil with the underground!

Basic Existentialist Concepts

Subjectivity Existentialism focuses on our consciousness of the world, other people, and ourselves rather than on external objects taken as things apart from consciousness. With its emphasis on the subjective side of our thoughts, perceptions, feelings, and actions, existentialism not only explores the variety of human experiences, but also reveals how the objects, people, and events we perceive are colored by our own subjective patterns.

Dostoyevsky's underground man makes no attempt to be objective about either the officer who clatters his sword or the normal, "healthy" people of action; instead he takes greater interest in how he feels about them, because his feelings reflect what he thinks about himself. This is another important theory in existentialism (developed by Sartre in particular)—namely, that we are not only conscious but also self-conscious. Human beings are aware of being conscious whenever we are conscious of the things, people, and events we experience in the world. This self-reflective dimension of subjectivity means that consciousness is not a simple recording of events occurring in the external world or in our sense organs but a complex activity that generates ideas about ourselves as much as it entertains ideas about other things.

Individuality Existentialists object to philosophical theories, organized religions, and political movements that treat human beings solely in terms of what is common to them. What makes each individual unique is important to existentialism. Because each individual regards her own life as central and valuable, who she is cannot be captured by theories (such as Hegelianism and Marxism) that treat individuals as just so many members of a larger group or economic class. Such theories reduce the individual to a replaceable part of a larger whole and ignore the subjective, self-conscious sense an individual has of herself. In contrast, existentialism treats individuals as valuable in their own right.

Individuality is not only a matter of an individual's uniqueness but also a function of an individual's volition. Individuals who are truly individualistic make their own choices instead of conforming to society. Dostoyevsky and Kierkegaard, another nineteenth-century precursor of existentialism, argue that this ability to exercise one's own choice, in opposition to societal pressures or to universal moral laws, is the most valuable feature of our identity as an individual (our "most advantageous advantage," as Dostoyevsky puts it). Later existentialists such as Sartre and Beauvoir develop this point further by arguing that each individual is who she is as a result of her freely chosen actions; an individual's identity is nothing other than her choices.

Questions for Discussion

1. Is the underground man perverse, or does he express the secret thoughts that all of us have?

2. Why does he claim that there is an impasse between thought and action?

3. Is there a necessary connection between alienation and intense consciousness? Are nonconformists the most intelligent?

4. Who knows what is most beneficial for an individual—the individual him- or herself or the doctors, psychologists, and economists who study the causes of human well-being?

5. Is "living according to our own stupid will" an intelligent or a stupid way to live? Will it harm ourselves or others?

Chapter 2

Jean-Paul Sartre's Nausea

Introduction: Lived Experience

Jean-Paul Sartre (1905–1980) was one of the most influential philosophers of the twentieth century. Starting in the 1930s, he took up a line of inquiry begun by the German philosophers Heidegger and Jaspers that came to be labeled *existentialism.* His contributions to this line of inquiry—in the form of philosophical treatises, novels, plays, short stories, and essays—not only defined the basic tenets of existentialism, but also offered defiant symbols of freedom at a time when it was under attack by Nazism.

Sartre's earliest work applies a philosophical method known as *phenomenology,* which is used to describe and analyze our own consciousness. This inward turning method goes one step further than the description of innermost thoughts and feelings that Dostoyevsky's underground man undertakes. Phenomenology describes conscious experiences as accurately as possible, without presuming that these experiences provide data about the external world. If we attend to the qualitative features of our experiences instead of jumping to the conclusion that our experiences provide information about a world outside of ourselves, then we can discover the basic structures of our own consciousness. Phenomenology investigates our experiences as we actually live them—as lived experiences—rather than as the supposed by-products of external forces that affect our sense organs.

In *Nausea,* the narrator, Roquentin, slips almost naturally into the phenomenological method when he begins to describe his own experiences in their immediate, raw state. He does not take inanimate objects, such as stones and cardboard boxes, or even people for granted, but instead describes the peculiar ways these objects and people appear to him in his own lived experiences. His lived experiences are more like adventures that rise up in his consciousness than evidence for objects in the external world that exist apart from him. As the weeks pass, his experiences grow more chaotic, and his own questioning of what he is doing with his life grows more intense until he has a breakthrough in the park: He experiences a chestnut tree, not merely in terms of its apparent qualities—its colors, shapes, and textures—but also in terms of the brute fact of its being. The overflowing, unstoppable reality of the tree—the fact that it exists instead of not existing—is experienced by virtue of his phenomenologically sharpened awareness. Roquentin's nausea, like the underground man's sickness of too much consciousness, is discomforting, but it discloses the nature of existence more clearly than do our habitual ways of relating to the world.

Sartre's *Nausea* (Excerpts)[1]

Undated Pages

The best thing would be to write down events from day to day. Keep a diary to see clearly—let none of the nuances or small happenings escape even though they might seem to mean nothing. And above all, classify them. I must tell how I see this table, this street, the people, my packet of tobacco, since *those* are the things which have changed. I must determine the exact extent and nature of this change.

For instance, here is a cardboard box holding my bottle of ink. I should try to tell how I saw it *before* and now how I . . . Well, it's a parallelopiped rectangle, it opens—that's stupid, there's nothing I can say about it. This is what I have to avoid, I must not put in strangeness where there is none. I think that is the big danger in keeping a diary: you exaggerate everything. You continually force the truth because you're always looking for something. . . .

Naturally, I can write nothing definite about this Saturday and the day-before-business. I am already too far from it; the only thing I can say is that in neither case was there anything which could ordinarily be called an event. Saturday the children were playing ducks and drakes and, like them, I wanted to throw a stone into the sea. Just at that moment I stopped, dropped the stone and left. Probably I looked somewhat foolish or absent-minded, because the children laughed behind my back.

So much for external things. What has happened inside of me has not left any clear traces. I saw something which disgusted me, but I no longer know whether it was the sea or the stone. The stone was flat and dry, especially on one side, damp and muddy on the other. I held it by the edges with my fingers wide apart so as not to get them dirty.

. . . Anyhow, it was certain that I was afraid or had some other feeling of that sort. If I had only known what I was afraid of, I would have made a great step forward.

The strangest thing is that I am not at all inclined to call myself insane. I clearly see that I am not: all these changes concern objects. At least, that is what I'd like to be sure of.

TUESDAY, 30 JANUARY:

. . . I very much like to pick up chestnuts, old rags and especially papers. It is pleasant to me to pick them up, to close my hand on them; with a little encouragement I would carry them to my mouth the way children do. Anny went into a white rage when I picked up the corners of heavy, sumptuous papers, probably soiled by excrement. In summer or the beginning of autumn, you can find remnants of sun-baked newspapers in gardens, dry and fragile as dead leaves, so yellow you might think they had been washed with picric acid. In winter, some pages are pounded to pulp; crushed, stained, they return to the earth. Others quite new when covered with ice, all white, all throbbing, are like swans about to fly, but the earth has already caught them from below. They twist and tear themselves from the mud, only to be finally flattened out a little further on. It is good to pick up all that. Sometimes I simply feel them, looking at them closely; other times I tear them to hear their drawn-out crackling, or, if they are damp, I light them, not without difficulty; then I wipe my muddy hands on a wall or tree trunk.

So, today, I was watching the riding boots of a cavalry officer who was leaving his barracks. As I followed them with my eyes, I saw a piece of paper lying beside a puddle. I thought the officer was going to crush the paper into the mud with his heel, but no: he straddled paper and puddle in a single step. I went up to it: it was a lined page, undoubtedly torn from a school notebook. The rain had drenched and twisted it, it was covered with blisters and swellings like a burned hand. The red line of the margin was smeared into a pink splotch; ink had run in places. The bottom of the page disappeared beneath a crust of mud. I bent down, already rejoicing at the touch of this pulp, fresh and tender, which I should roll in my fingers into greyish balls.

I was unable.

I stayed bent down for a second, I read "Dictation: The White Owl," then I straightened up, empty-handed. I am no longer free, I can no longer do what I will.

Objects should not *touch* because they are not alive. You use them, put them back in place, you live among them: they are useful, nothing more. But they touch me, it is unbearable. I am afraid of being in contact with them as though they were living beasts.

Now I see: I recall better what I felt the other day at the seashore when I held the pebble. It was a sort of sweetish sickness. How unpleasant it was! It came from the stone, I'm sure of it, it passed from the stone to my hand. Yes, that's it, that's just it—a sort of nausea in the hands.

FRIDAY:

. . . I get up. I move through this pale light. I see it change beneath my hands and on the sleeves of my coat: I cannot describe how much it disgusts me. I yawn. I light the lamp on the table: perhaps its light will be able to combat the light of day. But no: the lamp makes nothing more than a pitiful pond around its base. I turn it out; I get up. There is a white hole in the wall, a mirror. It is a trap. I know I am going to let myself be caught in it. I have. The grey thing appears in the mirror. I go over and look at it, I can no longer get away.

It is the reflection of my face. Often in these lost days I study it. I can understand nothing of this face. The faces of others have some sense, some direction. Not mine. I cannot even decide whether it is handsome or ugly. I think it is ugly because I have been told so. But it doesn't strike me. At heart, I am even shocked that anyone can attribute qualities of this kind to it, as if you called a clod of earth or a block of stone beautiful or ugly.

Still, there is one thing which is pleasing to see, above the flabby cheeks, above the forehead; it is the beautiful red flame which crowns my head, it is my hair. That is pleasant to see. Anyhow, it is a definite colour: I am glad I have red hair. There it is in the mirror, it makes itself seen, it shines. I am still lucky: if my forehead was surmounted by one of the neutral heads of hair which are neither chestnut nor blond, my face would be lost in vagueness, it would make me dizzy.

My glance slowly and wearily travels over my forehead, my cheeks: it finds nothing firm, it is stranded. Obviously there are a nose, two eyes and a mouth, but none of it makes sense, there is not even a human expression. Yes, Anny and Vélines thought I looked so alive: perhaps I am too used to my face. When I was little, my Aunt Bigeois told me "If you look at yourself too long in the mirror, you'll see a monkey." I must have looked at myself even longer than that: what I see is well below the monkey, on the fringe of the vegetable world, at the level of jellyfish. It is alive, I can't say it isn't; but this was not the life that Anny contemplated: I see a slight tremor, I see the insipid flesh blossoming and palpitating with abandon. The eyes especially are horrible seen so close. They are glassy, soft, blind, red-rimmed, they look like fish scales.

I lean all my weight on the porcelain ledge, I draw my face closer until it touches the mirror. The eyes, nose and mouth disappear: nothing human is left. Brown wrinkles show on each side of the feverish swelled lips, crevices, mole holes. A silky white down covers the great slopes of the cheeks, two hairs protrude from the nostrils: it is a geological embossed map. And, in spite of everything, this lunar world is familiar to me. I cannot say I *recognize* the details. But the whole thing gives me an impression of something seen before which stupefies me: I slip quietly off to sleep.

I would like to take hold of myself: an acute, vivid sensation would deliver me. I plaster my left hand against my cheek, I pull the skin; I grimace at myself. An entire half of my face yields, the left half of the mouth twists and swells, uncovering a tooth, the eye opens on a white globe, on pink, bleeding flesh. That is not what I was looking for: nothing strong, nothing new; soft, flaccid, stale! I go to sleep with my eyes open, already the face is growing larger, growing in the mirror, an immense, light halo gliding in the light. . . .

I lose my balance and that wakes me. I find myself straddling a chair, still dazed. Do other men have as much difficulty in appraising their face? It seems that I see my own as I feel my body, through a dumb, organic sense. But the others? . . .

FRIDAY [TWO WEEKS LATER]:

. . . Frightened, I looked at these unstable beings which, in an hour, in a minute, were perhaps going to crumble: yes, I was there, living in the midst of these books full of knowledge describing the immutable forms of the animal species, explaining that the right quantity of energy is kept integral in the universe; I was there, standing in front of a window whose panes had a definite refraction index. But what feeble barriers! I suppose it is out of laziness that the world is the same day after day. Today it seemed to want to change. And then, *anything, anything* could happen.

. . . A real panic took hold of me. I didn't know where I was going. I ran along the docks, turned into the deserted streets in the Beauvoisis district; the houses watched my flight with their mournful eyes. I repeated with anguish: Where shall I go? where shall I go? *Anything* can happen. Sometimes, my heart pounding, I made a sudden right-about-turn: what was happening behind my back? Maybe it would start behind me and when I would turn around, suddenly, it would be too late. As long as I could stare at things nothing would happen: I looked at them as much as I could, pavements, houses, gaslights; my eyes went rapidly from one to the other, to catch them unawares, stop them in the midst of their metamorphosis. They didn't look too natural, but I told myself forcibly: this is a gaslight, this is a drinking fountain, and I tried to reduce them to their everyday aspect by the power of my gaze. . . .

MONDAY:

. . . The thing which was waiting was on the alert, it has pounced on me, it flows through me, I am filled with it. It's nothing: I am the Thing. Existence, liberated, detached, floods over me. I exist.

I exist. It's sweet, so sweet, so slow. And light: you'd think it floated all by itself. It stirs. It brushes by me, melts and vanishes. Gently, gently. There is bubbling water in my mouth. I swallow. It slides down my throat, it caresses me—and now it comes up again into my mouth. For ever I shall have a little pool of whitish water in my mouth—lying low—grazing my tongue. And this pool is still me. And the tongue. And the throat is me.

I see my hand spread out on the table. It lives—it is me. It opens, the fingers open and point. It is lying on its back. It shows me its fat belly. It looks like an animal turned upside down. The fingers are the paws. I amuse myself by moving them very rapidly, like the claws of a crab which has fallen on its back.

The crab is dead: the claws draw up and close over the belly of my hand. I see the nails—the only part of me that doesn't live. And once more. My hand turns over, spreads out flat on its stomach, offers me the sight of its back. A silvery back, shining a little—like a fish except for the red hairs on the knuckles. I feel my hand. I am these two beasts struggling at the end of my arms. My hand scratches one of its paws with the nail of the other paw; I feel its weight on the table which is not me. It's long, long, this impression of weight, it doesn't pass. There is no reason for it to pass. It becomes intolerable . . . I draw back my hand and put it in my pocket; but immediately I feel the warmth of my thigh through the stuff. I pull my hand out of my pocket and let it hang against the back of the chair. Now I feel a weight at the end of my arm. It pulls a little, softly, insinuatingly it exists. I don't *insist:* no matter where I put it it will go on existing; I can't suppress it, nor can I suppress the rest of my body, the sweaty warmth which soils my shirt, nor all this warm obesity which turns lazily, as if someone were stirring it with a spoon, nor all the sensations going on inside, going, coming, mounting from my side to my armpit or quietly vegetating from morning to night, in their usual corner.

I jump up: it would be much better if I could only stop thinking. Thoughts are the dullest things. Duller than flesh. They stretch out and there's no end to them and they leave a funny taste in the mouth. Then there are words, inside the thoughts, unfinished words, a sketchy sentence which constantly returns: "I have to fi . . . I ex . . . Dead . . . M. de Rollebon is dead . . . I am not . . . I ex . . ." It goes, it goes . . . and there's no end to it. It's worse than the rest because I feel responsible and have complicity in it. For example, this sort of painful rumination: I *exist,* I am the one who keeps it up. I. The body lives by itself once it has begun. But *thought—I* am the one who continues it, unrolls it, slowly. . . . If I could keep myself from thinking! I try, and succeed: my head seems to fill with smoke . . . and then it starts again: "Smoke . . . not to think . . . don't want to think . . . I think I don't want to think. I mustn't think that I don't want to think. Because that's still a thought." Will there never be an end to it?

My thought is *me:* that's what I can't stop. I exist because I think . . . and I can't stop myself from thinking. At this very moment—it's frightful—if I exist, it is because I am horrified at existing. *I am the one* who pulls myself from the nothingness to which I aspire: the hatred, the disgust of existing, there are as many ways to *make* myself exist, to thrust myself into existence. Thoughts are born at the back of me, like sudden giddiness, I feel them being born behind my head . . . if I yield, they're going to come round in front of me, between my eyes—and I always yield, the thought grows and grows and there it is, immense, filling me completely and renewing my existence.

Wednesday:

. . . Here is the Saint-Elémir tramway, I turn round and the objects turn with me, pale and green as oysters.

Useless, it was useless to get in since I don't want to go anywhere.

Bluish objects pass the windows. In jerks all stiff and brittle, people, walls; a house offers me its black heart through open windows; and the windows pale, all that is black becomes blue, blue this great yellow brick house advancing uncertainly, trembling, suddenly stopping and taking a nose dive. A man gets on and sits down opposite to me. The yellow house starts up again, it leaps against the windows, it is so close that you can only see part of it, it is obscured. The windows rattle. It rises, crushing, higher than you can see, with hundreds of windows opened on black hearts; it slides along the car brushing past it; night has come between the rattling windows. It slides interminably, yellow as mud, and the windows are sky blue. Suddenly it is no longer there, it has stayed behind, a sharp, grey illumination fills the car and spreads everywhere with inexorable justice: it is the sky; through the windows you can still see layer on layer of sky because we're going up Eliphar Hill and you can see clearly between the two slopes, on the right as far as the sea, on the left as far as the airfield. No smoking—not even a *gitane.*

I lean my hand on the seat but pull it back hurriedly: it exists. This thing I'm sitting on, leaning my hand on, is called a seat. They made it purposely for people to sit on, they took leather, springs and cloth, they went to work with the idea of making a seat and when they finished, *that* was what they had made. They carried it here, into this car and the car is now rolling and jolting with its rattling windows, carrying this red thing in its bosom. I murmur: "It's a seat," a little like an exorcism.

But the word stays on my lips: it refuses to go and put itself on the thing. It stays what it is, with its red plush, thousands of little red paws in the air, all still, little dead paws. This enormous belly turned upward, bleeding, inflated—bloated with all its dead paws, this belly floating in this car, in this grey sky, is not a seat. It could just as well be a dead donkey tossed about in the water, floating with the current, belly in the air in a great grey river, a river of floods; and I could be sitting on the donkey's belly, my feet dangling in the clear water. Things are divorced from their names. They are there, grotesque, headstrong, gigantic and it seems ridiculous to call them seats or say anything at all about them: I am in the midst of things, nameless things. Alone, without words, defenceless, they surround me, are beneath me, behind me, above me. They demand nothing, they don't impose themselves: they are there. Under the cushion on the seat there is a thin line of shadow, a thin black line running along the seat, mysteriously and mischievously, almost a smile. I know very well that it isn't a smile and yet it exists, it runs under the whitish windows, under the jangle of glass, obstinately, obstinately behind the blue images which pass in a throng, like the inexact memory of a smile, like a half forgotten word of which you can only remember the first syllable and the best thing you can do is turn your eyes away and think about something else, about that man half-lying down on the seat opposite me, there. His blue-eyed, terracotta face. The whole right side of his body has sunk, the right arm is stuck to the body, the right side barely lives, it lives with difficulty, with avarice, as if it were paralysed. But on the whole left side there is a little parasitic existence, which proliferates; a chance: the arm begins to tremble and then is raised up and the hand at the end is stiff. Then the hand begins to tremble too and when it reaches the height of the skull, a finger stretches out and begins scratching the scalp with a nail. A sort of voluptuous grimace comes to inhabit the right side of the mouth and the left side stays dead. The windows rattle, the arm shakes, the nail scratches, scratches, the mouth smiles under the staring eyes and the man tolerates, hardly noticing it, this tiny existence which swells his right side, which has borrowed his right arm and right cheek to bring itself into being. The conductor blocks my path.

"Wait until the car stops."

But I push him aside and jump out of the tramway. I couldn't stand any more. I could no longer stand things being so close. I push open a gate, go in, airy creatures are bounding and leaping and perching on the peaks. Now I recognize myself, I know where I am: I'm in the park. I drop onto a bench between great black tree-trunks, between the black, knotty hands reaching towards the sky. A tree scrapes at the earth under my feet with a black nail. I would so like to let myself go, forget myself, sleep. But I can't, I'm suffocating: existence penetrates me everywhere, through the eyes, the nose, the mouth. . . .

And suddenly, suddenly, the veil is torn away, I have understood, I have *seen*.

6:00 P.M.

I can't say I feel relieved or satisfied; just the opposite, I am crushed. Only my goal is reached: I know what I wanted to know; I have understood all that has happened to me since January. The Nausea has not left me and I don't believe it will leave me so soon; but I no longer have to bear it, it is no longer an illness or a passing fit: it is I.

So I was in the park just now. The roots of the chestnut tree were sunk in the ground just under my bench. I couldn't remember it was a root any more. The words had vanished and with them the significance of things, their methods of use, and the feeble points of reference which men have traced on their surface. I was sitting, stooping forward, head bowed, alone in front of this black, knotty mass, entirely beastly, which frightened me. Then I had this vision.

It left me breathless. Never, until these last few days, had I understood the meaning of "existence." I was like the others, like the ones walking along the seashore, all dressed in their spring finery. I said, like them, "The ocean is green; that white speck up there *is* a seagull," but I didn't feel that it existed or that the seagull was an "existing seagull" ; usually existence hides itself. It is there, around us, in us, it is *us,* you can't say two words without mentioning it, but you can never touch it. When I believed I was thinking about it, I must believe that I was thinking nothing, my head was empty, or there was just one word in my head, the word "to be." Or else I was thinking . . . how can I explain it? I was thinking of *belonging,* I was telling myself that the sea belonged to the class of green objects, or that the green was a part of the quality of the sea. Even when I looked at things, I was miles from dreaming that they existed: they looked like scenery to me. I picked them up in my hands, they served me as tools, I foresaw their resistance. But that all happened on the surface. If anyone had asked me what existence was, I would have answered, in good faith, that it was nothing, simply an empty form which was added to external things without changing anything in their nature. And then all of a sudden, there it was, clear as day: existence had suddenly unveiled itself. It had lost the harmless look of an abstract category: it was the very paste of things, this root was kneaded into existence. Or rather the root, the park gates, the bench, the sparse grass, all that had vanished: the diversity of things, their individuality, were only an appearance, a veneer. This veneer had melted, leaving soft, monstrous masses, all in disorder—naked, in a frightful, obscene nakedness.

I kept myself from making the slightest movement, but I didn't need to move in order to see, behind the trees, the blue columns and the lamp posts of the bandstand and the Velleda, in the midst of a mountain of laurel. All these objects . . . how can I explain? They inconvenienced me; I would have liked them to exist less strongly, more dryly, in a more abstract way, with more reserve. The chestnut tree pressed itself against my eyes. Green rust covered it half-way up; the bark, black and swollen, looked like boiled leather. The sound of the water in the Masqueret Fountain sounded in my ears, made a nest there, filled them with signs; my nostrils overflowed with a green, putrid odour. All things, gently, tenderly, were letting themselves drift into existence like those relaxed women who burst out laughing and say: "It's good to laugh," in a wet voice; they were parading, one in front of the other, exchanging abject secrets about their existence. I realized that there was no half-way house between non-existence and this flaunting abundance. If you existed, you had to *exist all the way,* as far as mouldiness, bloatedness, obscenity were concerned. In another world, circles, bars of music keep their pure and rigid lines. But existence is a deflection. Trees, night-blue pillars, the happy bubbling of a fountain, vital smells, little heat-mists floating in the cold air, a red-haired man digesting on a bench: all this somnolence, all these meals digested together, had its comic side . . . Comic . . . no: it didn't go as far as that, nothing that exists can be comic; it was like a floating analogy, almost entirely elusive, with certain aspects of vaudeville. We were a heap of living creatures, irritated, embarrassed at ourselves, we hadn't the slightest reason to be there, none of us, each one, confused, vaguely alarmed, felt in the way in relation to the others. *In the way:* it was the only relationship I could establish between these trees, these gates, these stones. In vain I tried to *count* the chestnut trees, to *locate* them by their relationship to the Velleda, to compare their height with the height of the plane trees: each of them escaped the relationship in which I tried to enclose it, isolated itself, and overflowed. Of these relations (which I insisted on maintaining in order to delay the crumbling of the human world, measures, quantities, and directions)—I felt myself to be the arbitrator; they no longer had their teeth into things. *In the way,* the chestnut tree there, opposite me, a little to the left. *In the way,* the Velleda . . .

And I—soft, weak, obscene, digesting, juggling with dismal thoughts—I, too, was *In the way.* Fortunately, I didn't feel it, although I realized it, but I was uncomfortable because I was afraid of feeling it (even now I am afraid—afraid that it might catch me behind my head and lift me up like a wave). I dreamed vaguely of killing myself to wipe out at least one of these superfluous lives. But even my death would have been *In the way. In the way,* my corpse, my blood on these stones, between these plants, at the back of this smiling garden. And the decomposed flesh would have been *In the way* in the earth which would receive my bones, at last, cleaned, stripped, peeled, proper and clean as teeth, it would have been *In the way:* I was *In the way* for eternity.

The word absurdity is coming to life under my pen; a little while ago, in the garden, I couldn't find it, but neither was I looking for it, I didn't need it: I thought without words, *on* things, *with* things. Absurdity was not an idea in my head, or the sound of a voice, only this long serpent dead at my feet, this wooden serpent. Serpent or claw or root or vulture's talon, what difference does it make. And without formulating anything clearly, I understood that I had found the key to Existence, the key to my Nauseas, to my own life. In fact, all that I could grasp beyond that returns to this fundamental absurdity. Absurdity: another word; I struggle against words; down there I touched the thing. But I wanted to fix the absolute character of this absurdity here. A movement, an event in the tiny coloured world of men is only relatively absurd: by relation to the accompanying circumstances. A madman's ravings, for example, are absurd in relation to the situation in which he finds himself, but not in relation to his delirium. But a little while ago I made an experiment with the absolute or the absurd. This root—there was nothing in relation to which it was absurd. Oh, how can I put it in words? Absurd: in relation to the stones, the tufts of yellow grass, the dry mud, the tree, the sky, the green benches. Absurd, irreducible; nothing—not even a profound, secret upheaval of nature—could explain it. Evidently I did not know everything. I had not seen the seeds sprout, or the tree grow. But faced with this great wrinkled paw, neither ignorance nor knowledge was important: the world of explanations and reasons is not the world of existence. A circle is not absurd, it is clearly explained by the rotation of a straight segment around one of its extremities. But neither does a circle exist. This root, on the other hand, existed in such a way that I could not explain it. Knotty, inert, nameless, it fascinated me, filled my eyes, brought me back unceasingly to its own existence. In vain to repeat: "This is a root"—it didn't work any more. I saw clearly that you could not pass from its function as a root, as a breathing pump, *to that,* to this hard and compact skin of a sea lion, to this oily, callous, headstrong look. The function explained nothing: it allowed you to understand generally that it was a root, but not *that one* at all. This root, with its colour, shape, its congealed movement, was . . . below all explanation. Each of its qualities escaped it a little, flowed out of it, half solidified, almost became a thing; each one was *In the way* in the root and the whole stump now gave me the impression of unwinding itself a little, denying its existence to lose itself in a frenzied excess. I scraped my heel against this black claw: I wanted to peel off some of the bark. For no reason at all, out of defiance, to make the bare pink appear absurd on the tanned leather: to *play* with the absurdity of the world. But, when I drew my heel back, I saw that the bark was still black.

Black? I felt the word deflating, emptied of meaning with extraordinary rapidity. Black? The root *was not* black, there was no black on this piece of wood—there was . . . something else: black, like the circle, did not exist. I looked at the root: was it *more than* black or *almost* black? But I soon stopped questioning myself because I had the feeling of knowing where I was. Yes, I had already scrutinized innumerable objects, with deep uneasiness. I had already tried—vainly—to think something *about* them: and I had already felt their cold, inert qualities elude me, slip through my fingers. . . . Suspicious: that's what they were, the sounds, the smells, the tastes. When they ran quickly under your nose like startled hares and you didn't pay too much attention, you might believe them to be simple and reassuring, you might believe that there was real blue in the world, real red, a real perfume of almonds or violets. But as soon as you held on to them for an instant, this feeling of comfort and security gave way to a deep uneasiness: colours, tastes, and smells were never real, never themselves and nothing but themselves. The simplest, most indefinable quality had too much content, in relation to itself, in its heart. That black against my foot, it didn't look like black, but rather the confused effort to imagine black by someone who had never seen black and who wouldn't know how to stop, who would have imagined an ambiguous being beyond colours. It *looked* like a colour, but also . . . like a bruise or a secretion, like an oozing—and something else, an odour, for example, it melted into the odour of wet earth, warm, moist wood, into a black odour that spread like varnish over this sensitive wood, in a flavour of chewed, sweet fibre. I did not simply *see* this black: sight is an abstract invention, a simplified idea, one of man's ideas. That black, amorphous, weakly presence, far surpassed sight, smell and taste. But this richness was lost in confusion and finally was no more because it was too much.

This moment was extraordinary. I was there, motionless and icy, plunged in a horrible ecstasy. But something fresh had just appeared in the very heart of this ecstasy; I understood the Nausea, I possessed it. To tell the truth, I did not formulate my discoveries to myself. But I think it would be easy for me to put them in words now. The essential thing is contingency. I mean that one cannot define existence as necessity. To exist is simply *to be there;* those who exist let themselves be encountered, but you can never deduce anything from them. I believe there are people who have understood this. Only they tried to overcome this contingency by inventing a necessary, causal being. But no necessary being can explain existence: contingency is not a delusion, a probability which can be dissipated; it is the absolute, consequently, the perfect free gift. All is free, this park, this city and myself. When you realize that, it turns your heart upside down and everything begins to float . . . here is Nausea; here there is what . . . others try to hide from themselves with their idea of their rights. But what a poor lie: no one has any rights; they are entirely free, like other men, they cannot succeed in not feeling superfluous. And in themselves, secretly, they are *superfluous,* that is to say, amorphous, vague, and sad.

How long will this fascination last? I *was* the root of the chestnut tree. Or rather I was entirely conscious of its existence. Still detached from it—since I was conscious of it—yet lost in it, nothing but it. An uneasy conscience which, notwithstanding, let itself fall with all its weight on this piece of dead wood. Time had stopped: a small black pool at my feet; it was impossible for something to come *after* that moment. I would have liked to tear myself from that atrocious joy, but I did not even imagine it would be possible; I was inside; the black stump did *not move,* it stayed there, in my eyes, as a lump of food sticks in the windpipe. I could neither accept nor refuse it. At what a cost did I raise my eyes? Did I raise them? Rather did I not obliterate myself for an instant in order to be reborn in the following instant with my head thrown back and my eyes raised upward? In fact, I was not even conscious of the transformation. But suddenly it became impossible for me to think of the existence of the root. It was wiped out, I could repeat in vain: it exists, it is still there, under the bench, against my right foot, it no longer meant anything. Existence is not something which lets itself be thought of from a distance: it must invade you suddenly, master you, weigh heavily on your heart like a great motionless beast—or else there is nothing more at all.

There was nothing more, my eyes were empty and I was spellbound by my deliverance. Then suddenly it began to move before my eyes in light, uncertain motions: the wind was shaking the top of the tree.

It did not displease me to see a movement, it was a change from these motionless beings who watched me like staring eyes, I told myself, as I followed the swinging of the branches: movements never quite exist, they are passages, intermediaries between two existences, moments of weakness, I expected to see them come out of nothingness, progressively ripen, blossom: I was finally going to surprise beings in the process of being born.

No more than three seconds, and all my hopes were swept away. I could not attribute the passage of time to these branches groping around like blind men. This idea of passage was still an invention of man. The idea was too transparent. All these paltry agitations, drew in on themselves, isolated. They overflowed the leaves and branches everywhere. They whirled about these empty hands, enveloped them with tiny whirlwinds. Of course a movement was something different from a tree. But it was still an absolute. A thing. My eyes only encountered completion. The tips of the branches rustled with existence which unceasingly renewed itself and which was never born. The existing wind rested on the tree like a great bluebottle, and the tree shuddered. But the shudder was not a nascent quality, a passing from power to action; it was a thing; a shudder-thing flowed into the tree, took possession of it, shook it and suddenly abandoned it, going further on to spin about itself. All was fullness and all was active, there was no weakness in time, all, even the least perceptible stirring, was made of existence. And all these existents which bustled about this tree came from nowhere and were going nowhere. Suddenly they existed, then suddenly they existed no longer: existence is without memory; of the vanished it retains nothing—not even a memory. Existence everywhere, infinitely, in excess, for ever and everywhere; existence—which is limited only by existence. I sank down on the bench, stupified, stunned by this profusion of beings without origin: everywhere blossomings, hatchings out, my ears buzzed with existence, my very flesh throbbed and opened, abandoned itself to the universal burgeoning. It was repugnant. But why, I thought, why so many existences, since they all look alike? What good are so many duplicates of trees? So many existences missed, obstinately begun again and again missed—like the awkward efforts of an insect fallen on its back? (I was one of those efforts.) That abundance did not give the effect of generosity, just the opposite. It was dismal, ailing, embarrassed at itself. Those trees, those great clumsy bodies . . . I began to laugh because I suddenly thought of the formidable springs described in books, full of crackings, burstings, gigantic explosions. There were those idiots who came to tell you about will-power and struggle for life. Hadn't they ever seen a beast or a tree? This plane-tree with its scaling bark, this half-rotten oak, they wanted me to take them for rugged youthful endeavor surging towards the sky. And that root? I would have undoubtedly had to represent it as a voracious claw tearing at the earth, devouring its food?

Impossible to see things that way. Weaknesses, frailties, yes. The trees floated. Gushing towards the sky? Or rather a collapse; at any instant I expected to see tree-trunks shrivel like weary wands, crumple up, fall on the ground in a soft, folded, black heap. *They did not want* to exist, only they could not help themselves. So they quietly minded their own business; the sap rose up slowly through the structure, half reluctant, and the roots sank slowly into the earth. But at each instant they seemed on the verge of leaving everything there and obliterating themselves. Tired and old, they kept on existing, against the grain, simply because they were too weak to die, because death could only come to them from the outside: strains of music alone can proudly carry their own death within themselves like an internal necessity: only they don't exist. Every existing thing is born without reason, prolongs itself out of weakness and dies by chance. I leaned back and closed my eyes. But the images, forewarned, immediately leaped up and filled my closed eyes with existences: existence is a fullness which man can never abandon. . . .

Had I dreamed of this enormous presence? It was there, in the garden, toppled down into the trees, all soft, sticky, soiling everything, all thick, a jelly. And I was inside, I with the garden. I was frightened, furious, I thought it was so stupid, so out of place, I hated this ignoble mess. Mounting up, mounting up as high as the sky, spilling over, filling everything with its gelatinous slither, and I could see depths upon depths of it reaching far beyond the limits of the garden, the houses, and Bouville, as far as the eye could reach. I was no longer in Bouville, I was nowhere, I was floating. I was not surprised, I knew it was the World, the naked World suddenly revealing itself, and I choked with rage at this gross, absurd being. You couldn't even wonder where all that sprang from, or how it was that a world came into existence, rather than nothingness. It didn't make sense, the World was everywhere, in front, behind. There had been nothing *before* it. Nothing. There had never been a moment in which it could not have existed. That was what worried me: of course there was no *reason* for this floating larva to exist. *But it was impossible* for it not to exist. It was unthinkable: to imagine nothingness you had to be there already, in the midst of the World, eyes wide open and alive; nothingness was only an idea in my head, an existing idea floating in this immensity: this nothingness had not come *before* existence, it was an existence like any other and appeared after many others. I shouted "filth! what rotten filth!" and shook myself to get rid of this sticky filth, but it held fast and there was so much, tons and tons of existence, endless: I stifled at the depths of this immense weariness. And then suddenly the park emptied as through a great hole, the World disappeared as it had come, or else I woke up—in any case, I saw no more of it; nothing was left but the yellow earth around me, out of which dead branches rose upward.

I got up and went out. Once at the gate, I turned back. Then the garden smiled at me. I leaned against the gate and watched for a long time. The smile of the trees, of the laurel, *meant* something; that was the real secret of existence. I remembered one Sunday, not more than three weeks ago, I had already detected everywhere a sort of conspiratorial air. Was it in my intention? I felt with boredom that I had no way of understanding. No way. Yet it was there, waiting, looking at one. It was there on the trunk of the chestnut tree . . . it was *the* chestnut tree. Things—you might have called them thoughts—which stopped halfway, which were forgotten, which forgot what they wanted to think and which stayed like that, hanging about with an odd little sense which was beyond them. That little sense annoyed me: *I could not* understand it, even if I could have stayed leaning against the gate for a century; I had learned all I could know about existence. I left, I went back to the hotel and I wrote. . . .

Basic Existentialist Concepts

Contingency The name *existentialism* derives from the word *existence*, which denotes the primary concern of the thinkers who make up the existentialist movement. Existentialists investigate what makes us real rather than nonexistent, as well as what kind of reality other things in the world have. But existentialists do not merely conduct an inventory of the different things that exist; they inquire into the very meaning of being: What does it mean to exist rather than not exist?

Sartre and other atheistic existentialists argue that an important part of the meaning of being is contingency. All things, people, and events in the world did not have to exist, but they do happen to exist. There is no reason that necessitates their presence in the world, and it is just as likely that they could never have existed at all. As Sartre puts it, "Every existing thing is born without reason, prolongs itself out of weakness and dies by chance."

For-itself In his inquiry into the meaning of being, Sartre distinguishes two kinds of reality: *For-itself* and *In-itself*. Whatever exists and is conscious—not only conscious of other things but also of itself—is For-itself. Whatever is real but is not conscious is In-itself. Basically, human beings are For-itself, but it is a bit more complicated, because these categories are not exclusive: There are facets of our reality, such as elements of our bodies, that are In-itself, even though we are For-itself insofar as we are conscious.

What it means for a human being to exist rather than not exist is to be conscious of the world and of oneself in the world. Because our consciousness is always self-consciousness as well as awareness of other things, events, and people, we exist for ourselves in our conscious life—that is, each of us is For-itself. In contrast to the kind of reality that stones and boxes have, our kind of reality includes self-reflexive awareness, which makes it possible for us to think about ourselves. To be For-itself is to exist for oneself as a topic of one's own contemplation and as a matter of one's own concern.

In-itself The distinction Sartre draws between For-itself and In-itself is not a distinction between two entirely separable groups of beings, because he, like other existentialists, argues that we humans are *in the world*—acting, working, and building with all of the various things the world contains. We interact with the things of the world, experiencing them as we act. Our lived experience of them is not that of a self-contained, disengaged subject isolated from objects, but of someone amidst things that are coded by the activities and tasks we undertake when we use them.

Even though the nonconscious beings that are In-itself are not inert or disconnected from human employments, they are self-enclosed in the properties they have. They have no will or idea to change themselves. The meaning of their being real rather than nonexistent is to be what they are, characterized by whatever qualities they have, and located wherever they are (*in the way*) among other things. Although nonconscious beings affect other beings causally, they are neither conscious nor intentional in such causal interactions. Although nonconscious beings change over time (e.g., plants grow), they have no conception of what they will become, let alone of what they could become—and it is this latter conception of what one could become that marks the For-itself as so very different from the In-itself.

Questions for Discussion

1. Is the narrator hallucinating when he describes how stones, houses, and his own hands appear to him to be alive?

2. Are you the face that appears in the mirror? Are you the unstoppable stream of your own thoughts? When you become aware of yourself, are you aware of being For-itself?

3. What are the most important insights that the narrator has when he experiences the chestnut tree in the park?

4. Are all beings "in the way" of other beings, or is this only true of beings that are In-itself?

5. Why do words become emptied of meaning when things are experienced directly in their overflowing plenitude of being?

Chapter 3

Jean-Paul Sartre's The Flies

Introduction: Existence Precedes Essence

In his nonfictional, philosophical writings, Sartre defined the word *existence* as a technical philosophical term that applied only to the kind of reality human beings have. (*Existentialism* derives from this narrower meaning of *existence.*) "Existence precedes essence" means that a human being exists before he or she has an essence. An essence is what something is; it is the character, nature, or function of something; it is what defines the thing and distinguishes it from other kinds of things. In the case of a human being, the essence is *who* he or she is.

According to Sartre, human beings do not have fixed, full-fledged essences at birth, whereas nonhuman things (such as pens and computers) are stamped with an essence from the first moment they come into being. Instead of having an essence at birth, we are free. We each create our own individual essence—our character—through the way we exist as human beings, choosing and then freely acting on our choices. We are also capable of revising or reinventing our essence if we change the course of our actions. This means that each individual creates his or her own personality, habits, tendencies, preferences, talents, and character flaws.

The Flies offers a case study of an individual creating his own essence: Orestes decides to define himself, through his actions, as the avenger of his father's death and as the liberator of the people of Argos. In Sartre's version of this ancient story, Orestes was not born or fated to be an avenger or liberator. He makes himself one after discovering he is free.

At the beginning of the play, Orestes enters Argos, the city where he was born and where his father, King Agamemnon, was murdered. At this point, Orestes has no intention of avenging his father's death; he and his tutor pretend to be travelers from Corinth in order to avoid suspicion. What they encounter in Argos is a populace burdened by guilt. The townspeople use religion to justify their sense of guilt and to avoid facing their own complicity in the murder of Agamemnon by Aegistheus and Queen Clytemnestra. In contrast, Orestes knows no guilt: He enters Argos "free as air"—a young man who naively believes that freedom is merely doing what one wishes, without feeling responsible for one's actions or feeling committed to other people.

But after he meets his sister, Electra, and understands her need to be free, his sense of his own freedom changes radically. He comes to realize that freedom means acting according to one's own choices—not according to religious or social norms—and taking full responsibility for one's actions. It also means acting in ways that can liberate others by modeling freedom for them. His discovery of this existential sense of freedom transforms him and leads him to act.

Sartre's *The Flies* (Excerpts)[1]

Characters in the Play

ZEUS
ORESTES
ELECTRA
ÆGISTHEUS
CLYTEMNESTRA
THE TUTOR
FIRST FURY
SECOND FURY
THIRD FURY
THE HIGH PRIEST
A YOUNG WOMAN
AN OLD WOMAN
AN IDIOT BOY
FIRST SOLDIER
SECOND SOLDIER
MEN AND WOMEN, TOWNSFOLK OF ARGOS
FURIES, SERVANTS, PALACE GUARDS

Act I

A public square in Argos, dominated by a statue of ZEUS, *god of flies and death. The image has white eyes and blood-smeared cheeks.*

A procession of OLD WOMEN *in black, carrying urns, advances; they make libations to the statue. An* IDIOT BOY *is squatting in the background.* ORESTES *enters, accompanied by* THE TUTOR.

* * *

ORESTES: Listen, my good women.

[*The* OLD WOMEN *swing round, emitting little squeals.*]

THE TUTOR: Would you kindly tell us—[*The* OLD WOMEN *spit on the ground and move back a pace.*] Steady, good ladies, steady. I only want a piece of simple information. We are travelers and we have lost our way. [*Dropping their urns, the* WOMEN *take to their heels.*] Stupid old hags! You'd think I had intentions on their virtue! [*Ironically*] Ah, young master, truly this has been a pleasant journey. And how well inspired you were to come to this city of Argos, when there are hundreds of towns in Greece and Italy where the drink is good, the inns are hospitable, and the streets full of friendly, smiling people! But these uncouth hillmen—one would suppose they'd never seen a foreigner before. A hundred times and more I've had to ask our way, and never once did I get a straight answer. And then the grilling heat. This Argos is a nightmare city. Squeals of terror everywhere, people who panic the moment they set eyes on you, and scurry to cover, like black beetles, down the glaring streets. Pfoo! I can't think how you bear it—this emptiness, the shimmering air, that fierce sun overhead. What's deadlier than the sun?

ORESTES: I was born here.

THE TUTOR: So the story goes. But, if I were you, I wouldn't brag about it.

ORESTES: I was born here—and yet I have to ask my way, like any stranger. Knock at that door.

THE TUTOR: What do you expect? That someone will open it? Only look at those

1 From *No Exit and the Flies* by Jean-Paul Sartre, translated by Stuart Gilbert.

freedom / responsibility + guilt / past + future

houses and tell me how they strike you. You will observe there's not a window anywhere. They open on closed courtyards, I suppose, and turn their backsides to the street. [ORESTES *makes a fretful gesture.* Very good, sir. I'll knock—but nothing will come of it.

[*He knocks. Nothing happens. He knocks again, and the door opens a cautious inch.*]

A VOICE: What do you want?

THE TUTOR: Just a word of information. Can you tell me where—? [*The door is slammed in his face.*] Oh, the devil take you! Well, my lord Orestes, is that enough, or must I try elsewhere? If you wish, I'll knock at every door.

ORESTES: No, that's enough.

THE TUTOR: Well, I never! There's someone here. [*He goes up to the* IDIOT BOY.] Excuse me, sir . . .

THE IDIOT: Hoo! Hoo! Hoo!

THE TUTOR [*bowing again*]: My noble lord . . .

THE IDIOT: Hoo!

THE TUTOR: Will Your Highness deign to show us where Ægistheus lives?

THE IDIOT: Hoo!

THE TUTOR: Ægistheus, King of Argos.

THE IDIOT: Hoo! Hoo! Hoo!

[ZEUS *passes by, back stage.*]

THE TUTOR: We're out of luck. The only one who doesn't run away is a half-wit. [ZEUS *retraces his steps.*] Ah, that's odd! He's followed us here.

ORESTES: Who?

THE TUTOR: That bearded fellow.

ORESTES: You're dreaming.

THE TUTOR: I tell you, I saw him go by.

ORESTES: You must be mistaken.

THE TUTOR: Impossible. Never in my life have I seen such a beard—or, rather, only one: the bronze beard on the chin of Zeus Ahenobarbos at Palermo. Look, there he is again. What can he want of us?

ORESTES: He is only a traveler like ourselves.

THE TUTOR: Only that? We met him on the road to Delphi. And when we took the boat at Itea, there he was, fanning that great beard in the bows. At Nauplia we couldn't move a step without having him at our heels, and now—here he is again! Do you think that chance explains it? [*He brushes the flies off his face.*] These flies in Argos are much more sociable than its townsfolk. Just look at them! [*Points to the* IDIOT BOY.] There must be a round dozen pumping away at each of his eyes, and yet he's smiling quite contentedly; probably he likes having his eyes sucked. That's not surprising; look at that yellow muck oozing out of them. [*He flaps his hands at the flies.*] Move on, my little friends. Hah! They're on you now. Allow me! [*He drives them away.*] Well, this should please you—you who are always complaining of being a stranger in your native land. These charming insects, anyhow, are making you welcome; one would think they know who you are. [*He whisks them away.*] Now leave us in peace, you buzzers. We know you like us, but we've had enough of you. . . . Where can they come from? They're as big as bumble-bees and noisy as a swarm of locusts.

[*Meanwhile* ZEUS *has approached them.*]

ZEUS: They are only bluebottles, a trifle larger than usual. Fifteen years ago a mighty stench of carrion drew them to this city, and since then they've been getting fatter and fatter. Give them another fifteen years, and they'll be as big as toads.

[*A short silence.*]

THE TUTOR: Pray, whom have I the honor of addressing?

ZEUS: Demetrios is my name, and I hail from Athens.

ORESTES: Did I not see you on the boat, a fortnight go?

ZEUS: Yes, and I saw you, too.

[*Hideous shrieks come from the palace.*]

THE TUTOR: Listen to that! I don't know if you will agree with me, young master, but I think we'd do better to leave this place.

ORESTES: Keep quiet!

ZEUS: You have nothing to fear. It's what they call Dead Men's Day today. Those cries announce the beginning of the ceremony.

ORESTES: You seem well posted on the local customs.

ZEUS: Yes, I often visit Argos. As it so happened, I was here on the great day of Agamemnon's homecoming when the Greek fleet, flushed with victory, anchored in the Nauplia roads. From the top of the rampart one saw the bay dappled with their white sails. [*He drives the flies away.*] There were no flies then. Argos was only a small country town, basking in the sun, yawning the years away. Like everyone else I went up to the sentry-path to see the royal procession, and I watched it for many an hour wending across the plain. At sundown on the second day Queen Clytemnestra came to the ramparts, and with her was Ægistheus, the present King. The people of Argos saw their faces dyed red by the sunset, and they saw them leaning over the battlements, gazing for a long while seawards. And the people thought: "There's evil brewing." But they kept silence. Ægistheus, you should know, was the Queen's lover. A hard, brutal man, and even in those days he had the cast of melancholy. . . . But you're looking pale, young sir.

ORESTES: It's the long journey I have made, and this accursed heat. But pray go on; you interest me.

ZEUS: Agamemnon was a worthy man, you know, but he made one great mistake. He put a ban on public executions. That was a pity. A good hanging now and then—that entertains folk in the provinces and robs death of its glamour. . . . So the people here held their tongues; they looked forward to seeing, for once, a violent death. They still kept silent when they saw their King entering by the city gates. And when Clytemnestra stretched forth her graceful arms, fragrant and white as lilies, they still said nothing. Yet at that moment a word, a single word, might have sufficed. But no one said it; each was gloating in imagination over the picture of a huge corpse with a shattered face.

ORESTES: And you, too, said nothing?

ZEUS: Does that rouse your indignation? Well, my young friend, I like you all the better for it; it proves your heart's in the right place. No, I admit I, too, held my peace. I'm a stranger here, and it was no concern of mine. And next day when it started, when the folks of Argos heard their King screaming his life out in the palace, they still kept silence, but they rolled their eyes in a sort of ecstasy, and the whole town was like a woman in heat.

ORESTES: So now the murderer is on the throne. For fifteen years he has enjoyed the fruits of crime. And I thought the gods were just!

ZEUS: Steady, my friend! Don't blame the gods too hastily. Must they always punish? Wouldn't it be better to use such breaches of the law to point a moral?

ORESTES: And is that what they did?

ZEUS: They sent the flies.

THE TUTOR: The flies? How do the flies come in?

ZEUS: They are a symbol. But if you want to know what the gods did, look around you. See that old creature over there, creeping away like a beetle on her little black feet, and hugging the walls. Well, she's a good specimen of the squat black vermin that teem in every cranny of this town. Now watch me catch our specimen, it's well worth inspection. Here it is. A loathsome object, you'll agree. . . . Hah! You're blinking now. Still, you're an Argive and you should be used to the white-hot rapiers of the sun. . . . Watch her wriggling, like a hooked fish! . . . Now, old lady, let's hear your tale of woe. I see you're in black from head to foot. In mourning for a whole regiment of sons, is that it? Tell us, and I'll release you—perhaps. For whom are you in mourning?

OLD WOMAN: Sir, I am not in mourning. Everyone wears black at Argos.

ZEUS: Everyone wears black? Ah, I see. You're in mourning for your murdered King.

OLD WOMAN: Whisht! For God's sake, don't talk of that.

ZEUS: Yes, you're quite old enough to have heard those huge cries that echoed and reechoed for a whole morning in the city streets. What did you do about it?

OLD WOMAN: My good man was in the fields, at work. What could I do, a woman alone? I bolted my door.

ZEUS: Yes, but you left your window not quite closed, so as to hear the better, and, while you peeped behind the curtains and held your breath, you felt a little tingling itch between your loins, and didn't you enjoy it!

OLD WOMAN: Oh, please stop, sir!

ZEUS: And when you went to bed that night, you had a grand time with your man. A real gala night.

OLD WOMAN: A what? . . . No, my lord, that was a dreadful, dreadful night.

ZEUS: A real gala, I tell you, and you've never been able to blot out its memory.

OLD WOMAN: Mercy on us! Are you—are you one of the Dead?

ZEUS: I dead? You're crazy, woman. . . . Anyhow, don't trouble your head who I am; you'd do better to think of yourself, and try to earn forgiveness by repenting of your sins.

OLD WOMAN: Oh, sir, I do repent, most heartily I repent. If you only knew how I repent, and my daughter too, and my son-in-law offers up a heifer every year, and my little grandson has been brought up in a spirit of repentance. He's a pretty lad, with flaxen hair, and he always behaves as good as gold. Though he's only seven, he never plays or laughs, for thinking of his original sin.

ZEUS: Good, you old bitch, that's as it should be—and be sure you die in a nice bitchy odor of repentance. It's your one hope of salvation. [*The* OLD WOMAN *runs away.*] Unless I'm much mistaken, my masters, we have there the real thing, the good old piety of yore, rooted in terror.

ORESTES: What man are you?

ZEUS: Who cares what I am? We were talking of the gods. Well now, should they have struck Ægistheus down?

ORESTES: They should. . . . They should. . . . Oh, how would I know what they should have done? What do I care, anyhow? I'm a stranger here. . . . Does Ægistheus feel contrition?

ZEUS: Ægistheus? I'd be much surprised. But what matter? A whole city's repenting on his account. And it's measured by the bushel, is repentance. [*Eerie screams in the palace.*] Listen! Lest they forget the screams of the late King in his last agony, they keep this festival of death each year when the day of the King's murder comes round. A herdsman from the hills—he's chosen for his lung-power—is set to bellow in the Great Hall of the palace. [ORESTES *makes a gesture of disgust.*] Bah! That's nothing. I wonder what you'll say presently, when they let the Dead loose. Fifteen years ago, to a day, Agamemnon was murdered. And what a change has come over the light-hearted folk of Argos since that day; how near and dear to me they are at present!

ORESTES: Dear to you?

ZEUS: Pay no heed, young man. That was a slip of the tongue. Near and dear to the gods, I meant.

ORESTES: You surprise me. Then those blood-smeared walls, these swarms of flies, this reek of shambles and the stifling heat, these empty streets and yonder god with his gashed face, and all those creeping, half-human creatures beating their breasts in darkened rooms, and those shrieks, those hideous, blood-curdling shrieks—can it be that Zeus and his Olympians delight in these?

ZEUS: Young man, do not sit in judgment on the gods. They have their secrets—and their sorrows.

[*A short silence.*]

ORESTES: Am I right in thinking Agamemnon had a daughter? A daughter named Electra?

ZEUS: Yes. She lives there, in the palace—that building yonder.

ORESTES: So that's the palace? . . . And what does Electra think of—all this?

ZEUS: Oh, she's a mere child. There was a son, too, named Orestes. But he's dead, it seems.

ORESTES: Dead? Well, really . . .

THE TUTOR: Of course he's dead, young master. I thought you knew it. Don't you remember what they told us at Nauplia—about Ægistheus' having him murdered, soon after Agamemnon's death?

ZEUS: Still, some say he's alive. The story

goes that the men ordered to kill the child had pity on him and left him in the forest. Some rich Athenians found him there and took him home. For my part, I'd rather he were dead.

ORESTES: Pray, why?

ZEUS: Suppose that one day he appeared in this city, and—

ORESTES: Continue, please.

ZEUS: As you wish. . . . Well, I'd say this to him. "My lad—" I'd say, "My lad," as he's your age or thereabouts—if he's alive, of course. By the way, young lord, may I know your name?

ORESTES: Philebus is my name, and I hail from Corinth. I am traveling to improve my mind, and this old slave accompanying me used to be my tutor.

ZEUS: Thank you. Well, I'd say something like this. "My lad, get you gone! What business have you here? Do you wish to enforce your rights? Yes, you're brave and strong and spirited. I can see you as a captain in an army of good fighters. You have better things to do than reigning over a dead-and-alive city, a carrion city plagued by flies. These people are great sinners but, as you see, they're working out their atonement. Let them be, young fellow, let them be; respect their sorrowful endeavor, and begone on tiptoe. You cannot share in their repentance, since you did not share their crime. Your brazen innocence makes a gulf between you and them. So if you have any care for them, be off! Be off, or you will work their doom. If you hinder them on their way, if even for a moment you turn their thoughts from their remorse, all their sins will harden on them—like cold fat. They have guilty consciences, they're afraid—and fear and guilty consciences have a good savor in the nostrils of the gods. Yes, the gods take pleasure in such poor souls. Would you oust them from the favor of the gods? What, moreover, could you give them in exchange? Good digestions, the gray monotony of provincial life, and the boredom—ah, the soul-destroying boredom—of long days of mild content. Go your way, my lad, go your way. The repose of cities and men's souls hangs on a thread; tamper with it and you bring disaster. [*Looking him in the eyes*] A disaster which will recoil on you.

ORESTES: Yes? So that is what you'd say? Well, if I were that young man, I'd answer—[*They eye each other truculently.* THE TUTOR *coughs.*] No, I don't know how I'd answer you. Perhaps you're right, and anyhow it's no concern of mine.

ZEUS: Good. I only hope Orestes would show as much sense. . . . Well, peace be with you, my friend; I must go about my business.

ORESTES: Peace be with you.

ZEUS: By the way, if those flies bother you, here's a way of getting rid of them. You see that swarm buzzing round your head? Right. Now watch! I flick my wrist—so—and wave my arm once, and then I say: Abraxas, galla, galla, tsay, tsay. See! They're falling down and starting to crawl on the ground like caterpillars.

ORESTES: By Jove!

ZEUS: Oh, that's nothing. Just a parlor trick. I'm a fly-charmer in my leisure hours. Good day to you. We shall meet again.

[*Exit* ZEUS.]

THE TUTOR: Take care. That man knows who you are.

ORESTES: "Man," you say. But *is* he a man?

THE TUTOR: What else should he be? You grieve me, my young master. Have all my lessons, all my precepts, the smiling skepticism I taught you, been wasted on your ears? "Is he a man?" you ask. There's nothing else but men—what more would you have? And that bearded fellow is a man, sure enough; probably one of Ægistheus' spies.

ORESTES: A truce to your philosophy! It's done me too much harm already.

THE TUTOR: Harm? Do you call it doing harm to people when one emancipates their minds? Ah, how you've changed! Once I read you like an open book. . . . But at least you might tell me your plans. Why bring me to this city, and what's your purpose here?

ORESTES: Did I say I had a purpose? But that's enough. Be silent now. [*He takes some steps towards the palace.*] This is *my* palace. My father's birthplace. And it's there a whore and her paramour foully butchered him. I, too, was born there. I was nearly three when that usurper's bravoes carried me away. Most likely we went out by that door. One of them held me in his arms, I had my eyes wide open, and no doubt I was crying. And yet I have no memories, none whatever. I am looking at a huge, gloomy building, solemn and pretentious in the worst provincial taste. I am looking at it, but I *see* it for the first time.

THE TUTOR: No memories, master? What ingratitude, considering that I gave ten years of my life to stocking you with them! And what of all the journeys we have made together, all the towns we visited? And the course in archæology I composed specially for you? No memories, indeed! Palaces, shrines, and temples—with so many of them is your memory peopled that you could write a guide-book of all Greece.

ORESTES: Palaces—that's so. Palaces, statues, pillars—stones, stones, stones! Why, with all those stones in my head, am I not heavier? While you are about it, why not remind me of the three hundred and eighty-seven steps of the temple at Ephesus? I climbed them, one by one, and I remember each. The seventeenth, if my memory serves me, was badly broken. And yet—! Why, an old, mangy dog, warming himself at the hearth, and struggling to his feet with a little whimper to welcome his master home—why, that dog has more memories than I! At least he recognizes his master. *His* master. But what can I call mine?

THE TUTOR: And what of your culture, Lord Orestes? What of that? All that wise lore I culled for you with loving care, like a bouquet, matching the fruits of my knowledge with the finest flowers of my experience? Did I not, from the very first, set you a-reading all the books there are, so as to make clear to you the infinite diversity of men's opinions? And did I not remind you, time and again, how variable are human creeds and customs? So, along with youth, good looks, and wealth, you have the wisdom of far riper years; your mind is free from prejudice and superstition; you have no family ties, no religion, and no calling; you are free to turn your hand to anything. But you know better than to commit yourself—and there lies your strength. So, in a word, you stand head and shoulders above the ruck and, what's more, you could hold a chair of philosophy or architecture in a great university. And yet you cavil at your lot!

ORESTES: No, I do not cavil. What should I cavil at? You've left me free as the strands torn by the wind from spiders' webs that one sees floating ten feet above the ground. I'm light as gossamer and walk on air. I know I'm favored, I appreciate my lot at its full value. [*A pause.*] Some men are born bespoken; a certain path has been assigned them, and at its end there is something they *must* do, a deed allotted. So on and on they trudge, wounding their bare feet on the flints. I suppose that strikes *you* as vulgar—the joy of going somewhere definite. And there are others, men of few words, who bear deep down in their hearts a load of dark imaginings; men whose whole life was changed because one day in childhood, at the age of five or seven— Right; I grant you these are no great men. When I was seven, I know I had no home, no roots. I let sounds and scents, the patter of rain on housetops, the golden play of sunbeams, slip past my body and fall round me—and I knew these were for others, I could never make them *my* memories. For memories are luxuries reserved for people who own houses, cattle, fields, and servants. Whereas I—! I'm free as air, thank God. My mind's my own, gloriously aloof. [*He goes nearer to the palace.*] I might have lived there. I'd not have read any of your books; perhaps I'd not have learned to read. It's rare for a Greek prince to know how to read. But I'd have come in and gone out by that door ten thousand times. As a child I'd have played with its leaves, and when I pushed at them with all my little might, they'd have creaked without yielding, and I'd have taken the measure of my weakness. Later on, I'd have pushed them open furtively by night and gone out after girls. And some years later, when I came of age, the slaves would have flung the doors wide open and I'd have crossed the threshold on horseback. My old wooden door! I'd have been able to find your keyhole with my eyes shut. And that notch there—I might have made it showing off, the first day they let me hold a spear. [*He steps back.*] Let's see. That's the Dorian style, isn't it? And what do you make of that gold inlay? I saw the like at Dodona; a pretty piece of craftsmanship. And now I'm going to say something that will rejoice you. This is not *my* palace, nor *my* door. And there's nothing to detain us here.

THE TUTOR: Ah, that's talking sense. For what would you have gained by living in Argos? By now your spirit would be broken, you'd be wallowing in repentance.

ORESTES: Still, it would be *my* repentance. And this furnace heat singeing my hair would be *mine*. Mine, too, the buzz of all these flies. At this moment I'd be lying naked in some dark room at the back of the palace, and watching a ribbon of red light lengthen across the floor. I'd be waiting for sundown; waiting for the cool dusk of an Argos evening to rise like perfume from the parched earth; an Argos evening like many a thousand others, familiar yet ever new, another evening that should be *mine*. . . . Well, well, my worthy pedagogue, let's be off. We've no business to be luxuriating in others' heat.

THE TUTOR: Ah, my young lord, how you've eased my mind! During these last few months—to be exact, ever since I revealed to you the secret of your birth—I could see you changing day by day, and it gave me many a sleepless night. I was afraid—

ORESTES: Of what?

THE TUTOR: No, it will anger you.

ORESTES: Speak.

THE TUTOR: Be it so. Well, though from one's earliest years one has been trained to skeptic irony, one can't help having foolish fancies now and then. And I wondered if you weren't hatching some wild scheme to oust Ægistheus and take his place.

ORESTES [*thoughtfully*]: To oust Ægistheus. Ah— [*A pause.*] No, my good slave, you need not fear; the time for that is past. True, nothing could please me better than to grip that sanctimonious ruffian by the beard and drag him from my father's throne. But what purpose would it serve? These folk are no concern of mine. I have not seen one of their children come into the world, nor been present at their daughters' weddings; I don't share their remorse, I don't even know a single one of them by name. That bearded fellow was right; a king should share his subjects' memories. So we'll let them be, and begone on tiptoe. . . . But, mind you, if there were something I could do, something to give me the freedom of the city; if, even by a crime, I could acquire their memories, their hopes and fears, and fill with these the void within me, yes, even if I had to kill my own mother—

THE TUTOR: Hush! For heaven's sake, hush!

ORESTES: Yes, these are idle dreams. Let's be off. Now go and see if we can get some horses here, and we'll move on to Sparta, where I have good friends.

[ELECTRA *comes forward, carrying a large ashcan. She goes up to the statue of* ZEUS, *without seeing them.*]

ELECTRA: Yes, you old swine, scowl away at me with your goggle eyes and your fat face all smeared with raspberry juice—scowl away, but you won't scare me, not you! They've been to worship you, haven't they?—those pious matrons in black dresses. They've been padding around you in their big creaky shoes. And you were pleased, old bugaboo, it warmed your silly wooden heart. You like them old, of course; the nearer they're to corpses, the more you love them. They've poured their choicest wines out at your feet, because it's your festival today, and the stale smell from their petticoats tickled your nostrils. [*She rubs herself against him.*] Now smell me for a change, smell the perfume of a fresh, clean body. But, of course, I'm young, I'm alive—and you loathe youth and life. I, too, am bringing you offerings, while all the others are at prayers. Here they are: ashes from the hearth, peelings, scraps of offal crawling with maggots, a chunk of bread too filthy even for our pigs. But your darling flies will love it, won't they, Zeus? A good feast-day to you, old idol, and let's hope it is your last. I'm not strong enough to pull you down. All I can do is to spit at you. But some day he will come, the man I'm waiting for, carrying a long, keen sword. He'll look you up and down and chuckle, with his hands on his hips, like this, and his head thrown back. Then he'll draw his sword and chop you in two, from top to bottom—like this! So the two halves of Zeus will fall apart, one to the left, one to the right, and everyone will see he's made of common wood. Just a lump of cheap white deal, the terrible God of Death! And all that frightfulness, the blood on his face, his dark-green eyes, and all the rest—they'll see it was only a coat of paint. *You,* anyhow, you know you're white inside, white as a child's body, and you know, too, that a sword can rip you limb from limb, and you won't even bleed. Just a log of deal—anyhow it will serve to light our fires next winter. [*She notices* ORESTES.] Oh!

ORESTES: Don't be alarmed.

ELECTRA: I'm not alarmed. Not a bit. Who are you?

ORESTES: A stranger.

ELECTRA: Then you are welcome. All that's foreign to this town is dear to me. Your name?

ORESTES: Philebus. I've come from Corinth.

ELECTRA: Ah? From Corinth. My name's Electra.

ORESTES: Electra—[*To* THE TUTOR] Leave us.
[*Exit* THE TUTOR.]

ELECTRA: Why are you looking at me like that?

ORESTES: You're very beautiful. Not at all like the people in these parts.

ELECTRA: I beautiful? Can you really mean it? As beautiful as the Corinthian girls?

ORESTES: Yes.

ELECTRA: Well, here they never tell me that I'm beautiful. Perhaps they don't want me to know it. Anyhow, what use would beauty be to me? I'm only a servant.

ORESTES: What! You a servant?

ELECTRA: The least of the servants in the palace. I wash the King's and the Queen's underlinen. And how dirty it is, all covered with spots and stains! Yes, I have to wash everything they wear next their skin, the shifts they wrap their rotting bodies in, the nightdresses Clytemnestra has on when the King shares her bed. I shut my eyes and scrub with all my might. I have to wash up, too. You don't believe me? See my hands, all chapped and rough. Why are you looking at them in that funny way? Do they, by any chance, look like the hands of a princess?

ORESTES: Poor little hands. No, they don't look like a princess's hands. . . . But tell me more. What else do they make you do?

ELECTRA: Every morning I've to empty the ash-can. I drag it out of the palace, and then—well you saw what I do with the refuse. That big fellow in wood is Zeus, God of Death and Flies. The other day, when the High Priest came here to make his usual bows and scrapings, he found himself treading on cabbage-stumps and rotten turnips and mussel-shells. He looked startled, I can tell you! I say! You won't tell on me, will you?

ORESTES: No.

ELECTRA: Really I don't care if you do. They can't make things much worse for me than they are already. I'm used to being beaten. Perhaps they'd shut me up in one of the rooms in the tower. That wouldn't be so bad; at least I wouldn't have to see their faces. Just imagine what I get by way of thanks at bedtime, when my day's work is done. I go up to a tall, stout lady with dyed hair, with thick lips and very white hands, a queen's hands, that smell of honey. Then she puts her hands on my shoulders and dabs my forehead with her lips and says: "Good night, Electra. Good night." Every evening. Every evening I have to feel that woman slobbering on my face. Ugh! Like a piece of raw meat on my forehead. But I hold myself up, I've never fallen yet. She's my mother, you know. If I was up in the tower, she wouldn't kiss me any more.

ORESTES: Have you never thought of running away?

ELECTRA: I haven't the courage; I daren't face the country roads at night all by myself.

ORESTES: Is there no one, no girl friend of yours, who'd go with you?

ELECTRA: No, I'm quite alone. Ask any of the people here, and they'll tell you I'm a pest, a public nuisance. I've no friends.

ORESTES: Not even an old nurse, who saw you into the world and has kept a little affection for you?

ELECTRA: Not even an old nurse. Mother will tell you; I freeze even the kindest hearts—that's how I am.

ORESTES: Do you propose to spend your life here?

ELECTRA [*excitedly*]: My life? Oh no, no! Of course not! Listen. I'm waiting for—for something.

ORESTES: Something, or someone?

ELECTRA: That's my secret. Now it's your turn to speak. You're good-looking, too. Will you be here long?

ORESTES: Well, I'd thought of leaving today. But, as it is—

ELECTRA: Yes?

ORESTES: As it is, I'm not so sure.

ELECTRA: Is Corinth a pretty place?

ORESTES: Very pretty.

ELECTRA: Do you like it? Are you proud of Corinth?

ORESTES: Yes.

ELECTRA: How strange that sounds! I can't imagine myself being proud of my home town. Tell me what it feels like.

ORESTES: Well— No, I don't know. I can't explain.

ELECTRA: You can't? I wonder why. [*A short silence.*] What's Corinth like? Are there shady streets and squares? Places where one can stroll in the cool of the evening?

ORESTES: Yes.

ELECTRA: And everyone comes out of doors? People go for walks together?

ORESTES: Almost everyone is out and about at sundown.

ELECTRA: Boys and girls together?

ORESTES: Oh yes, one often sees them going for walks together.

ELECTRA: And they always find something to say to each other? They like each other's company, and one hears them laughing in the streets quite late at night?

ORESTES: Yes.

ELECTRA: I suppose you think I'm very childish. But it's so hard for me to picture a life like that—going for walks, laughing and singing in the streets. Everybody here is sick with fear. Everyone except me. And I—

ORESTES: Yes? And you?

ELECTRA: Oh, I—I'm sick with—hatred. And what do they do all day, the girls at Corinth?

ORESTES: Well, they spend quite a while making themselves pretty; then they sing or play on lutes. Then they call on their friends, and at night they go to dances.

ELECTRA: But don't they have any worries?

ORESTES: Only quite little ones.

ELECTRA: Yes? Now listen well, please. Don't the people at Corinth feel remorse?

ORESTES: Sometimes. Not very often.

ELECTRA: So they do what they like and, afterwards, don't give another thought to it?

ORESTES: That's their way.

ELECTRA: How strange! [*A short silence.*] Please tell me something else; I want to know it because of—of someone I'm expecting. Suppose one of the young fellows you've been telling about, who walk and laugh with girls in the evenings—suppose one of these young men came home after a long journey and found his father murdered, and his mother living with the murderer, and his sister treated like a slave—what would he do, that young man from Corinth? Would he just take it for granted and slink out of his father's house and look for consolation with his girl friends? Or would he draw his sword and hurl himself at the assassin, and slash his brains out? . . . Why are you silent? . . .

[ZEUS *enters, back stage, and takes cover to listen to them.*]

ORESTES: Electra, I'm Orestes, your brother. I, too, am of the house of Atreus, and my place is at your side.

ELECTRA: No. You're not my brother;

you're a stranger. Orestes is dead, and so much the better for him. From now on I'll do homage to his shade, along with my father's and my sister's. You, Philebus, claim to be of our house. So be it! But can you truly say that you are one of *us*? Was *your* childhood darkened by the shadow of a murder? No, more likely you were a quiet little boy with happy, trustful eyes, the pride of your adoptive father. Naturally you could trust people—they always had a smile for you—just as you could trust the solid friendly things around you: tables, beds, and stairs. And because you were rich, and always nicely dressed, and had lots of toys, you must have often thought the world was quite a nice world to live in, like a big warm bath in which one can splash and loll contentedly. My childhood was quite different. When I was six I was a drudge, and I mistrusted everything and everyone. [*A short pause.*] So go away, my noble-souled brother. I have no use for noble souls; what I need is an accomplice.

ORESTES: How could I leave you alone; above all, now that you've lost even your last hope? . . . What do you propose to do here?

ELECTRA: That's my business. Good-by, Philebus.

ORESTES: So you're driving me away? [*He takes some steps, then halts and faces her.*] Is it my fault if I'm not the fierce young swashbuckler you expected? Him you'd have taken by the hand at once and said: "Strike!" Of me you asked nothing. But, good heavens, why should I be outcast by my own sister—when I've not even been put to the test?

ELECTRA: No, Philebus, I could never lay such a load upon a heart like yours; a heart that has no hatred in it.

ORESTES: You are right. No hatred; but no love, either. You, Electra, I might have loved. And yet—I wonder. Love or hatred calls for self-surrender. He cuts a fine figure, the warm-blooded, prosperous man, solidly entrenched in his well-being, who one fine day surrenders all to love—or to hatred; himself, his house, his land, his memories. But who am I, and what have I to surrender? I'm a mere shadow of a man; of all the ghosts haunting this town today, none is ghostlier than I. The only loves I've known were phantom loves, rare and vacillating as will-o'-the-wisps. The solid passions of the living were never mine. Never! [*A short silence.*] But, oh, the shame of it. Here I am, back in the town where I was born, and my own sister disavows me. And now—where shall I go? What city must I haunt?

ELECTRA: Isn't there some pretty girl waiting for you—somewhere in the world?

ORESTES: Nobody is waiting for me anywhere. I wander from city to city, a stranger to all others and to myself, and the cities close again behind me like the waters of a pool. If I leave Argos, what trace of my coming will remain, except the cruel disappointment of your hope?

ELECTRA: You told me about happy towns—

ORESTES: What do I care for happiness? I want my share of memories, my native soil, my place among the men of Argos. [*A short silence.*] Electra, I shall not leave Argos.

ELECTRA: Please, please, Philebus, go away. If you have any love for me, go. It hurts me to think what may come to you here—nothing but evil, that I know—and your innocence would ruin all my plans.

ORESTES: I shall not go.

ELECTRA: How can you think I'd let you stay beside me—you with your stubborn uprightness—to pass silent judgment on my acts? Oh, why are you so obstinate? Nobody wants you here.

ORESTES: It's my one chance, and you, Electra—surely you won't refuse it to me? Try to understand. I want to be a man who belongs to some place, a man among comrades. Only consider. Even the slave bent beneath his load, dropping with fatigue and staring dully at the ground a foot in front of him—why, even that poor slave can say he's in *his* town, as a tree is in a forest, or a leaf upon the tree. Argos is all around him, warm, compact, and comforting. Yes, Electra, I'd gladly be that slave and enjoy that feeling of drawing the city round me like a blanket and curling myself up in it. No, I shall not go.

ELECTRA: Even if you stayed a hundred years among us, you'd still be a stranger here, and lonelier than if you were tramping the high-roads of Greece. The townspeople would be watching you all the time from the corner of an eye, and they'd lower their voices when you came near.

ORESTES: Is it really so hard to win a place among you? My sword can serve the city, and I have gold to help the needy.

ELECTRA: We are not short of captains, or of charitable souls.

ORESTES: In that case—[*He takes some steps away from her, with lowered eyes.* ZEUS *comes forward and gazes at him, rubbing his hands.* ORESTES *raises his eyes heavenwards.*] Ah, if only I knew which path to take! O Zeus, our Lord and King of Heaven, not often have I called on you for help, and you have shown me little favor; yet this you know: that I have always tried to act aright. But now I am weary and my mind is dark; I can no longer distinguish right from wrong. I need a guide to point my way. Tell me, Zeus, is it truly your will that a king's son, hounded from this city, should meekly school himself to banishment and slink away from his ancestral home like a whipped cur? I cannot think it. And yet—and yet you have forbidden the shedding of blood. . . . What have I said? Who spoke of bloodshed? . . . O Zeus, I beseech you, if meek acceptance, the bowed head and lowly heart are what you would have of me, make plain your will by some sign; for no longer can I see my path.

ZEUS [*aside*]: Ah, that's where I can help, my young friend. Abraxas, abraxas, tsou, tsou.

[*Light flashes out round the stone.*]

ELECTRA [*laughing*]: Splendid! It's raining miracles today! See what comes of being a pious young man and asking counsel of the gods. [*She is convulsed with laughter and can hardly get the words out.*] Oh, noble youth, Philebus, darling of the gods! "Show me a sign," you asked. "Show me a sign." Well, now you've had your sign—a blaze of light round that precious, sacred stone of theirs. So off you go to Corinth! Off you go!

ORESTES [*staring at the stone*]: So that is the Right Thing. To live at peace—always at perfect peace. I see. Always to say "Excuse me," and "Thank you." That's what's wanted, eh? [*He stares at the stone in silence for some moments.*] The Right Thing. *Their* Right Thing. [*Another silence.*] Electra!

ELECTRA: Hurry up and go. Don't disappoint your fatherly old friend, who has bent down from Olympus to enlighten you. [*She stops abruptly, a look of wonder on her face.*] But—but what's come over you?

ORESTES [*slowly, in a tone he has not used till now*]: There is another way.

ELECTRA [*apprehensively*]: No, Philebus, don't be stubborn. You asked the gods for orders; now you have them.

ORESTES: Orders? What do you mean? Ah yes, the light round that big stone. But it's not for me, that light; from now on I'll take no one's orders, neither man's nor god's.

ELECTRA: You're speaking in riddles.

ORESTES: What a change has come on everything, and, oh, how far away you seem! Until now I felt something warm and living round me, like a friendly presence. That something has just died. What emptiness! What endless emptiness, as far as eye can reach! [*He takes some steps away from her.*] Night is coming on. The air is getting chilly, isn't it? But what was it—what was it that died just now?

ELECTRA: Philebus—

ORESTES: I say there is another path—*my* path. Can't you see it? It starts here and leads down to the city. I must go down—do you understand?—I must go down into the depths, among you. For you are living, all of you, at the bottom of a pit. [*He goes up to* ELECTRA.] You are *my* sister, Electra, and that city is *my* city. *My* sister. [*He takes her arm.*]

ELECTRA: Don't touch me. You're hurting me, frightening me—and I'm *not* yours.

ORESTES: I know. Not yet. I'm still too—too light. I must take a burden on my shoulders, a load of guilt so heavy as to drag me down, right down into the abyss of Argos.

ELECTRA: But what—what do you mean to do?

ORESTES: Wait. Give me time to say farewell to all the lightness, the aery lightness that was mine. Let me say good-by to my youth. There are evenings at Corinth and at Athens, golden evenings full of songs and scents and laughter; these I shall never know again. And mornings, too, radiant with promise. Good-by to them all, good-by. . . . Come, Electra, look at our city. There it lies, rose-red in the sun, buzzing with men and flies, drowsing its doom away in the languor of a summer afternoon. It fends me off with its high walls, red roofs, locked doors. And yet it's mine for the taking; I've felt that since this morning. You, too, Electra, are mine for the taking—and I'll take you, too. I'll turn into an ax and hew those walls asunder, I'll rip open the bellies of those stolid houses and there will steam up from the gashes a stench of rotting food and incense. I'll be an iron wedge driven into the city, like a wedge rammed into the heart of an oak tree.

ELECTRA: Oh, how you've changed! Your eyes have lost their glow; they're dull and smoldering. I'm sorry for that, Philebus; you were so gentle. But now you're talking like the Orestes of my dreams.

ORESTES: Listen! All these people quaking with fear in their dark rooms, with their dear departed round them—supposing I take over all their crimes. Supposing I set out to win the name of "guilt-stealer," and heap on myself all their remorse; that of the woman unfaithful to her husband, of the tradesman who let his mother die, of the usurer who bled his victims white? Surely once I am plagued with all those pangs of conscience, innumerable as the flies of Argos—surely then I shall have earned the freedom of your city. Shall I not be as much at home within your red walls as the red-aproned butcher in his shop, among the carcasses of flayed sheep and cattle?

ELECTRA: So you wish to atone for us?

ORESTES: To atone? No. I said I'd house your penitence, but I did *not* say what I'd do with all those cackling fowls; maybe I'll wring their necks.

ELECTRA: And how can you take over our sense of guilt?

ORESTES: Why, all of you ask nothing better than to be rid of it. Only the King and Queen force you to nurse it in your foolish hearts.

ELECTRA: The King and Queen—Oh, Philebus!

ORESTES: The gods bear witness that I had no wish to shed their blood.

[*A long silence.*]

ELECTRA: You're too young, too weak.

ORESTES: Are you going to draw back—*now?* Hide me somewhere in the palace, and lead me tonight to the royal bedchamber—and then you'll see if I am too weak!

ELECTRA: Orestes!

ORESTES: Ah! For the first time you've called me Orestes.

ELECTRA: Yes. I know you now. You are indeed Orestes. I didn't recognize you at first, I'd expected somebody quite different. But this throbbing in my blood, this sour taste on my lips—I've had them in my dreams, and I know what they mean. So at last you have come, Orestes, and your resolve is sure. And here I am beside you—just as in my dreams—on the brink of an act beyond all remedy. And I'm frightened; that, too, was in my dreams. How long I've waited for this moment, dreading and hoping for it! From now on, all the moments will link up, like the cogs in a machine, and we shall never rest again until they both are lying on their backs, with faces like crushed mulberries. In a pool of blood. To think it's you who are going to shed it, you with those gentle eyes! I'm sorry now, sorry that never again I'll see that gentleness, never again see Philebus. Orestes, you are my elder brother, and head of our house: fold me in your arms, protect me. Much suffering, many perils lie ahead of both of us.

[ORESTES *takes her in his arms.* ZEUS *leaves his hiding-place and creeps out on tiptoe.*]

CURTAIN

Act II, Scene Two

. . . [ORESTES *returns, his sword dripping blood.* ELECTRA *runs to him and flings herself into his arms.*]

ELECTRA: Orestes! . . . Oh! . . .

ORESTES: You're frightened. Why?

ELECTRA: I'm not frightened. I'm drunk. Drunk with joy. What did she say? Did she beg for mercy long?

ORESTES: Electra. I shall not repent of what I have done, but I think fit not to speak of it. There are some memories one does not share. It is enough for you to know she's dead.

ELECTRA: Did she die cursing us? That's all I want you to tell me. Did she curse us?

ORESTES: Yes. She died cursing us.

ELECTRA: Take me in your arms, beloved, and press me to your breast. How dark the night is! I never knew such darkness; those torches have no effect on it. . . . Do you love me?

ORESTES: It is not night; a new day is dawning. We are free, Electra. I feel as if I'd brought you into life and I, too, had just been born. Yes, I love you, and you belong to me. Only yesterday I was empty-handed, and today I have *you.* Ours is a double tie of blood; we two come of the same race and we two have shed blood.

ELECTRA: Let go your sword. Give me that hand, your strong right hand. [*She clasps and kisses it.*] Your fingers are short and square, made to grasp and hold. Dear hand! It's whiter than mine. But how heavy it became to strike down our father's murderers! Wait! [*She takes a torch and holds it near* ORESTES.] I must light up your face; it's getting so dark that I can hardly see you. And I *must* see you; when I stop seeing you, I'm afraid of you. I daren't take my eyes off you. I must tell myself again and again that I love you. But—how strange you look!

ORESTES: I am free, Electra. Freedom has crashed down on me like a thunderbolt.

ELECTRA: Free? But I—I don't feel free. And you—can you undo what has been done? Something has happened and we are no longer free to blot it out. Can you prevent our being the murderers of our mother—for all time?

ORESTES: Do you think I'd wish to prevent it? I have done *my* deed, Electra, and that deed was good. I shall bear it on my shoulders as a carrier at a ferry carries the traveler to the farther bank. And when I have brought it to the farther bank I shall take stock of it. The heavier it is to carry, the better pleased I shall be; for that burden is my freedom. Only yesterday I walked the earth haphazard; thousands of roads I tramped that brought me nowhere, for they were other men's roads. Yes, I tried them all; the haulers' tracks along the riverside, the mule-paths in the mountains, and the broad, flagged highways of the charioteers. But none of these was mine. Today I have one path only, and heaven knows where it leads. But it is *my* path. . . . What is it, Electra?

ELECTRA: I can't see you any more. Those torches give no light. I hear your voice, but it hurts me, it cuts like a knife. Will it always be as dark as this—always, even in the daytime? . . . Oh, Orestes! There they are!

ORESTES: Who?

ELECTRA: There they are! Where have they come from? They're hanging from the ceiling like clusters of black grapes; the walls are alive with them; they're swirling down across the torchlight and it's their shadows that are hiding your face from me.

ORESTES: The flies—

ELECTRA: Listen! The sound of their wings is like a roaring furnace. They're all round us, Orestes, watching, biding their time. Presently they'll swoop down on us and I shall feel thousands of tiny clammy feet crawling over me. Oh, look! They're growing bigger, bigger; now they're as big as bees. We'll never escape them, they'll follow us everywhere in a dense cloud. Oh God, now I can see their eyes, millions of beady eyes all staring at us!

ORESTES: What do the flies matter to us?

ELECTRA: They're the Furies, Orestes, the goddesses of remorse.

VOICE [*from behind the door*]: Open! Open! . . . If you don't, we'll smash the door in.

[*Heavy thuds. They are battering at the door.*]

ORESTES: Clytemnestra's cries must have

brought them here. Come! Lead me to Apollo's shrine. We will spend the night there, sheltered from men and flies. And tomorrow I shall speak to my people.

CURTAIN

. . . THE FURIES [*shrieking and laughing*]: Murderer! Murderer! Butcher!

ORESTES: Electra, behind that door is the outside world. A world of dawn. Out there the sun is rising, lighting up the roads. Soon we shall leave this place, we shall walk those sunlit roads, and these hags of darkness will lose their power. The sunbeams will cut through them like swords.

ELECTRA: The sun—

FIRST FURY: You will never see the sun again, Electra. We shall mass between you and the sun like a swarm of locusts; you will carry darkness round your head wherever you go.

ELECTRA: Oh, let me be! Stop torturing me!

ORESTES: It's your weakness gives them their strength. Mark how they dare not speak to me. A nameless horror has descended on you, keeping us apart. And yet why should this be? What have you lived through that I have not shared? Do you imagine that my mother's cries will ever cease ringing in my ears? Or that my eyes will ever cease to see her great sad eyes, lakes of lambent darkness in the pallor of her face? And the anguish that consumes you—do you think it will ever cease ravaging my heart? But what matter? I am free. Beyond anguish, beyond remorse. Free. And at one with myself. No, you must not loathe yourself, Electra. Give me your hand. I shall never forsake you.

ELECTRA: Let go of my hand! Those hell-hounds frighten me, but you frighten me more.

FIRST FURY: You see! You see! . . . That's quite true, little doll; you're less afraid of us than of that man. Because you need us, Electra. You are our child, our little girl. You need our nails to score your skin, our teeth to bite your breast, and all our savage love to save you from your hatred of yourself. Only the suffering of your body can take your mind off your suffering soul. So come and let us hurt you. You have only those two steps to come down, and we will take you in our arms. And when our kisses sear your tender flesh, you'll forget all in the cleansing fires of pain.

THE FURIES: Come down to us! Come down! [*Slowly they dance round her, weaving their spell.* ELECTRA *rises to her feet.*]

ORESTES [*gripping her arm*]: No, no, for pity's sake. Don't go to them. Once they get you, all is lost.

ELECTRA [*freeing herself violently*]: Let go! Oh, how I hate you! [*She goes down the steps, and the* Furies *fling themselves on her.*] Help! [ZEUS *enters.*]

ZEUS: Kennel up!

FIRST FURY: The master!

[*The* FURIES *slink off reluctantly, leaving* ELECTRA *lying on the ground.*]

ZEUS: Poor children. [*He goes up to* ELECTRA.] So to this you've come, unhappy pair? My heart is torn between anger and compassion. Get up, Electra. So long as I am here, my Furies will not hurt you. [*He helps her to rise and gazes at her face.*] Ah, what a cruel change! In a night, a single night, all the wild-rose bloom has left your cheeks. In one night your body has gone to ruin, lungs, gall, and liver all burnt out. The pride of headstrong youth—see what it has brought you to, poor child.

ORESTES: Stop talking in that tone, fellow. It is unbecoming for the king of the gods.

ZEUS: And you, my lad, drop that haughty tone. It's unbecoming for a criminal atoning for his crime.

ORESTES: I am no criminal, and you have no power to make me atone for an act I don't regard as a crime.

ZEUS: So you may think, but wait awhile. I shall cure you of that error before long.

ORESTES: Torture me to your heart's content; I regret nothing. . . .

ZEUS: So you take pride in being an outcast, do you? But the solitude you're doomed to, most cowardly of murderers, is the solitude of scorn and loathing.

ORESTES: The most cowardly of murders is he who feels remorse.

ZEUS: Orestes, I created you, and I created all things. Now see! [*The walls of the temple draw apart, revealing the firmament, spangled with wheeling stars.* ZEUS *is standing in the background. His voice becomes huge—amplified by loud-speakers—but his form is shadowy.*] See those planets wheeling on their appointed ways, never swerving, never clashing. It was I who ordained their courses, according to the law of justice. Hear the music of the spheres, that vast, mineral hymn of praise, sounding and resounding to the limits of the firmament. [*Sounds of music.*] It is my work that living things increase and multiply, each according to his kind. I have ordained that man shall always beget man, and dog give birth to dog. It is my work that the tides with their innumerable tongues creep up to lap the sand and draw back at the appointed hour. I make the plants grow, and my breath fans round the earth the yellow clouds of pollen. You are not in your own home, intruder; you are a foreign body in the world, like a splinter in flesh, or a poacher in his lordship's forest. For the world is good; I made it according to my will, and I am Goodness. But you, Orestes, you have done evil, the very rocks and stones cry out against you. The Good is everywhere, it is the coolness of the wellspring, the pith of the reed, the grain of flint, the weight of stone. Yes, you will find it even in the heart of fire and light; even your own body plays you false, for it abides perforce by my law. Good is everywhere, in you and about you; sweeping through you like a scythe, crushing you like a mountain. Like an ocean it buoys you up and rocks you to and fro, and it enabled the success of your evil plan, for it was in the brightness of the torches, the temper of your blade, the strength of your right arm. And that of which you are so vain, the Evil that you think is your creation, what is it but a reflection in a mocking mirror, a phantom thing that would have no being but for Goodness. No, Orestes, return to your saner self; the universe refutes you, you are a mite in the scheme of things. Return to Nature, Nature's thankless son. Know your sin, abhor it, and tear it from you as one tears out a rotten, noisome tooth. Or else—beware lest the very seas shrink back at your approach, springs dry up when you pass by, stones and rocks roll from your path, and the earth crumbles under your feet.

ORESTES: Let it crumble! Let the rocks revile me, and flowers wilt at my coming. Your whole universe is not enough to prove me wrong. You are the king of gods, king of stones and stars, king of the waves of the sea. But you are not the king of man.

[*The walls draw together.* ZEUS *comes into view, tired and dejected, and he now speaks in his normal voice.*]

ZEUS: Impudent spawn! So I am not your king? Who, then, made you?

ORESTES: You. But you blundered; you should not have made me free.

ZEUS: I gave you freedom so that you might serve me.

ORESTES: Perhaps. But now it has turned against its giver. And neither you nor I can undo what has been done.

ZEUS: Ah, at last! So this is your excuse?

ORESTES: I am not excusing myself.

ZEUS: No? Let me tell you it sounds much like an excuse, this freedom whose slave you claim to be.

ORESTES: Neither slave nor master. I *am* my freedom. No sooner had you created me than I ceased to be yours.

ELECTRA: Oh, Orestes! By all you hold most holy, by our father's memory, I beg you do not add blasphemy to your crime!

ZEUS: Mark her words, young man. And hope no more to win her back by arguments like these. Such language is somewhat new to her ears—and somewhat shocking.

ORESTES: To my ears, too. And to my lungs, which breathe the words, and to my tongue, which shapes them. In fact, I can hardly understand myself. Only yesterday you were still a veil on my eyes, a clot of wax in my ears; yesterday, indeed, I had an excuse. *You* were my excuse for being alive, for you had put me in the world to fulfill your purpose, and the world was an old pander prating to me about your goodness, day in, day out. And then you forsook me.

ZEUS: *I* forsook you? How?

ORESTES: Yesterday, when I was with Electra, I felt at one with Nature, this Nature of your making. It sang the praises of Good—*your* Good—in siren tones, and lavished intimations. To lull me into gentleness, the fierce light mellowed and grew tender as a lover's eyes. And, to teach me the forgiveness of offenses, the sky grew bland as a pardoner's face. Obedient to your will, my youth rose up before me and pleaded with me like a girl who fears her lover will forsake her. That was the last time, the last, I saw my youth. Suddenly, out of the blue, freedom crashed down on me and swept me off my feet. Nature sprang back, my youth went with the wind, and I knew myself alone, utterly alone in the midst of this well-meaning little universe of yours. I was like a man who's lost his shadow. And there was nothing left in heaven, no right or wrong, nor anyone to give me orders.

ZEUS: What of it? Do you want me to admire a scabby sheep that has to be kept apart; or the leper mewed in a lazar-house? Remember, Orestes, you once were of my flock, you fed in my pastures among my sheep. Your vaunted freedom isolates you from the fold; it means exile.

ORESTES: Yes, exile.

ZEUS: But the disease can't be deeply rooted yet; it began only yesterday. Come back to the fold. Think of your loneliness; even your sister is forsaking you. Your eyes are big with anguish, your face is pale and drawn. The disease you're suffering from is inhuman, foreign to my nature, foreign to yourself. Come back. I am forgetfulness, I am peace.

ORESTES: Foreign to myself—I know it. Outside nature, against nature, without excuse, beyond remedy, except what remedy I find within myself. But I shall not return under your law; I am doomed to have no other law but mine. Nor shall I come back to nature, the nature you found good; in it are a thousand beaten paths all leading up to you—but I must blaze my trail. For I, Zeus, am a man, and every man must find out his own way. Nature abhors man, and you too, god of gods, abhor mankind.

ZEUS: That is true; men like you I hold in abhorrence.

ORESTES: Take care; those words were a confession of your weakness. As for me, I do not hate you. What have I to do with you, or you with me? We shall glide past each other, like ships in a river, without touching. You are God and I am free; each of us is alone, and our anguish is akin. How can you know I did not try to feel remorse in the long night that has gone by? And to sleep? But no longer can I feel remorse, and I can sleep no more.

[*A short silence.*]

ZEUS: What do you propose to do?

ORESTES: The folk of Argos are my folk. I must open their eyes.

ZEUS: Poor people! Your gift to them will be a sad one; of loneliness and shame. You will tear from their eyes the veils I had laid on them, and they will see their lives as they are, foul and futile, a barren boon.

ORESTES: Why, since it is their lot, should I deny them the despair I have in me?

ZEUS: What will they make of it?

ORESTES: What they choose. They're free; and human life begins on the far side of despair. . . .

BASIC EXISTENTIALIST CONCEPTS:

Freedom Sartre's equation of existence and freedom is the key to his claim that human beings have a special kind of reality—existence—that distinguishes them from nonhuman things. Existence involves *freedom* of thought and action: Both our ability to be self-conscious and our ability to launch ourselves into action are aspects of human freedom.

Our freedom of thought is most manifest in the way each individual is free to interpret herself and her actions. Someone could decide to ignore certain actions she committed in the past when she thinks about who she is; or she could decide to obsess about these same actions; or she could decide to consider the actions as ingredients, balanced by her other actions, of who she is.

Our freedom of action is the ability to choose an action and to act on our choice. Admittedly, there are circumstances that restrict what we are capable of doing, but each individual is still the director of the actions she performs rather than the puppet who undergoes these actions. Existentialists do not believe in the causal determinism of human actions.

These two aspects of freedom are closely connected in Sartre's existentialism because our self-consciousness is not only awareness of who I am but also of who I shall be; my future self, the one who will result from my future actions, is as much a part of who I am as my past self. Because existence precedes essence, my future self is not already made or programmed to turn out in a specific way; instead, it will be my free creation. Sartre's emphasis on freedom is not a recommendation that we do whatever we feel like doing, whenever we feel like it. He does not recommend acting on personal whim. Instead, Sartre's philosophical writings develop the idea of freedom as autonomy, which is the ability to guide and govern oneself by freely adopting principles or maxims. Autonomy is the freedom of being a self-legislator—someone who creates and follows laws governing one's own actions.

Responsibility Because we are free and create our own individual essence through our actions, we are also responsible for who we actually become. Freedom and *responsibility* go hand in hand in existentialist theory.

Being free means that no other cause—be it a physical force, an instinct, social conditioning, or God—determines our actions. No other person or force can step in and take control of our conscious actions unless we freely choose to allow it. Consequently, what each of us does depends on our own choice. We are each responsible for our choices and our actions.

Responsibility has two, mutually reinforcing aspects: authorship of one's own actions and authorship of one's own character. Our actions create our essence or individual character. Not only the more enduring facets of our personality—such as our habits, talents, and character flaws—but also the more transient properties—such as our emotions, attitudes, desires, and value judgments—arise from our actions. We are each responsible for who we are as individuals.

Project Sartre introduces the concept of the *project* to account for the originating context of an individual's actions. The project is an individual's most basic choice of who he is in relation to the world. It is both proclamation and propulsion: It proposes a self-made plan for who he will become in the future, and it also commits him to activity.

A project is not simply a goal, but a projection of oneself into the future. It motivates an individual to undertake actions, and it also unites his actions so that they will not be haphazard but will build on one another and coalesce into a single, effective course of action. Orestes' project of being a liberator for the people of Argos is an example of this concept. When he decides on this project, he undertakes actions that help free the people from their guilt. Yet his project of being a liberator means that he takes responsibility not only for his actions but also for becoming the kind of character—a leader—who will change the world through such actions.

Anguish For existentialists, not all truths are known through rational understanding; some are disclosed through an individual's moods. Existential moods, such as anguish and despair, are not simply painful psychological processes that get in the way of understanding oneself and the world: They provide self-reflective evidence about human existence.

Anguish is a mood that reveals to the individual how her freedom makes her responsible for the values embodied in her actions. Anguish is unlike fear, which alerts her to danger in the external world; instead, anguish is anxiety before herself, as she senses that nothing other than her own will makes her choose how to act.

Why is one's own freedom experienced emotionally in such a disturbing way? First, it is because anguish reveals the groundlessness of an individual's choices to her. Her mood shows her that nothing is set, forever unchangeable, in her life: Nothing dictates her choices to her, and nothing forces her into a state of allegiance to her past choices—she can always change her mind about how she wants to live her life.

Second, it is because anguish discloses the intersubjective consequences of each individual's freedom. Nothing other than our own individual will makes us choose and act the ways we do, but we live in the world with others, who respond to the ways we choose and act. According to Sartre, an individual not only establishes what is valuable for herself by choosing which actions to perform, but also sets an example for others, because her actions occur in the public domain. Others regard her actions and may even imitate them, because our human tendency is to fall into conformity to others. Thus an individual's responsibility extends to others, because she not only chooses for herself but also chooses for others insofar as her actions are publicly available as potential examples for others.

Questions for Discussion

1. What do the flies—and, later in the play, the Furies—symbolize? Why are they allied with Zeus?

2. Orestes changes radically from the character he was at the beginning of the play. Does he experience anguish?

3. Why does Orestes experience the abyss of freedom rather than the certitude of divine commands when he interprets Zeus' lightning?

4. Is Orestes' act of killing immoral? Why or why not?

5. How is an individual's freedom related to the freedom of others? Could Orestes be free if he did not also try to free others?

Chapter 4

Albert Camus' The Stranger

Introduction: Existential Estrangement

Albert Camus (1913–1960) was a central figure in the French existentialist movement. Fascinated with the question of how individuals act in the face of the absurd, Camus created several characters who act in ways that run counter to societal expectations. His main characters are not merely individuals who are different from others—they are strangers who are out of place and alienated.

For Camus, we are not at home in the universe but are extraneous to it. The universe has no overall design that marks out a special place for us; no divine architect watches out for us and provides for us. We are stranded in a universe that is not of our own making and that is often intractable and bizarre.

But it is not hostility on the part of nature that makes us strangers in the universe, because nature has so many enjoyable facets—a sparkling sea, the warmth of the sun, a gentle closing of the day in the light of dusk—that make us love our life on earth. Primarily it is the inevitability of death that makes us strangers in the universe. We wish to remain here forever but this possibility is denied us. We are strangers because no one can settle down in this world: Death always comes and takes us much too soon, making all of us "transients" on the move through an all-too-temporary life.

The theme of death making individuals into strangers is sounded early and frequently in Camus' early work *The Stranger*. The novel begins with the death of the main character's mother, reaches its dramatic peak with his act of committing murder, and ends with his fantasies about his own death by execution. The main character, Meursault, is both an orphan abandoned in the universe and a death-row criminal alienated from a society full of suspicion and hatred for those who are different. Orphan and criminal, abandonment and ostracism—these are the extreme conditions of a stranger.

The following excerpt is from the last chapter of *The Stranger*. Meursault awaits his execution after he was found guilty of murder. At his trial, the prosecutor emphasized Meursault's many lapses in conforming to social norms: Meursault did not cry at his mother's funeral; he befriended a neighbor of unsavory character; and he expressed no guilt for his crime, but only frustration at his own mistake. Condemned for his nonconformity as well as for his actual action, Meursault spends his time in prison reflecting upon the "brutal certitude" of death.

Camus' *The Stranger* (Excerpts)[1]

. . . I have just refused, for the third time, to see the prison chaplain. I have nothing to say to him, don't feel like talking—and shall be seeing him quite soon enough, anyway. The only thing that interests me now is the problem of circumventing the machine, learning if the inevitable admits a loophole.

They have moved me to another cell. In this one, lying on my back, I can see the sky, and there is nothing else to see. All my time is spent in watching the slowly changing colors of the sky, as day moves on to night. I put my hands behind my head, gaze up, and wait.

This problem of a loophole obsesses me; I am always wondering if there have been cases of condemned prisoners' escaping from the implacable machinery of justice at the last moment, breaking through the police cordon, vanishing in the nick of time before the guillotine falls. Often and often I blame myself for not having given more attention to accounts of public executions. One should always take an interest in such matters. There's never any knowing what one may come to. Like everyone else I'd read descriptions of executions in the papers. But technical books dealing with this subject must certainly exist; only I'd never felt sufficiently interested to look them up. And in these books I might have found escape stories. Surely they'd have told me that in one case, anyhow, the wheels had stopped; that once, if only once, in that inexorable march of events, chance or luck had played a happy part. Just once! In a way I think that single instance would have satisfied me. My emotion would have done the rest. The papers often talk of "a debt owed to society"—a debt which, according to them, must be paid by the offender. But talk of that sort doesn't touch the imagination. No, the one thing that counted for me was the possibility of making a dash for it and defeating their bloodthirsty rite; of a mad stampede to freedom that would anyhow give me a moment's hope, the gambler's last throw. Naturally, all that "hope" could come to was to be knocked down at the corner of a street or picked off by a bullet in my back. But, all things considered, even this luxury was forbidden me; I was caught in the rattrap irrevocably.

Try as I might, I couldn't stomach this brutal certitude. For really, when one came to think of it, there was a disproportion between the judgment on which it was based and the unalterable sequence of events starting from the moment when that judgment was delivered. The fact that the verdict was read out at eight P.M. rather than at five, the fact that it might have been quite different, that it was given by men who change their underclothes, and was credited to so vague an entity as the "French people"—for that matter, why not to the Chinese or the German people?—all these facts seemed to deprive the court's decision of much of its gravity. Yet I could but recognize that, from the moment the verdict was given, its effects became as cogent, as tangible, as, for example, this wall against which I was lying, pressing my back to it.

When such thoughts crossed my mind, I remembered a story Mother used to tell me about my father. I never set eyes on him. Perhaps the only things I really knew about him were what Mother had told me. One of these was that he'd gone to see a murderer executed. The mere thought of it turned his stom-

1 From *The Stranger* by Albert Camus, translated by Stuart Gilbert. Copyright © 1946 by Alfred Al Knopf, Inc. Reprinted by permission of Alfred A. Knopf, a Division of Random House, Inc.

ach. But he'd seen it through and, on coming home, was violently sick. At the time, I found my father's conduct rather disgusting. But now I understood; it was so natural. How had I failed to recognize that nothing was more important than an execution; that, viewed from one angle, it's the only thing that can genuinely interest a man? And I decided that, if ever I got out of jail, I'd attend every execution that took place. I was unwise, no doubt, even to consider this possibility. For, the moment I'd pictured myself in freedom, standing behind a double rank of policemen—on the right side of the line, so to speak—the mere thought of being an onlooker who comes to see the show, and can go home and vomit afterward, flooded my mind with a wild, absurd exultation. It was a stupid thing to let my imagination run away with me like that; a moment later I had a shivering fit and had to wrap myself closely in my blanket. But my teeth went on chattering; nothing would stop them.

Still, obviously, one can't be sensible all the time. Another equally ridiculous fancy of mine was to frame new laws, altering the penalties. What was wanted, to my mind, was to give the criminal a chance, if only a dog's chance; say, one chance in a thousand. There might be some drug, or combination of drugs, which would kill the patient (I thought of him as "the patient") nine hundred and ninety times in a thousand. That he should know this was, of course, essential. For after taking much thought, calmly, I came to the conclusion that what was wrong about the guillotine was that the condemned man had no chance at all, absolutely none. In fact, the patient's death had been ordained irrevocably. It was a foregone conclusion. If by some fluke the knife didn't do its job, they started again. So it came to this, that—against the grain, no doubt—the condemned man had to hope the apparatus was in good working order! This, I thought, was a flaw in the system; and, on the face of it, my view was sound enough. On the other hand, I had to admit it proved the efficiency of the system. It came to this; the man under sentence was obliged to collaborate mentally, it was in his interest that all should go off without a hitch.

Another thing I had to recognize was that, until now, I'd had wrong ideas on the subject. For some reason I'd always supposed that one had to go up steps and climb on to a scaffold, to be guillotined. Probably that was because of the 1789 Revolution; I mean, what I'd learned about it at school, and the pictures I had seen. Then one morning I remembered a photograph the newspapers had featured on the occasion of the execution of a famous criminal. Actually the apparatus stood on the ground; there was nothing very impressing about it, and it was much narrower than I'd imagined. It struck me as rather odd that picture had escaped my memory until now. What had struck me at the time was the neat appearance of the guillotine; its shining surfaces and finish reminded me of some laboratory instrument. One always has exaggerated ideas about what one doesn't know. Now I had to admit it seemed a very simple process, getting guillotined; the machine is on the same level as the man, and he walks toward it as he steps forward to meet somebody he knows. In a sense, that, too, was disappointing. The business of climbing a scaffold, leaving the world below, so to speak, gave something for a man's imagination to get hold of. But, as it was, the machine dominated everything; they killed you discreetly, with a hint of shame and much efficiency.

There were two other things about which I was always thinking: the dawn and my appeal. However, I did my best to keep my mind off these thoughts. I lay down, looked up at the sky, and forced myself to study it. When the light began to turn green I knew that night was coming. Another thing I did to deflect the course of my thoughts was to listen to my heart. I couldn't imagine that this faint throbbing which had been with me for so long would ever cease. Imagination has never been one of my strong points. Still, I tried to picture a moment when the beating of my heart no longer echoed in my head. But, in vain. The dawn and my appeal were still there. And I ended by believing it was a silly thing to try to force one's thoughts out of their natural groove.

They always came for one at dawn; that much I knew. So, really, all my nights were spent in waiting for that dawn. I have never liked being taken by surprise. When something happens to me I want to be ready for it. That's why I got into the habit of sleeping off and on in the daytime and watching through the night for the first hint of daybreak in the dark dome above. The worst period of the night was that vague hour when, I knew, they usually come; once it was after midnight I waited, listening intently. Never before had my ears perceived so many noises, such tiny sounds. Still, I must say I was lucky in one respect; never during any of those periods did I hear footsteps. Mother used to say that however miserable one is, there's always something to be thankful for. And each morning, when the sky brightened and light began to flood my cell, I agreed with her. Because I might just as well have heard footsteps, and felt my heart shattered into bits. Even though the faintest rustle sent me hurrying to the door and, pressing an ear to the rough, cold wood, I listened so intently that I could hear my breathing, quick and hoarse like a dog's panting—even so there was an end; my heart hadn't split, and I knew I had another twenty-four hours' respite.

Then all day there was my appeal to think about. I made the most of this idea, studying my effects so as to squeeze out the maximum of consolation. Thus, I always began by assuming the worst; my appeal was dismissed. That meant, of course, I was to die. Sooner than others, obviously. "But," I reminded myself, "it's common knowledge that life isn't worth living, anyhow." And, on a wide view, I could see that it makes little difference whether one dies at the age of thirty or threescore and ten—since, in either case, other men and women will continue living, the world will go on as before. Also, whether I died now or forty years hence, this business of dying had to be got through, inevitably. Still, somehow this line of thought wasn't as consoling as it should have been; the idea of all those years of life in hand was a galling reminder! However, I could argue myself out of it, by picturing what would have been my feelings when my term was up, and death had cornered me. Once you're up against it, the precise manner of your death has obviously small importance. Therefore—but it was hard not to lose the thread of the argument leading up to that "therefore"—I should be prepared to face the dismissal of my appeal.

At this stage, but only at this stage, I had, so to speak, the *right*, and accordingly I gave myself leave, to consider the other alternative; that my appeal was successful. And then the trouble was to calm down that sudden rush of joy racing through my body and even bringing tears to my eyes. But it was up to me to bring my nerves to heel and steady my mind; for, even in considering this possibility, I had to keep some order in my thoughts, so as to make my consolations, as regards the first alternative, more plausible. When I'd succeeded, I had earned a good hour's peace of mind; and that, anyhow, was something.

It was at one of these moments that I refused once again to see the chaplain. I was lying down and could mark the summer evening coming on by a soft golden glow spreading across the sky. I had just turned down my appeal, and felt my blood circulating with slow, steady throbs. No, I didn't want to see the chaplain. . . .Then I did something I hadn't done for quite a while; I fell to thinking about Marie. She hadn't written for ages; probably, I surmised, she had grown tired of being the mistress of a man sentenced to death. Or she might be ill, or dead. After all, such things happen. How could I have known about it, since, apart from our two bodies, separated now, there was no link between us, nothing to remind us of each other? Supposing she were dead, her memory would mean nothing; I couldn't feel an interest in a dead girl. This seemed to me quite normal; just as I realized people would soon forget me once I was dead. I couldn't even say that this was hard to stomach; really, there's no idea to which one doesn't get acclimatized in time.

My thoughts had reached this point when the chaplain walked in, unannounced. I couldn't help giving a start on seeing him. He noticed this evidently, as he promptly told me not to be alarmed. I reminded him that usually his visits were at another hour, and for a pretty grim occasion. This, he replied, was just a friendly visit; it had no concern with my appeal, about which he knew nothing. Then he sat down on my bed, asking me to sit beside him. I refused—not because I had anything against him; he seemed a mild, amiable man.

He remained quite still at first, his arms resting on his knees, his eyes fixed on his hands. They were slender but sinewy hands, which made me think of two nimble little animals. Then he gently rubbed them together. He stayed so long in the same position that for a while I almost forgot he was there.

All of a sudden he jerked his head up and looked me in the eyes.

"Why," he asked, "don't you let me come to see you?"

I explained that I didn't believe in God.

"Are you really so sure of that?"

I said I saw no point in troubling my head about the matter; whether I believed or didn't was, to my mind, a question of so little importance.

He then leaned back against the wall, laying his hands flat on his thighs. Almost without seeming to address me, he remarked that he'd often noticed one fancies one is quite sure about something, when in point of fact one isn't. When I said nothing, he looked at me again, and asked:

"Don't you agree?"

I said that seemed quite possible. But, though I mightn't be so sure about what interested me, I was absolutely sure about what didn't interest me. And the question he had raised didn't interest me at all.

He looked away and, without altering his posture, asked if it was because I felt utterly desperate that I spoke like this. I explained that it wasn't despair I felt, but fear—which was natural enough.

"In that case," he said firmly, "God can help you. All the men I've seen in your position turned to Him in their time of trouble."

Obviously, I replied, they were at liberty to do so, if they felt like it. I, however, didn't want to be helped, and I hadn't time to work up interest for something that didn't interest me.

He fluttered his hands fretfully; then, sitting up, smoothed out his cassock. When this was done he began talking again, addressing me as "my friend." It wasn't because I'd been condemned to death, he said, that he spoke to me in this way. In his opinion, every man on the earth was under sentence of death.

There, I interrupted him; that wasn't the same thing, I pointed out, and, what's more, could be no consolation.

He nodded. "Maybe. Still, if you don't die soon, you'll die one day. And then the same question will arise. How will you face that terrible, final hour?"

I replied that I'd face it exactly as I was facing it now.

Thereat he stood up, and looked me straight in the eyes. It was a trick I knew well. I used to amuse myself trying it on Emmanuel and Celeste, and nine times out of ten they'd look away uncomfortably. I could see the chaplain was an old hand at it, as his gaze never faltered. And his voice was quite steady when he said: "Have you no hope at all? Do you really think that when you die you die outright, and nothing remains?"

I said: "Yes."

He dropped his eyes and sat down again. He was truly sorry for me, he said. It must make life unbearable for a man, to think as I did.

The priest was beginning to bore me, and, resting a shoulder on the wall, just beneath the little skylight, I looked away. Though I didn't trouble much to follow what he said, I gathered he was questioning me again. Presently his tone became agitated, urgent, and, as I realized that he was genuinely distressed, I began to pay more attention.

He said he felt convinced my appeal would succeed, but I was saddled with a load of guilt, of which I must get rid. In his view man's justice was a vain thing; only God's justice mattered. I pointed out that the former had condemned me. Yes, he agreed, but it hadn't absolved me from my sin. I told him that I wasn't conscious of any "sin"; all I knew was that I'd been guilty of a criminal offense. Well, I was paying the penalty of that offense, and no one had the right to expect anything more of me.

Just then he got up again, and it struck me that if he wanted to move in this tiny cell, almost the only choice lay between standing up and sitting down. I was staring at the floor. He took a single step toward me, and halted, as if he didn't dare to come nearer. Then he looked up through the bars at the sky.

"You're mistaken, my son," he said gravely. "There's more that might be required of you. And perhaps it *will* be required of you.

"What do you mean?"

"You might be asked to see . . ."

"To see what?"

Slowly the priest gazed round my cell, and I was struck by the sadness of his voice when he replied:

"These stone walls. I know it only too well, are steeped in human suffering. I've never been able to look at them without a shudder. And yet—believe me, I am speaking from the depths of my heart—I *know* that even the wretchedest amongst you have sometimes seen, taking form against that grayness, a divine face. It's that face you are asked to see."

This roused me a little. I informed him that I'd been staring at those walls for months; there was nobody, nothing in the world, I knew better than I knew them. And once upon a time; perhaps, I used to try to see a face. But it was a sun-gold face, lit up with desire—Marie's face. I had no luck; I'd never seen it, and now I'd given up trying. Indeed, I'd never seen anything "taking form," as he called it, against those gray walls.

The chaplain gazed at me with a sort of sadness. I now had my back to the wall and light was flowing over my forehead. He muttered some words I didn't catch; then abruptly asked if he might kiss me. I said, "No." Then he turned, came up to the wall, and slowly drew his hand along it.

"Do you really love these earthly things so very much?" he asked in a low voice.

I made no reply.

For quite a while he kept his eyes averted. His presence was getting more and more irksome, and I was on the point of telling him to go, and leave me in peace, when all of a sudden he swung round on me, and burst out passionately:

"No! No! I refuse to believe it. I'm sure you've often wished there was an afterlife."

Of course I had, I told him. Everybody has that wish at times. But that had no more importance than wishing to be rich, or to swim very fast, or to have a better-shaped mouth. It was in the same order of things. I was going on in the same vein, when he cut in with a question. How did I picture the life after the grave?

I fairly bawled out at him: "A life in which I can remember this life on earth. That's all I want of it." And in the same breath I told him I'd had enough of his company.

But, apparently, he had more to say on the subject of God. I went close up to him and made a last attempt to explain that I'd very little time left, and I wasn't going to waste it on God.

Then he tried to change the subject by asking me why I hadn't once addressed him as "Father," seeing that he was a priest. That irritated me still more, and I told him he wasn't my father; quite the contrary, he was on the others' side.

"No, no, my son," he said, laying his hand on my shoulder. "I'm on *your* side, though you don't realize it—because your heart is hardened. But I shall pray for you."

Then, I don't know how it was, but something seemed to break inside me, and I started yelling at the top of my voice. I hurled insults at him, I told him not to waste his rotten prayers on me; it was better to burn than to disappear. I'd taken him by the neckband of his cassock, and, in a sort of ecstasy of joy and rage, I poured out on him all the thoughts that had been simmering in my brain. He seemed so cocksure, you see. And yet none of his certainties was worth one strand of a woman's hair. Living as he did, like a corpse, he couldn't even be sure of being alive. It might look as if my hands were empty. Actually, I was sure of myself, sure about everything, far surer than he; sure of my present life and of the death that was coming. That, no doubt, was all I had; but at least that certainty was something I could get my teeth into—just as it had got its teeth into me. I'd been right, I was still right, I was always right. I'd passed my life in a certain way, and I might have passed it in a different way, if I'd felt like it. I'd acted thus, and I hadn't acted otherwise; I hadn't done *x*, whereas I had done *y* or *z*. And what did that mean? That, all the time, I'd been waiting for this present moment, for that dawn, tomorrow's or another day's, which was to justify me. Nothing, nothing had the least importance, and I knew quite well why. He, too, knew why. From the dark horizon of my future a sort of slow, persistent breeze had been blowing toward me, all my life long, from the years that were to come. And on its way that breeze had levelled out all the ideas that people tried to foist on me in the equally unreal years I then was living through. What difference could they make to me, the deaths of others, or a mother's love, or his God; or the way a man decides to live, the fate he thinks he chooses, since one and the same fate was bound to "choose" not only me but thousands of millions of privileged people who, like him, called themselves my brothers. Surely, surely he must see that? Every man alive was privileged; there was only one class of men, the privileged class. All alike would be condemned to die one day; his turn, too, would come like the others'. And what difference could it make if, after being charged with murder, he were executed because he didn't weep at his mother's funeral, since it all came to the same thing in the end? . . .

I had been shouting so much that I'd lost my breath, and just then the jailers rushed in and started trying to release the chaplain from my grip. One of them made as if to strike me. The chaplain quietened them down, then gazed at me for a moment without speaking. I could see tears in his eyes. Then he turned and left the cell.

Once he'd gone, I felt calm again. But all this excitement had exhausted me and I dropped heavily on to my sleeping plank. I must have had a longish sleep, for, when I woke, the stars were shining down on my face. Sounds of the countryside came faintly in, and cool night air, veined with smells of earth and salt, fanned my cheeks. The marvelous peace of the sleepbound summer night flooded through me like a tide. Then, just on the edge of daybreak, I heard a steamer's siren. People were starting on a voyage to a world which had ceased to concern me forever. Almost for the first time in many months I thought of my mother. And now, it seemed to me, I understood why at her life's end she had taken on a "fiancé"; why she'd played at making a fresh start. There, too, in that Home where lives were flickering out, the dusk came as a mournful solace. With death so near, Mother must have felt like someone on the brink of freedom, ready to start life all over again. No one, no one in the world had any right to weep for her. And I, too, felt ready to start life all over again. It was as if that great rush of anger had washed me clean, emptied me of hope, and, gazing up at the dark sky spangled with its signs and stars, for the first time, the first, I laid my heart open to the benign indifference of the universe. To feel it so like myself, indeed, so brotherly, made me realize that I'd been happy, and that I was happy still. For all to be accomplished, for me to feel less lonely, all that remained to hope was that on the day of my execution there should be a huge crowd of spectators and that they should greet me with howls of execration.

Basic Existentialist Concepts

Alienation Existentialists inherited the concept of alienation from the nineteenth-century philosophers Hegel and Marx, but they converted it into a more personal sense of feeling separated and alone. Existential *alienation* is felt in at least three ways: as alienation from nature, alienation from others, and alienation from the continuance of life.

Feeling distant from nature, an individual fails to understand the world into which he is thrown. Scientific accounts of natural processes do not forge a real sense of kinship with nature or a confident belief that the world is a logically ordered domain. Instead, the world often appears hostile to human interests and often seems incomprehensible by human faculties. In *The Stranger*, Meursault is alienated from nature because it contains irrational, invasive, and irresistible forces over which he has no control. He moves through the world surprised by unexpected happenings. For example, when he pulls the trigger and shoots a man on the beach, he is so surprised by the event that it seems to him to have been caused by forces beyond his control—the heat pouring down from the sky, the blinding light reflected off the other man's knife blade.

The second sense of alienation, alienation from others, occurs because even though we live among others, we do not have access to one another's inner thoughts and feelings. Our individual freedom also creates differences between what we and what others find meaningful in the world. Meursault, for example, is frequently misunderstood by others, despite his success at his job and his involvement in friendships and a romantic relationship. Even more significantly, Meursault simply does not conform to societal norms of appropriate behavior. His alienation from others has disastrous consequences at his trial, where he is condemned to death—not for killing—but for failing to behave in socially acceptable ways at his mother's funeral.

The third meaning of existential alienation is the most important of all in Camus' view because it is fundamental to absurdity: In a world shaped by death, everyone is a stranger. The universe is indifferent to whether we are born or whether we die; its "benign indifference" is the typical attitude taken toward strangers—an attitude of not caring one way or the other. Thus we are alienated from life itself, from the life that we wish would continue eternally, because death is our master.

Authenticity Many existentialist philosophers criticized our tendency to settle into a life dictated by the prevailing opinions and values of the majority. (For example, Kierkegaard inveighed against "the public," Nietzsche against "the herd," and Heidegger against "the they.") Falling under the influence of mass opinion, we become inauthentic because we neither seek nor create what is most meaningful to us as individuals. When we live the way that everyone else does, think the way that everyone else thinks, and hold the same values that everyone else holds, we do not use our freedom to create ourselves as unique individuals; instead we become slaves to a communal standard that, more often than not, is mediocre and repressive.

In contrast, *authenticity* is being true to oneself as a free individual. It involves fully acknowledging one's own freedom and decisiveness in undertaking the particular actions that go into the creation of one's own essence. When we are authentic, we resolve to be what we freely choose to be; we make manifest what is truly important to ourselves as we act in the world. Authenticity is not always an easy way to live (it is quite rare, according to most existentialists); but it brings out the uniqueness of an individual and his or her deepest values.

In *The Stranger*, Camus' Meursault does not conform to societal norms, speaks truthfully about his own preferences and feelings, takes responsibility for his actions, and, even more importantly, understands the decisiveness of his own death. His idiosyncratic approach to life makes him a misfit, a stranger, in his society, but it also makes him authentic. He chooses to live in a way that is true to himself rather than lose himself in the crowd.

Questions for Discussion

1. Do we all seek a "loophole" from death in the way that Meursault sought a "loophole" from his execution? Do we all receive the death penalty?

2. If there is no afterlife, and this is the only life we have, does death then make our life meaningless?

3. How does intensified awareness of the inevitability of our death and of our alienation in the universe affect us? Why does Meursault feel happy at the end?

4. Do society's rituals for death mask our basic feelings about death?

5. Does religion distract us from our fear of death?

Chapter 5

Albert Camus' "The Myth of Sisyphus"

Introduction: The Absurd Hero

Among the heroes and heroines of existential literature is a particular kind of champion, one who may not succeed in a worldly way but may nonetheless succeed in advancing the cause of freedom. This is the absurd hero, who is characterized by Camus as someone who maintains full awareness of the absurdity of her life by rebelling against the forces that diminish freedom. Among these forces are death and religion. While knowing full well that there is no escape from death, the absurd hero rebels against death because death not only negates all actions and accomplishments that have been undertaken with freedom, but also negates all of the pleasures of life, such as swimming in the sea or watching a sunset. The absurd hero rebels against religion because it limits the individual's freedom, either with its standards of what is good and evil or with its presentation of a divine being who has power over human beings.

The absurd hero is epitomized by Camus' Sisyphus, who endures an absurd life that has been narrowed down to endless labor without results. What makes Sisyphus a hero is that he uses what freedom he has left to rebel against all restrictions on his freedom. Sisyphus' scorn for the gods, hatred of death, and passion for life form the heart of his revolt. His rebel spirit succeeds in overcoming the conditions and forces that make his life absurd because he is not only conscious of them, but also sneers at them.

Camus' "The Myth of Sisyphus (Excerpt)"[1]

The gods had condemned Sisyphus to ceaselessly rolling a rock to the top of a mountain, whence the stone would fall back of its own weight. They had thought with some reason that there is no more dreadful punishment than futile and hopeless labor.

If one believes Homer, Sisyphus was the wisest and most prudent of mortals. According to another tradition, however, he was disposed to practice the profession of highwayman. I see no contradiction in this. Opinions differ as to the reasons why he became the futile laborer of the

1 From *The Myth of Sisyphus and Other Essays* by Albert Camus, translated by Justin O'Brien.

underworld. To begin with, he is accused of a certain levity in regard to the gods. He stole their secrets. Aegina, the daughter of Aesopus, was carried off by Jupiter. The father was shocked by that disappearance and complained to Sisyphus. He, who knew of the abduction, offered to tell about it on condition that Aesopus would give water to the citadel of Corinth. To the celestial thunderbolts he preferred the benediction of water. He was punished for this in the underworld. Homer tells us also that Sisyphus had put Death in chains. Pluto could not endure the sight of his deserted, silent empire. He dispatched the god of war, who liberated Death from the hands of her conqueror.

It is said also that Sisyphus, being near to death, rashly wanted to test his wife's love. He ordered her to cast his unburied body into the middle of the public square. Sisyphus woke up in the underworld. And there, annoyed by an obedience so contrary to human love, he obtained from Pluto permission to return to earth in order to chastise his wife. But when he had seen again the face of this world, enjoyed water and sun, warm stones and the sea, he no longer wanted to go back to the infernal darkness. Recalls, signs of anger, warnings were of no avail. Many years more he lived facing the curve of the gulf, the sparkling sea, and the smiles of earth. A decree of the gods was necessary. Mercury came and seized the impudent man by the collar and, snatching him from his joys, led him forcibly back to the underworld, where his rock was ready for him.

You have already grasped that Sisyphus is the absurd hero. He *is,* as much through his passions as through his torture. His scorn of the gods, his hatred of death, and his passion for life won him that unspeakable penalty in which the whole being is exerted toward accomplishing nothing. This is the price that must be paid for the passions of this earth. Nothing is told us about Sisyphus in the underworld. Myths are made for the imagination to breathe life into them. As for this myth, one sees merely the whole effort of a body straining to raise the huge stone, to roll it and push it up a slope a hundred times over; one sees the face screwed up, the cheek tight against the stone, the shoulder bracing the clay-covered mass, the foot wedging it, the fresh start with arms outstretched, the wholly human security of two earth-clotted hands. At the very end of his long effort measured by skyless space and time without depth, the purpose is achieved. Then Sisyphus watches the stone rush down in a few moments toward that lower world whence he will have to push it up again toward the summit. He goes back down to the plain.

It is during that return, that pause, that Sisyphus interests me. A face that toils so close to stones is already stone itself! I see that man going back down with a heavy yet measured step toward the torment of which he will never know the end. That hour like a breathing-space which returns as surely as his suffering, that is the hour of consciousness. At each of those moments when he leaves the heights and gradually sinks toward the lairs of the gods, he is superior to his fate. He is stronger than his rock.

If this myth is tragic, that is because its hero is conscious. Where would his torture be, indeed, if at every step the hope of succeeding upheld him? The workman of today works every day in his life at the same tasks, and this fate is no less absurd. But it is tragic only at the rare moments when it becomes conscious. Sisyphus, proletarian of the gods, powerless and rebellious, knows the whole extent of his wretched condition: it is what he thinks of during his descent. The lucidity that was to constitute his torture at the same time crowns his victory. There is no fate that cannot be surmounted by scorn.

If the descent is thus sometimes performed in sorrow, it can also take place in joy. This word is not too much. Again I fancy Sisyphus returning toward his rock, and the sorrow was in the beginning. When the images of earth cling too tightly to memory, when the call of happiness becomes too insistent, it happens that melancholy rises in man's heart: this is the rock's victory, this is the rock itself. The boundless grief is too heavy to bear. These are our nights of Gethsemane. But crushing truths perish from being acknowledged. Thus, Œdipus at the outset obeys fate without knowing it. But from the moment he knows, his tragedy begins. Yet at the same moment, blind and desperate, he realizes that the only bond linking him to the world is the cool hand of a girl. Then a tremendous remark rings out: "Despite so many ordeals, my advanced age and the nobility of my soul make me conclude that all is well." Sophocles' Œdipus, like Dostoevsky's Kirilov, thus gives the recipe for the absurd victory. Ancient wisdom confirms modern heroism.

One does not discover the absurd without being tempted to write a manual of happiness. "What! by such narrow ways—?" There is but one world, however. Happiness and the absurd are two sons of the same earth. They are inseparable. It would be a mistake to say that happiness necessarily springs from the absurd discovery. It happens as well that the feeling of the absurd springs from happiness. "I conclude that all is well," says Œdipus, and that remark is sacred. It echoes in the wild and limited universe of man. It teaches that all is not, has not been, exhausted. It drives out of this world a god who had come into it with dissatisfaction and a preference for futile sufferings. It makes of fate a human matter, which must be settled among men.

All Sisyphus' silent joy is contained therein. His fate belongs to him. His rock is his thing. Likewise, the absurd man, when he contemplates his torment, silences all the idols. In the universe suddenly restored to its silence, the myriad wondering little voices of the earth rise up. Unconscious, secret calls, invitations from all the faces, they are the necessary reverse and price of victory. There is no sun without shadow, and it is essential to know the night. The absurd man says yes and his effort will henceforth be unceasing. If there is a personal fate, there is no higher destiny, or at least there is but one which he concludes is inevitable and despicable. For the rest, he knows himself to be the master of his days. At that subtle moment when man glances backward over his life, Sisyphus returning toward his rock, in that slight pivoting he contemplates that series of unrelated actions which becomes his fate, created by him, combined under his memory's eye and soon sealed by his death. Thus, convinced of the wholly human origin of all that is human, a blind man eager to see who knows that night has no end, he is still on the go. The rock is still rolling.

I leave Sisyphus at the foot of the mountain! One always finds one's burden again. But Sisyphus teaches the higher fidelity that negates the gods and raises rocks. He too concludes that all is well. This universe henceforth without a master seems to him neither sterile nor futile. Each atom of that stone, each mineral flake of that night-filled mountain, in itself forms a world. The struggle itself toward the heights is enough to fill a man's heart. One must imagine Sisyphus happy.

Basic Existentialist Concepts

Absurdity The French existentialists—Camus, Beauvoir, and Sartre—all regard absurdity as a central feature of human life, although they differ somewhat in their conceptions of it. What is the absurd? For all of them, the absurd not only evades our understanding but also undermines whatever we have grown accustomed to; it destabilizes whatever gives us a sense of security. It is like a thief stealing meaning away when we least expect it.

In *Nausea*, Sartre speaks of absurdity as the contingency and superfluity of everything that is real: Everything is *de trop* (overmuch) and *in the way*. No overall, preordained design stipulates that we and others should exist. Even the contents of the natural world are not conscripted into a logically ordered army of rational items. When the root of the chestnut tree becomes unhinged from the names and concepts by which reality is normally apprehended, the brute fact that it exists overflows Roquentin's senses and ability to grasp it.

For Camus, absurdity lies in the irrationality and chaos of the universe, especially in the way that death brings these on in human life. The universe itself is not oriented toward human concerns; it is "benignly indifferent" or even disruptive. Even we humans are not rational, often doing things without knowing why we do them. Evidence for absurdity includes unpredictable "twists of fate," irrational patterns of behavior, and moments of intense sense experience. Such oddities of human life are glimpses of the absurd.

But the main source of absurdity is death, according to Camus. Death makes human aspirations irrational because anything we achieve will be negated by death; death also overturns and destroys everything that we enjoy in life and find meaningful. Death makes every individual's life absurd because it is like a "dark wind" blowing from the future that levels down everything we accomplish in our lifetimes and everything we consider important. As Meursault argues in *The Stranger*, whether an individual is a great success or a criminal, a saint or a sinner, smart or dumb, rich or poor, death equalizes all individuals' lives to the same level: nothingness. No one escapes death, so what does it matter how an individual spends his or her life? It all comes to the same in the end.

Questions for Discussion

1. Why is Sisyphus' task of rolling the rock up the mountain absurd?

2. What are the passions that make Sisyphus an absurd hero?

3. Is there absurdity without consciousness? Can someone live an absurd life without being conscious of the absurdity of his or her life?

4. Is Sisyphus a successful rebel?

5. How does a religious conception of the world differ from Camus' conception of absurdity?

Chapter 6

Simone de Beauvoir's A Very Easy Death

Introduction: Autobiographical Consciousness

Simone de Beauvoir (1908–1986) is one of the most famous women philosophers of the twentieth century. The wide range of her writings includes the groundbreaking feminist treatise *The Second Sex*, philosophical works such as *The Ethics of Ambiguity*, novels that are expressive of existentialist concerns, literary and political essays, and, finally, autobiographical writings in which she reflects on the phases of her own life.

Like other existentialists, Beauvoir believed that human existence is an issue for each individual, as each questions herself about the meaning of her life. We do not simply persist alongside rocks and trees without ever asking, "Why am I alive?" or "How should I lead my life?" Instead, each of us wonders why we are here and what we are doing with our lives. This questioning of our own individual existence is not coincidental but is actually central to existing as a human being.

Autobiographical consciousness captures this inquiry into the meaning of one's own existence in a firsthand way. Because autobiographical consciousness is personal awareness of one's own life and reflection on the most important issues one faces, it inevitably raises the question of the meaning of one's own being. Beauvoir pursues this kind of autobiographical questioning in many of her works. In *A Very Easy Death*, she describes her own feelings and actions as her mother lay dying. Beauvoir recounts stories from her mother's and her own childhoods; she reports the emotional outbursts, confusions, and reconciliations that occur within the family around the deathbed; she details the physical processes of her mother's rotting, disintegrating flesh. As she focuses on what her mother seems to be going through, she also confronts her own feelings about the dying process—concluding that it was not an easy death for either of them.

Beauvoir's *A Very Easy Death* (Excerpts)[1]

At four o'clock in the afternoon of Thursday, 24 October 1963, I was in Rome, in my room at the Hotel Minerva; I was to fly home the next day and I was putting papers away when the telephone rang. It was Bost calling me from Paris: "Your mother has had an accident," he said. I thought: she has been knocked down by a car; she was climbing laboriously from the roadway to the pavement, leaning on her stick, and a car knocked her down. "She had a fall in the bathroom: she has broken the neck of her femur," said Bost. He lived in the same building as my mother. About ten o'clock the evening before, he had been going up the stairs with Olga, and they noticed three people ahead of them—a woman and two policemen. "It's the landing above the second floor," the woman was saying. Had something happened to Madame de Beauvoir? Yes. A fall. For two hours she had crawled across the floor before she could reach the telephone; she had asked a friend, Madame Tardieu, to have the door forced open. Bost and Olga followed them up to the flat. They found Maman lying on the floor in her red corduroy dressing-gown. Dr Lacroix, a woman doctor who was living in the house, diagnosed a fracture of the neck of the femur: Maman had been taken away by the emergency service of the Boucicaut hospital and she spent the night in the public ward. "But I'm taking her to the C nursing home," Bost told me. "That's where Professor B operates—he's one of the best bone surgeons. She was against it; she was afraid it would cost you too much. But I persuaded her in the end."

Poor Maman! I had lunched with her when I came back from Moscow five weeks before; she looked poorly, as usual. There had been a time, not very long ago, when she took pleasure in the thought that she did not look her age; now there could no longer be any mistake about it—she was a woman of seventy-seven, quite worn out. The arthritis in her hips, which had first appeared after the war, had grown worse year by year, in spite of massage and cures at Aix-les-Bains; it took her an hour to make her way round one block of houses. She had a good deal of pain and she slept badly in spite of the six aspirins she took every day. For the last two or three years, and especially since the last winter, I had always seen her with those dark rings round her eyes, her face thin and a pinched look about her nose. It was nothing serious, said D, her doctor—an upset liver and sluggish bowels. He prescribed some drugs; tamarind jelly for constipation. That day I had not been surprised at her feeling poorly. . . .

At about six o'clock I telephoned her at the nursing home. I told her that I was coming to see her. She answered in a wavering, doubtful voice. Professor B took over the telephone: he was going to operate on Saturday morning.

"You haven't written me a letter for two months!" she said, as I came towards her bed. I protested: we had seen each other; I had sent her a letter from Rome. She listened to me with an air of disbelief. Her forehead and hands were burning hot; her mouth was slightly twisted, she had difficulty in articulating and her mind was confused. Was this the effect of shock? Or had her fall been caused by a slight stroke? She had always had a nervous tic. (No, not always, but for a long while. Since when?) . . .

Professor B came to see her at the end of the day and I followed him into the corridor. Once she had recovered, he said, my mother would walk no worse than before. "She will be able to potter around again." Did he think she had had a fainting-fit? Not at all. He seemed disconcerted when I told him that her bowels had been giving her trouble. The Boucicat had reported a broken neck of the femur and he

[1] From *A Very Easy Death*, by Simone de Beauvoir, translated by Patrick O'Brien.

had confined himself to that: he would have her examined by a physician. . . .

"I have not slept so well for ages," she said to me on Monday. She had her normal look again; her voice was clear and her eyes were taking notice of the things around her. "Dr Lacroix ought to be sent some flowers." I promised to see to it. "And what about the policemen? Shouldn't they be given something? I put them to great trouble." I found it hard to convince her that it was not called for.

She leaned back against her pillows, looked straight at me and said very firmly, "I have been overdoing it, you know. I tired myself out—I was at the end of my tether. I would not admit that I was old. But one must face up to things; in a few days I shall be seventy-eight, and that is a great age. I must arrange my life accordingly. I am going to start a fresh chapter."

I gazed at her with admiration. For a great while she had insisted upon considering herself young. Once, when her son-in-law made a clumsy remark, she had crossly replied, "I know very well that I am old, and I don't like it at all: I don't care to be reminded of it." Suddenly, coming out of the fog she had been floating in these three days past, she found the strength to face her seventy-eight years, clear-sighted and determined. "I am going to start a fresh chapter." . . .

"I saw too many people yesterday, and they tired me," she told me on Sunday. She was in a bad mood. Her usual nurses were off duty; an inexperienced girl had upset the bed-pan full of urine; the bed and even the bolster had been soaked. She closed her eyes often, and her recollection was confused. Dr T could not make out the plates that Dr D had sent and the next day there was to be a fresh intestinal X-ray. "They will give me a barium enema, and it hurts," Maman told me. "And they are going to shake me about again and trundle me around: I should so like to be left in peace."

I pressed her damp, rather cold hand. "Don't think about it in advance. Don't worry. Worrying is bad for you." . . .

She expected many visitors on Monday and I was busy. I did not come until Tuesday morning. I opened the door and stopped dead. Maman, who was so thin, seemed to have grown still thinner and more shrivelled, wizened, dried up, a pinkish twig. In a somewhat bewildered voice she whispered, "They have dried me out completely." She had waited until the evening to be X-rayed and for twenty hours on end they had not allowed her to drink. The barium enema had not hurt; but the thirst and the anxiety had quite worn her out. Her face had dissolved: she was tense with unhappiness. What was the result of the X-rays? "We can't understand them," the nurses replied in frightened voices. I managed to see Dr T. The information the plates gave was still obscure: according to him there was no "pocket," but the bowel was contorted by spasms, nervous in origin, which had prevented it from working since the day before. My mother was obstinately sanguine; but for all that she was anxious and highly-strung—that was the explanation of her tics. She was too exhausted to see visitors and she asked me to telephone Father P, her confessor, and put him off. She scarcely spoke to me, and she could not manage a smile.

"I'll see you tomorrow evening," I said as I left. My sister was arriving during the night and she would go to the clinic in the morning. At nine in the evening my telephone rang. It was Professor B. "I should like to have a nightnurse for your mother: do you agree? She is not well. You thought of not coming until tomorrow evening; it would be better to be there in the morning." In the end he told me that there was a tumour blocking the small intestine: Maman had cancer.

Cancer. It was all about us. Indeed, it was patently obvious—those ringed eyes, that thinness. But her doctor had ruled out that hypothesis. And it is notorious that the parents are the last to admit that their son is mad; the children that their mother has cancer. We believed it all the less since that was what she had been afraid of all her life. When she was forty, if she knocked her chest against a piece of furniture she grew terribly frightened—"I shall have cancer of the breast." Last winter one of my friends had been operated upon for cancer of the stomach. "That is what is going to happen to me, too." I had shrugged: there is a very wide difference between cancer and a sluggishness of the bowels that is treated with tamarind jelly. We never imagined that Maman's obsession could possibly be justified. Yet—she told us this later—it was cancer that Francine Diato thought of: "I recognized that expression. And," she added, "that smell, too." Everything became clear. Maman's sudden illness in Alsace arose from her tumour. The tumour had caused her fainting-fit and her fall. And these two weeks of bed had brought on the blockage of the intestine that had been threatening for a long while.

. . . At about ten I met [my sister] Poupette outside the door of room 114. I repeated what Dr B had said. She told me that since the beginning of the morning a resuscitation expert, Dr N, had been working on Maman: he was going to put a tube into her nose to clean out her stomach. "But what's the good of tormenting her, if she is dying? Let her die in peace," said Poupette, in tears. I sent her down to Bost, who was waiting in the hall: he would take her to have some coffee. Dr N passed by me; I stopped him. White coat, white cap: a young man with an unresponsive face. "Why this tube? Why torture Maman, since there's no hope?" He gave me a withering look. "I am doing what has to be done." He opened the door. After a moment a nurse told me to come in.

The bed was back in its ordinary place in the middle of the room with its head against the wall. On the left there was an intravenous dripper, connected with Maman's arm. From her nose there emerged a tube of transparent plastic that passed through some complicated apparatus and ended in a jar. Her nose was pinched and her face had shrunk even more: it had the saddest air of submission. In a whisper she told me that the tube did not worry her too much, but that during the night she had suffered a great deal. She was thirsty and she was not allowed to drink: the nurse put a thin tube to her mouth with the other end in a glass of water; Maman moistened her lips, without swallowing. I was fascinated by the sucking motion, at once avid and restrained, of her lip, with its faint downy shadow, that rounded just as it had rounded in my childhood whenever Maman was cross or embarrassed. "Would you like me to have left that in her stomach?" said N aggressively, showing me the jar full of a yellowish substance. I did not reply. In the corridor he said "At dawn she had scarcely four hours left. I have brought her back to life." I did not venture to ask him "For what?"

Consultation of specialists. My sister at my side while a physician and a surgeon, Dr P, palpate the swollen abdomen. Maman groans under their fingers: she cries out. Morphine injection. She still groans. "Another injection," we beg. They are against it: too much morphine would paralyse the intestine. What are they hoping for then? . . . Are they thinking of operating? That is hardly possible, the surgeon tells me as he leaves the room; the patient is too weak. He walks away, and an elderly nurse, Mme Gontrand, who has heard him, bursts out, "Don't let her be operated on!" Then she claps her hand to her mouth. "If Dr N knew I had said that to you! I was speaking as if it were my own mother." I question her. "What will happen if they do operate on her?" But she has closed up again: she does not answer.

Maman had gone to sleep: I went away, leaving telephone numbers with Poupette. When she called me at Sartre's place at about five there was hope in her voice. "The surgeon wants to try the operation. The blood analyses are very encouraging; her strength has come back, and her heart will stand it. And after all, it is not absolutely sure that it is cancer: perhaps it is just peritonitis. If it is, she has a chance. Do you agree?"

Don't let them operate on her.

"Yes, I agree. When?"

"Be here by two. They will not tell her they are going to operate; they will say they are going to X-ray her again."

"Don't let them operate on her." A frail argument against the decision of a specialist; a frail argument against my sister's hopes. Maman might not wake up again? That was not the worst way out. And I did not imagine that a surgeon would take that risk: she would get over it. Would the operation hasten the development of the disease? No doubt that is what Mme Gontrand had meant. But with the intestinal obstruction at this stage Maman could not survive three days and I was terribly afraid that her death might be appalling.

An hour later the telephone, and Poupette sobbing, "Come at once. They have operated: they found a huge cancerous tumour . . ." Sartre went down with me; he took me in a taxi as far as the nursing-home. My throat was constricted with anguish. A male nurse showed me the lobby between the entrance-hall and the operating-theatre where my sister was waiting. She was so upset that I asked for a tranquillizer for her. She told me that the doctors had warned Maman in a very natural voice, that before X-raying her they would give her a sedative injection; Dr N had put her to sleep; Poupette had held Maman's hand right through the anaesthetizing, and I could imagine what a trial it had been for her, the sight of that old, ravaged body, quite naked—that body which was her mother's. Maman's eyes had turned up; her mouth had opened: Poupette would never be able to forget that face, either. They had wheeled her into the operating-theatre and Dr N had come out a moment later: four pints of pus in the abdomen, the peritoneum burst, a huge tumour, a cancer of the worst kind. The surgeon was removing everything that could be removed. . . .We discussed what we should say to Maman when she woke up. It was easy enough: the X-ray had shown that she had peritonitis and an operation had been decided upon at once.

Maman had just been taken up to her room, N told us. He was triumphant: she had been half-dead that morning and yet she had withstood a long and serious operation excellently. Thanks to the very latest methods of anaesthesia her heart, lungs, the whole organism had continued to function normally. There was no sort of doubt that he entirely washed his hands of the consequences of that feat. My sister had said to the surgeon, "Operate on Maman. But if it is cancer, promise me that you will not let her suffer." He had promised. What was his word worth? . . .

Poupette was living on her nerves. My blood-pressure mounted; a pulse throbbed in my head. What tried us more than anything were Maman's death-agonies, her resurrections, and our own inconsistency. In this race between pain and death we most earnestly hoped that death would come first. Yet when Maman was asleep with her face lifeless, we would anxiously gaze at the white bed-jacket to catch the faint movement of the black ribbon that held her watch: dread of the last spasm gripped us by the throat.

She was well when I left her in the early afternoon of Sunday. On Monday morning her wasted face terrified me; it was terribly obvious, the work of those mysterious colonies between her skin and her bones that were devouring her cells. At ten in the evening Poupette had secretly passed the nurse a piece of paper—"Should I call my sister?" The nurse shook her head: Maman's heart was holding out. But new forms of wretchedness were to come. Madame Gontrand showed me Maman's right side: water dripped from the pores of her skin; the sheet was soaked. She hardly urinated any more and her flesh was puffing up in an oedema. She looked at her hands, and in a puzzled way she moved her swollen fingers. "It is because you have to keep so still," I told her.

Tranquillized by equanil and morphia, she was aware of her sickness, but she accepted it patiently. "One day when I thought I was better already your sister said something that has been very useful to me: she said that I should be unwell again. So I know that it's normal." She saw Madame de Saint-Ange for a moment and said to her, "Oh, now I am coming along very well!" A smile uncovered her gums: already it was the macabre grin of a skeleton; at the same time her eyes shone with a somewhat feverish innocence. She was suddenly unwell after having eaten; I rang and rang for the nurse; what I had wanted was happening; she was dying and it filled me with panic. A tablet brought her round.

In the evening I imagined her dead, and it wrung my heart. "Things are going rather better locally," Poupette told me in the morning, and I regretted it bitterly. Maman was so well that she read a few pages of Simenon. In the night she suffered a great deal. "I hurt all over!" They gave her an injection of morphia. When she opened her eyes during the day they had an unseeing, glassy look and I thought, "This time it is the end." She went to sleep again. I asked N, "Is this the end?"

"Oh, no!" he said in a half-pitying, half triumphant tone, "she has been revived too well for that!"

So it was to be pain that would win? *Finish me off. Give me my revolver. Have pity on me.* She said, "I hurt all over." She moved her swollen fingers anxiously. Her confidence waned: "These doctors are beginning to irritate me. They are always telling me that I am getting better. And I feel myself getting worse."

I had grown very fond of this dying woman. As we talked in the half-darkness I assuaged an old unhappiness; I was renewing the dialogue that had been broken off during my adolescence and that our differences and our likenesses had never allowed us to take up again. And the early tenderness that I had thought dead for ever came to life again, since it had become possible for it to slip into simple words and actions.

I looked at her. She was there, present, conscious, and completely unaware of what she was living through. Not to know what is happening underneath one's skin is normal enough. But for her the outside of her body was unknown—her wounded abdomen, her fistula, the filth that issued from it, the blueness of her skin, the liquid that oozed out of her pores: she could not explore it with her almost paralysed hands, and when they treated her and dressed her wound her head was thrown back. She had not asked for a mirror again: her dying face did not exist for her. She rested and dreamed, infinitely far removed from her rotting flesh, her ears filled with the sound of our lies; her whole person was concentrated upon one passionate hope—getting well. I should have liked to spare her pointless unpleasantness: "You don't have to take this medicine any more." "It would be better to take it." And she gulped down the chalky liquid. She found it difficult to eat: "Don't force yourself: that's enough, don't eat any more." "Do you think so?" She looked at the dish, hesitated, "Give me a little more." In the end I spirited her plate away: "You finished it all up," I said. She compelled herself to swallow yoghourt in the afternoon. She often asked for fruit-juice. She moved her arms a little, and slowly, carefully raised her hands, cupping them together, and gropingly she seized the glass, which I still held. She drew up the beneficent vitamins through the little tube: a ghoul's mouth avidly sucking life.

Her eyes had grown huge in her wasted face; she opened them wide, fixed them; at the cost of an immense effort she wrenched herself from her dim private world to rise to the surface of those pools of dark light; she concentrated her whole being there; she gazed at me with a dramatic immobility—it was as though she had just discovered sight. "I can see you!" Every time she had to win it from the darkness again. By her eyes she clung to the world, as by her nails she clung to the sheet, so that she might not be engulfed. "Live! Live!"

How desolate I was, that Wednesday evening, in the cab that was taking me away! . . .

Friday passed uneventfully. On Saturday Maman slept all the time. "That's splendid," said Poupette to her. "You have rested."

"Today I have not lived," sighed Maman.

A hard task, dying, when one loves life so much. "She may hold out for two or three months," the doctors told us that evening. So we had to organize our lives and get Maman used to spending a few hours without us. As her husband had come to Paris the day before, my sister decided to leave Maman alone that night with Mademoiselle Cournot. She would come in the morning; Marthe would come at about half past two; and I would come at five.

At five I opened the door. The blind was down and it was almost entirely dark. Marthe was holding Maman's hand, and Maman was lying crumpled up, on her right side, with a pitiful, exhausted look: the bed-sores on her left buttock were completely raw and lying like this she suffered less, but the discomfort of her position was tiring her out. She had waited in extreme anxiety until eleven o'clock for Poupette and Lionel to come, because the nurses had forgotten to pin the bell-cord to her sheet: the push button was out of her reach and she had no way of calling anyone. Her friend, Madame Tardieu, had come to see her, but all the same Maman said to my sister, "You leave me in the power of the brutes!" (She hated the Sunday nurses.) Then she recovered enough spirit to say to Lionel, "So you hoped to be rid of mother-in-law? Well, it's not to be; not yet." She was alone for an hour after lunch and the tormenting anxiety seized upon her again. In a feverish voice she said to me, "I must not be left alone; I am still too weak. I must not be left in the power of the brutes!"

"We won't leave you anymore."

Marthe went away; Maman dozed off and woke with a start—her right buttock was hurting. Madame Gontrand changed her. Maman still complained: I wanted to ring again. "It would still be Madame Gontrand. She's no good." There was nothing imaginary about Maman's pains; they had exact organic causes. Yet below a certain threshold they could be soothed by the attentions of Mademoiselle Parent or Mademoiselle Martin; exactly the same things done by Madame Gontrand did not ease her. However, she went to sleep again. At half past six she took some soup and custard, and it gave her pleasure. Then suddenly she cried out, a burning pain in her left buttock. It was not at all surprising. Her flayed body was bathing in the uric acid that oozed from her skin; the nurses burnt their fingers when they changed her draw-sheet. I rang and rang, panic-stricken: how the interminable seconds dragged out! I held Maman's hand, I stroked her forehead, I talked. "They will give you an injection. It won't hurt any more. Just one minute more. Only one minute." All tense, on the edge of shrieking, she moaned, "It burns, it's awful; I can't stand it. I can't bear it any longer." And half sobbing, "I'm so utterly miserable," in that child's voice that pierced me to the heart. How completely alone she was! I touched her, I talked to her, but it was impossible to enter into her suffering. Her heart took to beating madly, her eyes turned back. I thought "She is dying," and she murmured, "I am going to faint." At last Madame Gontrand gave her an injection of morphia. It did not work. I rang again. I was terrified by the idea that the pain might have started in the morning, when Maman had no one with her and no means of calling anyone: there was no longer any question of leaving her alone for a moment. This time the nurses gave Maman equanil, changed her draw-sheet and put an ointment on her open places that left a metallic sheen on their hands. The burning went off; it had lasted only a quarter of an hour—an eternity. *He shrieked for hours.* "It's stupid," said Maman. "It's so stupid." Yes: so stupid as to make one weep. I could no longer understand the doctors, nor my sister nor myself. Nothing on earth could possibly justify these moments of pointless torment.

On Monday morning I talked to Poupette on the telephone: the end was near. The oedema was not being reabsorbed: the abdomen was not closing. The doctors had told the nurses that the only thing left to do was to daze Maman with sedatives.

At two o'clock I found my sister outside

door 114, almost out of her mind. She had said to Mademoiselle Martin, "Don't let Maman suffer as she did yesterday." "But Madame, if we give her such a lot of injections just for the bedsores, the morphia won't work when the time of the great pain comes." Questioned closely, she explained that generally speaking, in cases like Maman's, the patient died in hideous torment. *Have pity on me. Finish me off.* Had Dr P lied, then? Get a revolver somehow: kill Maman: strangle her. Empty romantic fantasies. But it was just as impossible for me to see myself listening to Maman scream for hours. "We'll go and talk to P." He came and we seized upon him. "You promised she wouldn't suffer." "She will not suffer." He pointed out that if they had wanted to prolong her life at any cost and give her an extra week of martyrdom, another operation would have been necessary, together with transfusions and resuscitating injections. Yes. That morning even N had said to Poupette, "We did everything that had to be done while there was still a chance. Now it would be mere sadism to try to delay her death." But this abstention was not enough for us. We asked P, "Will morphia stop the great pains?" "She will be given the doses that are called for."

He had spoken firmly and he gave us confidence. We grew calmer. . . .

She dropped off, and her breath was so imperceptible that I thought, "If only it could stop, without any violence." But the black ribbon rose and fell: the leap was not to be so easy. I woke her up at five, as she had insisted, to give her some yoghourt. "Your sister wants me to: it's good for me." She ate two or three spoonfuls: I thought of the food that is put on the graves of the dead in certain countries. I held her a rose to smell, one that Catherine had brought the day before—"The last of the Meyrignac roses." She only gave it a preoccupied glance. She sank down into sleep again: a burning pain in her buttock woke her violently. Morphia injection: no result. As I had done two days before I held her hand, urged her, "One minute more. The injection is going to work. In one minute it will be over."

"It's a Chinese torture," she said, in a flat, expressionless voice, too weakened even to protest.

I rang again; insisted; another injection. The Parent girl arranged the bed and moved Maman a little; she went to sleep again; her hands were deathly cold. The maid grumbled because I sent away the dinner that she brought at six o'clock: the implacable routine of clinics, where deathbeds and death itself are daily occurrences. At half past seven Maman said to me, "Ah! Now I feel well. Really well. It's a long time since I've felt so well." Jeanne's eldest daughter came, and she helped me give her a little soup and some coffee custard. It was difficult, because she coughed: she almost choked. Poupette and Mademoiselle Cournot advised me to leave. In all likelihood nothing would happen that night, and my being there would worry Maman. I kissed her, and with one of her hideous smiles she said to me, "I am glad you have seen me looking so well!"

I went to bed half an hour after midnight, dosed with sleeping-pills. I woke: the telephone was ringing. "There are only a few minutes left. Marcel is coming to fetch you in a car." Marcel—Lionel's cousin—drove me at great speed through a deserted Paris. We gulped down some coffee at a red-lit bar near the Porte Champerret. Poupette came to meet us in the garden of the nursing-home. "It's all over." We went up the stairs. It was so expected and so unimaginable, that dead body lying on the bed in Maman's place. Her hand was cold; so was her forehead. It was still Maman, and it was her absence for ever. There was a bandage holding up her chin, framing her face. My sister wanted to go and fetch clothes from the rue Blomet.

"What's the point?"

"Apparently that is what's done."

"We shan't do it."

I could not conceive putting a dress and shoes on Maman as though she was going out to dinner; and I did not think that she would have wanted it—she had often said that she was not in the least concerned with what happened to her body.

"Just dress her in one of her long nightgowns," I said to Mademoiselle Cournot.

"And what about her wedding-ring?" asked Poupette, taking it out of the table drawer. We put it on to her finger. Why? No doubt because that little round of gold belonged nowhere else on earth.

Poupette was utterly exhausted. After a last look at what was no longer Maman I quickly took her away. We had a drink with Marcel at the bar of the Dôme. She told us what had happened.

At nine o'clock N came out of the room and said angrily, "Another clip has given way. After all that has been done for her: how irritating!" He went off, leaving my sister dumbfounded. In spite of her icy hands Maman complained of being too hot, and she had some difficulty in breathing. She was given an injection and she went to sleep. Poupette undressed, got into bed and went through the motions of reading a detective story. Towards midnight Maman moved about. Poupette and the nurse went to her bedside. She opened her eyes. "What are you doing here? Why are you looking so worried? I am quite well." "You have been having a bad dream." As Mademoiselle Cournot smoothed the sheets she touched Maman's feet: there was the chill of death upon them. My sister wondered whether to call me. But at that time of night my presence would have frightened Maman, whose mind was perfectly clear. Poupette went back to bed. At one o'clock Maman stirred again. In a roguish voice she whispered the words of an old refrain that Papa used to sing, *You are going away and you will leave us.* "No, no," said Poupette, "I shan't leave you," and Maman gave a little knowing smile. She found it harder and harder to breathe. After another injection she murmured in a rather thick voice, "We must . . . keep . . . back . . . desh."

"We must keep back the desk?"

"No," said Maman. "Death." Stressing the word *death* very strongly. She added, "I don't want to die."

"But you are better now!"

After that she wandered a little. "I should have liked to have the time to bring out my book . . . She must be allowed to nurse whoever she likes."

My sister dressed herself: Maman had almost lost consciousness. Suddenly she cried, "I can't breathe!" Her mouth opened, her eyes stared wide, huge in that wasted, ravaged face: with a spasm she entered into coma.

"Go and telephone," said Mademoiselle Cournot.

Poupette rang me up: I did not answer. The operator went on ringing for half an hour before I woke. Meanwhile Poupette went back to Maman: already she was no longer there—her heart was beating and she breathed, sitting there with glassy eyes that saw nothing. And then it was over. "The doctors said she would go out like a candle: it wasn't like that, it wasn't like that at all," said my sister, sobbing.

"But, Madame," replied the nurse, "I assure you it was a very easy death." . . .

Sometimes, though very rarely, it happens that love, friendship or comradely feeling overcomes the loneliness of death: in spite of appearances, even when I was holding Maman's hand, I was not with her—I was lying to her. Because she had always been deceived, gulled, I found this ultimate deception revolting. I was making myself an accomplice of that fate which was so misusing her. Yet at the same time in every cell of my body I joined in her refusal, in her rebellion: and it was also because of that that her defeat overwhelmed me. Although I was not with Maman when she died, and although I had been with three people when they were actually dying, it was when I was at her bedside that I saw Death, the Death of the dance of death, with its bantering grin, the Death of fireside tales that knocks on the door, a scythe in its hand, the Death that comes from elsewhere, strange and inhuman: it had the very face of Maman when she showed her gums in a wide smile of unknowingness.

"He is certainly of an age to die." The sadness of the old; their banishment: most of them do not think that this age has yet come for them. I too made use of this cliché, and that when I was referring to my mother. I did not understand that one might sincerely weep for a relative, a grandfather aged seventy and more. If I met a woman of fifty overcome with sadness because she had just lost her mother, I thought her neurotic: we are all mortal; at eighty you are quite old enough to be one of the dead . . .

But it is not true. You do not die from being born, nor from having lived, nor from old age. You die from *something*. The knowledge that because of her age my mother's life must soon come to an end did not lessen the horrible surprise: she had sarcoma. Cancer, thrombosis, pneumonia: It is as violent and unforeseen as an engine stopping in the middle of the sky. My mother encouraged one to be optimistic when, crippled with arthritis and dying, she asserted the infinite value of each instant; but her vain tenaciousness also ripped and tore the reassuring curtain of everyday triviality. There is no such thing as a natural death: nothing that happens to a man is ever natural, since his presence calls the world into question. All men must die: but for every man his death is an accident and, even if he knows it and consents to it, an unjustifiable violation.

Basic Existentialist Concepts

Finitude For atheistic existentialists such as Beauvoir, human life is not merely ended by death; it is also structured by death. Death permeates every moment of a human life: As soon as we are born, we are ripe to die; as soon as we have accomplished something, death can take it away from us. In *The Stranger*, Camus' metaphor for death is not a final curtain but a steady, dark wind blowing from the future that penetrates every aspect of a human life.

This means that every decision and every moment of our life occurs within the context of a limited time frame. Death is not only the ever-present possibility that we may not have any future, but also a restrictive pressure on our present. Because we shall die, we do not have an infinite number of choices and we cannot perform an infinite number of actions. We are limited in the sense that every choice we make excludes other choices, and, because of death, there will not be time to take up all of these excluded alternatives later. Thus, we are finite not only because our years on earth are limited, but also because we cannot choose or do everything that is possible for us.

Existentialism's focus on death is not meant to be a morbid preoccupation but rather a reminder of how much death shapes and structures our lives and choices. With fuller awareness of our own finitude, we can make more authentic choices. For the existentialists, it is a way of intensifying our sense of our own freedom.

Lived Body The French existentialists rejected Cartesian dualism, which postulated the existence of two separable substances—mind and body. For these existentialists, my body is not an independent container or vehicle for my mind, but an inseparable part of who I am and the energies and attitudes through which I am involved in the world. In the terms of the philosopher Merleau-Ponty, I am a lived body, which is not simply a complex of physical organs and parts, but an embodied intentionality—that is, a dynamic complex of vital capacities for relating to other people and to the world outside me.

One's own flesh, then, is not matter that can be observed in the disinterested way that external objects can be scientifically observed. One's flesh is subjective, felt, and moving, never just observed. It is the generative occasion of one's existence, not simply the spatial locus of one's existence. For this reason, Beauvoir is critical of Dr. N, who treats her mother as a mechanical object that can be repaired through surgery and chemicals. Beauvoir finds such an attitude toward her mother cold because it does not consider her mother as a lived body.

Questions for Discussion

1. Because we cannot come back after our own death and describe what it was like, is a description of our mother's death the closest we can come to an autobiographical account of death?

2. Beauvoir provides detailed, repellent descriptions of her mother's physical condition (e.g., swollen abdomen, liquid oozing from her pores) and of the events occurring during Maman's hospital stay (e.g., spilling the bed pan, removal of four pints of pus from her abdomen). What purpose do such grisly details serve in Beauvoir's account of her mother's dying process?

3. Can we rebel against death if it is inevitable?

4. Why, according to Beauvoir, is there no such thing as a natural death?

5. If you could write your own obituary in a philosophically reflective style, what would it include?

Part Two

Existentialist Views on Relations with Others

7 *Jean-Paul Sartre's* No Exit
8 *Simone de Beauvoir's "The Woman Destroyed"*
9 *Richard Wright's "The Man Who Lived Underground"*

Q14

opening - existentialism is humanism, liberatarian humanist, creativity & freedom

humanism of existentialism express the power of humans to make freely willed choices independant of the influences of religion or society

existentialism to broad a concept - marxist & catholic provenance critics argue existentialis to pessimistic & anti humanist nihilistic

X3

1) Dangerous Permissiveness) dostesky - paper/exam
~~catholics~~ nietchze - god is dead / zuther - pg145

2) Disappointing negativity) worst of humanity) nietchze pg149) ③ sartre being with other pg46
~~catholics~~ salient focus herd look
\+

④ Individualistic Isolation) pure subjectivity ② alienation pg 50
* ↕ ~~catholic marxs~~ man isolated
no solidarity of men

③ Hopeless pessimism) absurdity pg55
nilhism alienation pg 50

Solutions - man creates own world - human subjectivity is not subjectivism & arbitrariness / promotes authenticity

freedom pg40 & responsibility, authenticity pg 41, project pg 71, transition values pg148

②
Close
Simon de beauvoir - paper + The ethics of ambiguity - argues embracing our own personal freedom requires us to fight for the freedom of all of humanity

① before Beauvoir
Sartre = denies existentialism is humanistic "man as end of higher value"
existentialism is man in process of self overcoming, transendence
no determinate final state or perfection on choice & responsibility.

"Humanism reminds us man fulfills himself not in turning inwards but seeking outside himself a goal,"

Chapter 7

Jean-Paul Sartre's No Exit

Introduction: Hell Is Other People

In his provocative assessment of relations with others as hellish, Sartre calls attention to two important philosophical issues concerning freedom. The first is the extent to which an individual's freedom is restricted by others' judgment of his actions; the second is the relation between the freedom to act and the definition of one's self-identity. These two issues are interconnected because an individual suffers not only when others restrict his freedom of action but also when others define him. Even though the individual acts freely and defines himself through his actions, his actions occur in the public world where they are judged by others. These judgments contribute to the definition of who the individual is.

In *Being and Nothingness*, Sartre describes interpersonal relations as conflictual. Each individual aims to be free and to avoid becoming subject to others' control. But the control that we typically exercise over one another is not brute, physical force, but the freedom to judge the other person as we wish. Because each of us is free, you and I are free to form opinions about one another. The other person wishes to shape and even control the opinion I form of him, but he is unable to do this. I wish to appear favorably in the other person's eyes, but I am unable to know what he truly thinks of me, let alone to dictate what he thinks. We engage in a psychological power struggle, each trying to be free from the other's judging power while retaining our freedom to judge the other.

Hell, then, is the unavoidable human situation of being free and of being with other people while being confined by their judgments of oneself. There is no way to reach a settlement between my own freedom to define myself and others' freedom to define me. Each of us is condemned to a hell of realizing that others do not think of us the way that we think of ourselves; we are unable to sustain an independent self-image because of our inescapable interactions with others.

A further meaning of hell in Sartre's *No Exit* is the finality of being defined by our actions. For Sartre, an individual is the sum total of his actions. Once we complete our actions, and especially once all of our actions come to a halt in death, they become our essence. There are no excuses or second chances: What we have done constitutes who we are as an individual. Hell is the inflexible situation of being bound by our own actions.

Sartre's *No Exit* (Excerpts)[1]

Characters in the Play

VALET

GARCIN

ESTELLE

INEZ

Scene

A drawing room in Second Empire style. A massive bronze ornament stands on the mantelpiece.

* * *

GARCIN [*enters, accompanied by the* ROOM VALET, *and glances around him*]: Hm! So here we are?

VALET: Yes, Mr. Garcin.

GARCIN: And this is what it looks like?

VALET: Yes.

GARCIN: Second Empire furniture, I observe. . . . Well, well, I dare say one gets used to it in time.

VALET: Some do. Some don't.

GARCIN: Are all the other rooms like this one?

VALET: How could they be? We cater for all sorts: Chinamen and Indians, for instance. What use would they have for a Second Empire chair?

GARCIN: And what use do you suppose I have for one? Do you know who I was? . . . Oh, well, it's no great matter. And, to tell the truth, I had quite a habit of living among furniture that I didn't relish, and in false positions. I'd even come to like it. A false position in a Louis-Philippe dining-room—you know the style?—well, that had its points, you know. Bogus in bogus, so to speak.

VALET: And you'll find that living in a Second Empire drawing-room has its points.

GARCIN: Really? . . . Yes, yes, I dare say. . . . [*He takes another look around.*] Still, I certainly didn't expect—this! You know what they tell us down there?

VALET: What about?

GARCIN: About [*makes a sweeping gesture*] this—er—residence.

VALET: Really, sir, how could you believe such cock-and-bull stories? Told by people who'd never set foot here. For, of course, if they had—

GARCIN: Quite so. [*Both laugh. Abruptly the laugh dies from* GARCIN'S *face.*] But, I say, where are the instruments of torture?

VALET: The what?

GARCIN: The racks and red-hot pincers and all the other paraphernalia?

VALET: Ah, you must have your little joke, sir!

GARCIN: My little joke? Oh, I see. No, I wasn't joking. [*A short silence. He strolls round the room.*] No mirrors, I notice. No windows. Only to be expected. And nothing breakable. [*Bursts out angrily.*] But, damn it all, they might have left me my toothbrush!

VALET: That's good! So you haven't yet got over your—what-do-you-call-it?—sense of human dignity? Excuse me smiling.

GARCIN [*thumping ragefully the arm of an armchair*]: I'll ask you to be more polite. I quite realize the position I'm in, but I won't tolerate . . .

VALET: Sorry, sir. No offense meant. But all our guests ask me the same questions. Silly questions, if you'll pardon me saying so. Where's the torture-chamber? That's the first thing they ask, all of them. They don't bother their heads about the bathroom requisites, that I can assure you. But after a bit, when they've got their nerve back, they start in about their toothbrushes and what-not. Good heavens, Mr. Garcin, can't you use your brains? What, I ask you, would be the point of brushing your teeth?

GARCIN [*more calmly*]: Yes, of course you're right. [*He looks around again.*] And why should one want to see oneself in a looking-glass? But that bronze contraption on the mantelpiece, that's another story. I suppose there will be

[1] From *No Exit and Three Other Plays* by Jean-Paul Sartre, translated by Stuart Gilbert.

times when I stare my eyes out at it. Stare my eyes out—see what I mean? . . . All right, let's put our cards on the table. I assure you I'm quite conscious of my position. Shall I tell you what it feels like? A man's drowning, choking, sinking by inches, till only his eyes are just above water. And what does he see? A bronze atrocity by—what's the fellow's name?—Barbedienne. A collector's piece. As in a nightmare. That's their idea, isn't it? . . . No, I suppose you're under orders not to answer questions; and I won't insist. But don't forget, my man, I've a good notion of what's coming to me, so don't you boast you've caught me off my guard. I'm facing the situation, facing it. [*He starts pacing the room again.*] So that's that; no toothbrush. And no bed, either. One never sleeps, I take it?

VALET: That's so.

GARCIN: Just as I expected. *Why* should one sleep? A sort of drowsiness steals on you, tickles you behind the ears, and you feel your eyes closing—but why sleep? You lie down on the sofa and—in a flash, sleep flies away. Miles and miles away. So you rub your eyes, get up, and it starts all over again.

VALET: Romantic, that's what you are.

GARCIN: Will you keep quiet, please! . . . I won't make a scene, I shan't be sorry for myself, I'll face the situation, as I said just now. Face it fairly and squarely. I won't have it springing at me from behind, before I've time to size it up. And you call that being "romantic"! . . . So it comes to this; one doesn't need rest. Why bother about sleep if one isn't sleepy? That stands to reason, doesn't it? Wait a minute, there's a snag somewhere; something disagreeable. Why, now, should it be disagreeable? . . . Ah, I see; it's life without a break.

VALET: What do you mean by that?

GARCIN: What do I mean? [*Eyes the* VALET *suspiciously.*] I thought as much. That's why there's something so beastly, so damn bad-mannered, in the way you stare at me. They're paralyzed.

VALET: What are you talking about?

GARCIN: Your eyelids. We move ours up and down. Blinking, we call it. It's like a small black shutter that clicks down and makes a break. Everything goes black; one's eyes are moistened. You can't imagine how restful, refreshing, it is. Four thousand little rests per hour. Four thousand little respites—just think! . . . So that's the idea. I'm to live without eyelids. Don't act the fool, you know what I mean. No eyelids, no sleep; it follows, doesn't it? I shall never sleep again. But then—how shall I endure my own company? Try to understand. You see, I'm fond of teasing, it's a second nature with me—and I'm used to teasing myself. Plaguing myself, if you prefer; I don't tease nicely. But I can't go on doing that without a break. Down there I had my nights. I slept. I always had good nights. By way of compensation, I suppose. And happy little dreams. There was a green field. Just an ordinary field. I used to stroll in it. . . . Is it daytime now?

VALET: Can't you see? The lights are on.

GARCIN: Ah yes, I've got it. It's *your* daytime. And outside?

VALET: Outside?

GARCIN: Damn it, you know what I mean. Beyond that wall.

VALET: There's a passage.

GARCIN: And at the end of the passage?

VALET: There's more rooms, more passages, and stairs.

GARCIN: And what lies beyond them?

VALET: That's all.

GARCIN: But surely you have a day off sometimes. Where do you go?

VALET: To my uncle's place. He's the head valet here. He has a room on the third floor.

GARCIN: I should have guessed as much. Where's the lightswitch?

VALET: There isn't any.

GARCIN: What? Can't one turn off the light?

VALET: Oh, the management can cut off the current if they want to. But I can't remember their having done so on this floor. We have all the electricity we want.

GARCIN: So one has to live with one's eyes open all the time?

VALET: To *live,* did you say?

GARCIN: Don't let's quibble over words.

With one's eyes open. Forever. Always broad daylight in my eyes—and in my head. [*Short silence.*] And suppose I took that contraption on the mantelpiece and dropped it on the lamp—wouldn't it go out?

VALET: You can't move it. It's too heavy.

GARCIN [*seizing the bronze ornament and trying to lift it*]: You're right? It's too heavy. [*A short silence follows.*]

VALET: Very well, sir, if you don't need me any more, I'll be off.

GARCIN: What? You're going? [*The* VALET *goes up to the door.*] Wait. [VALET *looks round.*] That's a bell, isn't it? [VALET *nods.*] And if I ring, you're bound to come?

VALET: Well, yes, that's so—in a way. But you can never be sure about that bell. There's something wrong with the wiring, and it doesn't always work. [GARCIN *goes to the bell-push and presses the button. A bell purrs outside.*]

GARCIN: It's working all right.

VALET [*looking surprised*]: So it is. *[He, too, presses the button.*] But I shouldn't count on it too much if I were you. It's—capricious. Well, I really must go now. [GARCIN *makes a gesture to detain him.*] Yes, sir?

GARCIN: No, never mind. [*He goes to the mantelpiece and picks up a paper-knife.*] What's this?

VALET: Can't you see? An ordinary paper-knife.

GARCIN: Are there books here?

VALET: No.

GARCIN: Then what's the use of this? [VALET *shrugs his shoulders.*] Very well. You can go. [VALET *goes out.*] [GARCIN *is by himself. He goes to the bronze ornament and strokes it reflectively. He sits down; then gets up, goes to the bell-push, and presses the button. The bell remains silent. He tries two or three times, without success. Then he tries to open the door, also without success. He calls the* VALET *several times, but gets no result. He beats the door with his fists, still calling. Suddenly he grows calm and sits down again. At the same moment the door opens and* INEZ *enters, followed by the* VALET.]

VALET: Did you call, sir?

GARCIN [*on the point of answering "Yes"—but then his eyes fall on* INEZ]: No.

VALET [*turning to* INEZ]: This is your room, madam. [INEZ *says nothing.*] If there's any information you require—? [INEZ *still keeps silent, and the* VALET *looks slightly huffed.*] Most of our guests have quite a lot to ask me. But I won't insist. Anyhow, as regards the toothbrush, and the electric bell, and that thing on the mantelshelf, this gentleman can tell you anything you want to know as well as I could. We've had a little chat, him and me. [VALET *goes out.*] [GARCIN *refrains from looking at* INEZ, *who is inspecting the room. Abruptly she turns to* GARCIN.]

INEZ: Where's Florence? [GARCIN *does not reply.*] Didn't you hear? I asked you about Florence. Where is she?

GARCIN: I haven't an idea.

INEZ: Ah, that's the way it works, is it? Torture by separation. Well, as far as I'm concerned, you won't get anywhere. Florence was a tiresome little fool, and I shan't miss her in the least.

GARCIN: I beg your pardon. Who do you suppose I am?

INEZ: You? Why, the torturer, of course.

GARCIN [*looks startled, then bursts out laughing*]: Well, that's a good one! Too comic for words. I the torturer! So you came in, had a look at me, and thought I was—er—one of the staff. Of course, it's that silly fellow's fault; he should have introduced us. A torturer indeed! I'm Joseph Garcin, journalist and man of letters by profession. And as we're both in the same boat, so to speak, might I ask you, Mrs.—?

INEZ [*testily*]: Not "Mrs." I'm unmarried.

GARCIN: Right. That's a start, anyway. Well, now that we've broken the ice, do you *really* think I look like a torturer? And, by the way, how does one recognize torturers when one sees them? Evidently you've ideas on the subject.

INEZ: They look frightened.

GARCIN: Frightened! But how ridiculous! Of whom should they be frightened? Of their victims?

INEZ: Laugh away, but I know what I'm

talking about. I've often watched my face in the glass.

GARCIN: In the glass? [*He looks around him.*] How beastly of them! They've removed everything in the least resembling a glass. [*Short silence.*] Anyhow, I can assure you I'm not frightened. Not that I take my position lightly; I realize its gravity only too well. But I'm not afraid.

INEZ [*shrugging her shoulders*]: That's your affair. [*Silence.*] Must you be here all the time, or do you take a stroll outside, now and then?

GARCIN: The door's locked.

INEZ: Oh! . . . That's too bad.

GARCIN: I can quite understand that it bores you having me here. And I, too—well, quite frankly, I'd rather be alone. I want to think things out, you know; to set my life in order, and one does that better by oneself. But I'm sure we'll manage to pull along together somehow. I'm no talker, I don't move much; in fact I'm a peaceful sort of fellow. Only, if I may venture on a suggestion, we should make a point of being extremely courteous to each other. That will ease the situation for us both.

INEZ: I'm not polite.

GARCIN: Then I must be polite for two.

[*A longish silence.* GARCIN *is sitting on a sofa, while* INEZ *paces up and down the room.*]

INEZ [*fixing her eyes on him*]: Your mouth!

GARCIN [*as if waking from a dream*]: I beg your pardon.

INEZ: Can't you keep your mouth still? You keep twisting it about all the time. It's grotesque.

GARCIN: So sorry. I wasn't aware of it.

INEZ: That's just what I reproach you with. [GARCIN'S *mouth twitches.*] There you are! You talk about politeness, and you don't even try to control your face. Remember you're not alone; you've no right to inflict the sight of your fear on me.

GARCIN [*getting up and going towards her*]: How about you? Aren't you afraid?

INEZ: What would be the use? There was some point in being afraid *before*; while one still had hope.

GARCIN [*in a low voice*]: There's no more hope—but it's still "before." We haven't yet begun to suffer.

INEZ: That's so. [*A short silence.*] Well? What's going to happen?

GARCIN: I don't know. I'm waiting.

[*Silence again.* GARCIN *sits down and* INEZ *resumes her pacing up and down the room.* GARCIN'S *mouth twitches; after a glance at* INEZ *he buries his face in his hands. Enter* ESTELLE *with the* VALET. ESTELLE *looks at* GARCIN, *whose face is still hidden by his hands.*]

ESTELLE [*to* GARCIN]: No. Don't look up. I know what you're hiding with your hands. I know you've no face left. [GARCIN *removes his hands.*] What! [*A short pause, then, in a tone of surprise*] But I don't know you!

GARCIN: I'm not the torturer, madam.

ESTELLE: I never thought you were. I—I thought someone was trying to play a rather nasty trick on me. [*To the* VALET] Is anyone else coming?

VALET: No madam. No one else is coming.

ESTELLE: Oh! Then we're to stay by ourselves, the three of us, this gentleman, this lady, and myself. [*She starts laughing.*]

GARCIN [*angrily*]: There's nothing to laugh about.

ESTELLE [*still laughing*]: It's those sofas. They're so hideous. And just look how they've been arranged. It makes me think of New Year's Day—when I used to visit that boring old aunt of mine, Aunt Mary. Her house is full of horrors like that. . . . I suppose each of us has a sofa of his own. Is this one mine? [*To the* VALET] But you can't expect me to sit on that one. It would be too horrible for words. I'm in pale blue and it's vivid green.

INEZ: Would you prefer mine?

ESTELLE: That claret-colored one, you mean? That's very sweet of you, but really—no, I don't think it'd be so much better What's the good of worrying, anyhow? We've got to take what comes to us, and I'll stick to the green one. [*Pause*] The only one which might do at a pinch, is that gentleman's. [*Another pause.*]

INEZ: Did you hear, Mr. Garcin?

GARCIN [*with a slight start*]: Oh—the sofa, you mean. So sorry. [*He rises.*] Please take it, madam.

ESTELLE: Thanks. [*She takes off her coat and drops it on the sofa. A short silence.*] Well, as we're to live together, I suppose we'd better introduce ourselves. My name's Rigault. Estelle Rigault. [GARCIN *bows and is going to announce his name, but* INEZ *steps in front of him.*]

INEZ: And I'm Inez Serrano. Very pleased to meet you.

GARCIN [*bowing again*]: Joseph Garcin.

VALET: Do you require me any longer?

ESTELLE: No, you can go. I'll ring when I want you.

[*Exit* VALET, *with polite bows to everyone.*]

INEZ: You're very pretty. I wish we'd had some flowers to welcome you with.

ESTELLE: Flowers? Yes, I loved flowers. Only they'd fade so quickly here, wouldn't they? It's so stuffy. Oh, well, the great thing is to keep as cheerful as we can, don't you agree? Of course, you, too, are—

INEZ: Yes. Last week. What about you?

ESTELLE: I'm—quite recent. Yesterday. As a matter of fact, the ceremony's not quite over. [*Her tone is natural enough, but she seems to be seeing what she describes.*] The wind's blowing my sister's veil all over the place. She's trying her best to cry. Come, dear! Make another effort. That's better. Two tears, two little tears are twinkling under the black veil. Oh dear! What a sight Olga looks this morning! She's holding my sister's arm, helping her along. She's not crying, and I don't blame her, tears always mess one's face up, don't they? Olga was my bosom friend, you know.

INEZ: Did you suffer much?

ESTELLE: No. I was only half conscious, mostly.

INEZ: What was it?

ESTELLE: Pneumonia. [*In the same tone as before*] It's over now, they're leaving the cemetery. Good-by. Good-by. Quite a crowd they are. My husband stayed at home. Prostrated with grief, poor man. [*To* INEZ] How about you?

INEZ: The gas stove.

ESTELLE: And you, Mr. Garcin?

GARCIN: Twelve bullets through my chest. [ESTELLE *makes a horrified gesture.*] Sorry! I fear I'm not good company among the dead.

ESTELLE: Please, please don't use that word. It's so—so crude. In terribly bad taste, really. It doesn't mean much, anyhow. Somehow I feel we've never been so much alive as now. If we've absolutely got to mention this—this state of things, I suggest we call ourselves—wait!—absentees. Have you been—been absent for long?

GARCIN: About a month.

ESTELLE: Where do you come from?

GARCIN: From Rio.

ESTELLE: I'm from Paris. Have you anyone left down there?

GARCIN: Yes, my wife. [*In the same tone as* ESTELLE *has been using*] She's waiting at the entrance of the barracks. She comes there every day. But they won't let her in. Now she's trying to peep between the bars. She doesn't yet know I'm—absent, but she suspects it. Now she's going away. She's wearing her black dress. So much the better, she won't need to change. She isn't crying, but she never did cry, anyhow. It's a bright sunny day and she's like a black shadow creeping down the empty street. Those big tragic eyes of hers—with that martyred look they always had. Oh, how she got on my nerves!

[*A short silence.* GARCIN *sits on the central sofa and buries his head in his hands.*]

INEZ: Estelle!

ESTELLE: Please, Mr. Garcin!

GARCIN: What is it?

ESTELLE: You're sitting on my sofa.

GARCIN: I beg your pardon. [*He gets up.*]

ESTELLE: You looked so—so far away. Sorry I disturbed you.

GARCIN: I was setting my life in order. [INEZ *starts laughing.*] You may laugh, but you'd do better to follow my example.

INEZ: No need. My life's in perfect order. It tidied itself up nicely of its own accord. So I needn't bother about it now.

GARCIN: Really? You imagine it's so simple as that. [*He runs his hand over his forehead.*] Whew! How hot it is here! Do you mind if—? [*He begins taking off his coat.*]

ESTELLE: How dare you! [*More gently*] No, please don't. I loathe men in their shirt-sleeves.

GARCIN [*putting on his coat again*]: All right. [*A short pause.*] Of course, I used to spend my nights in the newspaper office, and it was a regular Black Hole, so we never kept our coats on. Stiflingly hot it could be. [*Short pause. In the same tone, as previously*] Stifling, that it is. It's night now.

ESTELLE: That's so. Olga's undressing; it must be after midnight. How quickly the time passes, on earth!

INEZ: Yes, after midnight. They've sealed up my room. It's dark, pitch-dark, and empty.

GARCIN: They've strung their coats on the backs of the chairs. and rolled up their shirt-sleeves above the elbow. The air stinks of men and cigar-smoke. [*A short silence.*] I used to like living among men in their shirt-sleeves.

ESTELLE [*aggressively*]: Well, in that case our tastes differ. That's all it proves. [*Turning to* INEZ] What about you? Do you like men in their shirt-sleeves?

INEZ: Oh, I don't care much for men any way.

ESTELLE [*looking at the other two with a puzzled air*]: Really I can't imagine why they put us three together. It doesn't make sense.

INEZ [*stifling a laugh*]: What's that you said?

ESTELLE: I'm looking at you two and thinking that we're going to live together. . . . It's so absurd. I expected to meet old friends, or relatives.

INEZ: Yes, a charming old friend—with a hole in the middle of his face.

ESTELLE: Yes, him too. He danced the tango so divinely. Like a professional. . . . But why, why should we of all people be put together?

GARCIN: A pure fluke, I should say. They lodge folks as they can, in the order of their coming. [*To* INEZ] Why are you laughing?

INEZ: Because you amuse me, with your "flukes." As if they've left anything to chance. But I suppose you've got to reassure yourself somehow.

ESTELLE [*hesitantly*]: I wonder, now. Don't you think we may have met each other at some time in our lives?

INEZ: Never. I shouldn't have forgotten you.

ESTELLE: Or perhaps we have friends in common. I wonder if you know the Dubois-Seymours?

INEZ: Not likely.

ESTELLE: But *everyone* went to their parties.

INEZ: What's their job?

ESTELLE: Oh, they don't do anything. But they have a lovely house in the country, and hosts of people visit them.

INEZ: I didn't. I was a post-office clerk.

ESTELLE [*recoiling a little*]: Ah, yes. . . . Of course, in that case—[*A pause.*] And you, Mr. Garcin?

GARCIN: We've never met. I always lived in Rio.

ESTELLE: Then you must be right. It's mere chance that has brought us together.

INEZ: Mere chance? Then it's by chance this room is furnished as we see it. It's an accident that the sofa on the right is a livid green, and that one on the left's wine-red. Mere chance? Well, just try to shift the sofas and you'll see the difference quick enough. And that statue on the mantelpiece, do you think it's there by accident? And what about the heat here? How about that? [*A short silence.*] I tell you they've thought it all out. Down to the last detail. Nothing was left to chance. This room was all set for us.

ESTELLE: But really! Everything here's so hideous; all in angles, so uncomfortable. I always loathed angles.

INEZ [*shrugging her shoulders*]: And do you think *I* lived in a Second Empire drawing-room?

ESTELLE: So it was all fixed up beforehand?

INEZ: Yes. And they've put us together deliberately.

ESTELLE: Then it's not mere chance that *you* precisely are sitting opposite *me*? But what can be the idea behind it?

INEZ: Ask me another! I only know they're waiting.

ESTELLE: I never could bear the idea of anyone's expecting something from me. It always made me want to do just the opposite.

INEZ: Well, do it. Do it if you can. You don't even know what they expect.

ESTELLE [*stamping her foot*]: It's outrageous! So something's coming to me from you two? [*She eyes each in turn.*] Something nasty, I suppose. There are some faces that tell me everything at once. Yours don't convey anything.

GARCIN [*turning abruptly towards* INEZ]: Look here! Why are we together? You've given us quite enough hints, you may as well come out with it.

INEZ [*in a surprised tone*]: But I know nothing, absolutely nothing about it. I'm as much in the dark as you are.

GARCIN: We've *got* to know. [*Ponders for a while.*]

INEZ: If only each of us had the guts to tell—

GARCIN: Tell what?

INEZ: Estelle!

ESTELLE: Yes?

INEZ: What have you done? I mean, why have they sent you here?

ESTELLE [*quickly*]: That's just it. I haven't a notion, not the foggiest. In fact, I'm wondering if there hasn't been some ghastly mistake. [*To* INEZ] Don't smile. Just think of the number of people who—who become absentees every day. There must be thousands and thousands, and probably they're sorted out by—by understrappers, you know what I mean. Stupid employees who don't know their job. So they're bound to make mistakes sometimes. . . . Do stop smiling. [*To* GARCIN] Why don't you speak? If they made a mistake in my case, they may have done the same about you. [*To* INEZ] And you, too. Anyhow, isn't it better to think we've got here by mistake?

INEZ: Is that all you have to tell us?

ESTELLE: What else should I tell? I've nothing to hide. I lost my parents when I was a kid, and I had my young brother to bring up. We were terribly poor and when an old friend of my people asked me to marry him I said yes. He was very well off, and quite nice. My brother was a very delicate child and needed all sorts of attention, so really that was the right thing for me to do, don't you agree? My husband was old enough to be my father, but for six years we had a happy married life. Then two years ago I met the man I was fated to love. We knew it the moment we set eyes on each other. He asked me to run away with him, and I refused. Then I got pneumonia and it finished me. That's the whole story. No doubt, by certain standards, I did wrong to sacrifice my youth to a man nearly three times my age. [*To* GARCIN] Do *you* think that could be called a sin?

GARCIN: Certainly not. [*A short silence.*] And now, tell me, do you think it's a crime to stand by one's principles?

ESTELLE: Of course not. Surely no one could blame a man for that!

GARCIN: Wait a bit! I ran a pacifist newspaper. Then war broke out. What was I to do? Everyone was watching me, wondering: "Will he dare?" Well, I dared. I folded my arms and they shot me. Had I done anything wrong?

ESTELLE [*laying her hand on his arm*]: Wrong? On the contrary. You were—

INEZ [*breaks in ironically*]: —a hero! And how about your wife, Mr. Garcin?

GARCIN: That's simple. I'd rescued her from—from the gutter.

ESTELLE [*to* INEZ]: You see! You see!

INEZ: Yes, I see. [*A pause.*] Look here! What's the point of play-acting, trying to throw dust in each other's eyes? We're all tarred with the same brush.

ESTELLE [*indignantly*]: How dare you!

INEZ: Yes, we are criminals—murderers—all

three of us. We're in hell, my pets; they never make mistakes, and people aren't damned for nothing.

ESTELLE: Stop! For heaven's sake—

INEZ: In hell! Damned souls—that's us, all three!

ESTELLE: Keep quiet! I forbid you to use such disgusting words.

INEZ: A damned soul—that's you, my little plaster saint. And ditto our friend there, the noble pacifist. We've had our hour of pleasure, haven't we? There have been people who burned their lives out for our sakes—and we chuckled over it. So now we have to pay the reckoning.

GARCIN [*raising his fist*]: Will you keep your mouth shut, damn it!

INEZ [*confronting him fearlessly, but with a look of vast surprise*]: Well, well! [*A pause.*] Ah, I understand now. I know why they've put us three together.

GARCIN: I advise you to—to think twice before you say any more.

INEZ: Wait! You'll see how simple it is. Childishly simple. Obviously there aren't any physical torments—you agree, don't you? And yet we're in hell. And no one else will come here. We'll stay in this room together, the three of us, for ever and ever. . . . In short, there's someone absent here, the official torturer.

GARCIN [*sotto voce*]: I'd noticed that.

INEZ: It's obvious what they're after—an economy of man-power—or devil-power, if you prefer. The same idea as in the cafeteria, where customers serve themselves.

ESTELLE: What ever do you mean?

INEZ: I mean that each of us will act as torturer of the two others.

[*There is a short silence while they digest this information.*] . . .

GARCIN: You're crazy, both of you. Don't you see where this is leading us? For pity's sake, keep your mouths shut. [*Pause.*] Now let's all sit down again quite quietly; we'll look at the floor and each must try to forget the others are there.

[*A longish silence.* GARCIN *sits down. The women return hesitantly to their places. Suddenly* INEZ *swings round on him.*]

INEZ: To forget about the others? How utterly absurd! I *feel* you there, in every pore. Your silence clamors in my ears. You can nail up your mouth, cut your tongue out—but you can't prevent your *being there.* Can you stop your thoughts? I hear them ticking away like a clock, tick-tock, tick-tock, and I'm certain you hear mine. It's all very well skulking on your sofa, but you're everywhere, and every sound comes to me soiled, because you've intercepted it on its way. Why, you've even stolen my face; you know it and I don't! And what about her, about Estelle? You've stolen her from me, too; if she and I were alone do you suppose she'd treat me as she does? No, take your hands from your face, I won't leave you in peace—that would suit your book too well. You'd go on sitting there, in a sort of trance, like a yogi, and even if I didn't see her I'd feel it in my bones—that she was making every sound, even the rustle of her dress, for your benefit, throwing you smiles you didn't see. . . . Well, I won't stand for that, I prefer to choose my hell; I prefer to look you in the eyes and fight it out face to face.

GARCIN: Have it your own way. I suppose we were bound to come to this; they knew what they were about, and we're easy game. . . .

GARCIN: . . . So long as each of us hasn't made a clean breast of it—why they've damned him or her—we know nothing. Nothing that counts. You, young lady, you shall begin. Why? Tell us why. If you are frank, if we bring our specters into the open, it may save us from disaster. So—out with it! Why?

ESTELLE: I tell you I haven't a notion. They wouldn't tell me why.

GARCIN: That's so. They wouldn't tell me, either. But I've a pretty good idea. . . . Perhaps you're shy of speaking first? Right. I'll lead off. [*A short silence.*] I'm not a very estimable person.

INEZ: No need to tell us that. We know you were a deserter.

GARCIN: Let that be. It's only a side-issue. I'm here because I treated my wife abominably. That's all. For five years. Naturally, she's suffering still. There she is: the moment I mention her, I see her. It's Gomez who interests me, and it's she I see. Where's Gomez got to? For five years. There! They've given her back my things; she's sitting by the window, with my coat on her knees. The coat with the twelve bullet-holes. The blood's like rust; a brown ring round each hole. It's quite a museum-piece, that coat; scarred with history. And I used to wear it, fancy! . . . Now, can't you shed a tear, my love! Surely you'll squeeze one out—at last? No? You can't manage it? . . . Night after night I came home blind drunk, stinking of wine and women. She'd sat up for me, of course. But she never cried, never uttered a word of reproach. Only her eyes spoke. Big, tragic eyes. I don't regret anything. I must pay the price, but I shan't whine. . . . It's snowing in the street. Won't you cry, confound you? That woman was a born martyr, you know; a victim by vocation.

INEZ [*almost tenderly*]: Why did you hurt her like that?

GARCIN: It was so easy. A word was enough to make her flinch. Like a sensitive-plant. But never, never a reproach. I'm fond of teasing. I watched and waited. But no, not a tear, not a protest. I'd picked her up out of the gutter, you understand. . . . Now she's stroking the coat. Her eyes are shut and she's feeling with her fingers for the bullet-holes. What are you after? What do you expect? I tell you I regret nothing. The truth is, she admired me too much. Does that mean anything to you?

INEZ: No. Nobody admired *me*.

GARCIN: So much the better. So much the better for you. I suppose all this strikes you as very vague. Well, here's something you can get your teeth into. I brought a half-caste girl to stay in our house. My wife slept upstairs; she must have heard—everything. She was an early riser and, as I and the girl stayed in bed late, she served us our morning coffee.

INEZ: You brute!

GARCIN: Yes, a brute, if you like. But a well-beloved brute. [*A far-away look comes to his eyes.*] No, it's nothing. Only Gomez, and he's not talking about *me*. . . . What were you saying? Yes, a brute. Certainly. Else why should I be here? [*To* INEZ] Your turn.

INEZ: Well, I was what some people down there called "a damned bitch." Damned already. So it's no surprise, being here.

GARCIN: Is that all you have to say?

INEZ: No. There was that affair with Florence. A dead men's tale. With three corpses to it. He to start with; then she and I. So there's no one left, I've nothing to worry about; it was a clean sweep. Only that room. I see it now and then. Empty, with the doors locked. . . . No, they've just unlocked them. "To Let." It's to let; there's a notice on the door. That's—too ridiculous.

GARCIN: Three. Three deaths, you said?

INEZ: Three.

GARCIN: One man and two women?

INEZ: Yes.

GARCIN: Well, well. [*A pause.*] Did he kill himself?

INEZ: He? No, he hadn't the guts for that. Still, he'd every reason; we led him a dog's life. As a matter of fact, he was run over by a tram. A silly sort of end. . . . I was living with them; he was my cousin.

GARCIN: Was Florence fair?

INEZ: Fair? [*Glances at* ESTELLE.] You know, I don't regret a thing; still, I'm not so very keen on telling you the story.

GARCIN: That's all right. . . . So you got sick of him?

INEZ: Quite gradually. All sorts of little things got on my nerves. For instance, he made a noise when he was drinking—a sort of gurgle. Trifles like that. He was rather pathetic really. Vulnerable. Why are you smiling?

GARCIN: Because I, anyhow, am *not* vulnerable.

INEZ: Don't be too sure . . . I crept inside her skin, she saw the world through my eyes. When she left him, I had her on my hands. We shared a bed-sitting-room at the other end of the town.

GARCIN: And then?

INEZ: Then that tram did its job. I used to remind her every day: "Yes, my pet, we killed him between us." [*A pause.*] I'm rather cruel, really.

GARCIN: So am I.

INEZ: No, you're not cruel. It's something else.

GARCIN: What?

INEZ: I'll tell you later. When I say I'm cruel, I mean I can't get on without making people suffer. Like a live coal. A live coal in others' hearts. When I'm alone I flicker out. For six months I flamed away in her heart, till there was nothing but a cinder. One night she got up and turned on the gas while I was asleep. Then she crept back into bed. So now you know.

GARCIN: Well! Well!

INEZ: Yes? What's in your mind?

GARCIN: Nothing. Only that it's not a pretty story.

INEZ: Obviously. But what matter?

GARCIN: As you say, what matter? [*To* ESTELLE] Your turn. What have you done?

ESTELLE: As I told you, I haven't a notion. I rack my brain, but it's no use.

GARCIN: Right. Then we'll give you a hand. That fellow with the smashed face, who was he?

ESTELLE: Who—who do you mean?

INEZ: You know quite well. The man you were so scared of seeing when you came in.

ESTELLE: Oh, him! A friend of mine.

GARCIN: Why were you afraid of him?

ESTELLE: That's my business, Mr. Garcin.

INEZ: Did he shoot himself on your account?

ESTELLE: Of course not. How absurd you are!

GARCIN: Then why should you have been so scared? He blew his brains out, didn't he? That's how his face got smashed.

ESTELLE: Don't! Please don't go on.

GARCIN: Because of you. Because of you.

INEZ: He shot himself because of you.

ESTELLE: Leave me alone! It's—it's not fair, bullying me like that. I want to go! I want to go!

[*She runs to the door and shakes it.*]

GARCIN: Go if you can. Personally, I ask for nothing better. Unfortunately, the door's locked.

[ESTELLE *presses the bell-push, but the bell does not ring.* INEZ *and* GARCIN *laugh.* ESTELLE *swings round on them, her back to the door.*]

ESTELLE [*in a muffled voice*]: You're hateful, both of you.

INEZ: Hateful? Yes, that's the word. Now get on with it. That fellow who killed himself on your account—you were his mistress, eh?

GARCIN: Of course she was. And he wanted to have her to himself alone. That's so, isn't it?

INEZ: He danced the tango like a professional, but he was poor as a church mouse—that's right, isn't it?

[*A short silence.*]

GARCIN: Was he poor or not? Give me a straight answer.

ESTELLE: Yes, he was poor.

GARCIN: And then you had your reputation to keep up. One day he came and implored you to run away with him, and you laughed in his face.

INEZ: That's it. You laughed at him. And so he killed himself.

ESTELLE: Did you use to look at Florence in that way?

INEZ: Yes.

[*A short pause, then* ESTELLE *bursts out laughing.*]

ESTELLE: You've got it all wrong, you two. [*She stiffens her shoulders, still leaning against the door, and faces them. Her voice grows shrill, truculent.*] He wanted me to have a baby. So there!

GARCIN: And you didn't want one?

ESTELLE: I certainly didn't. But the baby came, worse luck. I went to Switzerland for five months. No one knew anything. It was a girl. Roger was with me when she was born. It pleased him no end, having a daughter. It didn't please *me*!

GARCIN: And then?

ESTELLE: There was a balcony overlooking the lake. I brought a big stone. He could see what I was up to and he kept on shouting: "Estelle, for God's sake, don't!" I hated him then. He saw it all. He was leaning over the balcony and he saw the rings spreading on the water—

GARCIN: Yes? And then?

ESTELLE: That's all. I came back to Paris—and he did as he wished.

GARCIN: You mean he blew his brains out?

ESTELLE: It was absurd of him, really, my husband never suspected anything. [*A pause.*] Oh, how I loathe you! [*She sobs tearlessly.*]

GARCIN: Nothing doing. Tears don't flow in this place.

ESTELLE: I'm a coward. A coward! [*Pause.*] If you knew how I hate you!

INEZ [*taking her in her arms*]: Poor child! [*To* GARCIN] So the hearing's over. But there's no need to look like a hanging judge.

GARCIN: A hanging judge? [*He glances around him.*] I'd give a lot to be able to see myself in a glass. [*Pause.*] How hot it is! [*Unthinkingly he takes off his coat.*] Oh, sorry! [*He starts putting it on again.*]

ESTELLE: Don't bother. You can stay in your shirt-sleeves. As things are—

GARCIN: Just so. [*He drops his coat on the sofa.*] You mustn't be angry with me, Estelle.

ESTELLE: I'm not angry with you.

INEZ: And what about me? Are you angry with me?

ESTELLE: Yes.

[*A short silence.*]

INEZ: Well, Mr. Garcin, now you have us in the nude all right. Do you understand things any better for that?

GARCIN: I wonder. Yes, perhaps a trifle better. [*Timidly*] And now suppose we start trying to help each other.

INEZ: I don't need help.

GARCIN: Inez, they've laid their snare damned cunningly—like a cobweb. If you make any movement, if you raise your hand to fan yourself, Estelle and I feel a little tug. Alone, none of us can save himself or herself; we're linked together inextricably. So you can take your choice. [*A pause.*] . . .

INEZ: Very well, have it your own way. I'm the weaker party, one against two. But don't forget I'm here, and watching. I shan't take my eyes off you, Garcin; when you're kissing her, you'll feel them boring into you. Yes, have it your own way, make love and get it over. We're in hell; my turn will come.

[*During the following scene she watches them without speaking.*]

GARCIN [*coming back to* ESTELLE *and grasping her shoulders*]: Now then. Your lips. Give me your lips.

A pause. He bends to kiss her, then abruptly straightens up.]

ESTELLE [*indignantly*]: Really! [*A pause.*] Didn't I tell you not to pay any attention to her?

GARCIN: You've got it wrong. [*Short silence.*] It's Gomez; he's back in the press-room. They've shut the windows; it must be winter down there. Six months since I—Well, I warned you I'd be absent-minded sometimes, didn't I? They're shivering, they've kept their coats on. Funny they should feel the cold like that, when I'm feeling so hot. Ah, this time he's talking about me.

ESTELLE: Is it going to last long? [*Short silence.*] You might at least tell me what he's saying.

GARCIN: Nothing. Nothing worth repeating. He's a swine, that's all. [*He listens attentively.*] A god-damned bloody swine. [*He turns to* ESTELLE.] Let's come back to—to ourselves. Are you going to love me?

ESTELLE [*Smiling*]: I wonder now!

GARCIN: Will you trust me?

ESTELLE: What a quaint thing to ask! Considering you'll be under my eyes all the time, and I don't think I've much to fear from Inez, so far as you're concerned.

GARCIN: Obviously. [*A pause. He takes his hands off* ESTELLE'S *shoulders.*] I was thinking of another kind of trust. [*Listens.*] Talk away, talk away, you swine. I'm not there to defend myself. [*To* ESTELLE] Estelle, you *must* give me your trust.

ESTELLE: Oh, what a nuisance you are! I'm giving you my mouth, my arms, my whole body—and everything could be so simple. . . . My trust! I haven't any to give, I'm afraid, and you're making me terribly embarrassed. You must have something pretty ghastly on your conscience to make such a fuss about my trusting you.

GARCIN: They shot me.

ESTELLE: I know. Because you refused to fight. Well, why shouldn't you?

GARCIN: I—I didn't exactly refuse. [*In a faraway voice*] I must say he talks well, he makes out a good case against me, but he never says what I should have done instead. Should I have gone to the general and said: "General, I decline to fight"? A mug's game; they'd have promptly locked me up. But I wanted to show my colors, my true colors, do you understand? I wasn't going to be silenced. [*To* ESTELLE] So I took the train. . . . They caught me at the frontier.

ESTELLE: Where were you trying to go?

GARCIN: To Mexico. I meant to launch a pacifist newspaper down there. [*A short silence.*] Well, why don't you speak?

ESTELLE: What could I say? You acted quite rightly, as you didn't want to fight. [GARCIN *makes a fretful gesture.*] But, darling, how on earth can I guess what you want me to answer?

INEZ: Can't you guess? Well, *I* can. He wants you to tell him that he bolted like a lion. For "bolt" he did, and that's what's biting him.

GARCIN: "Bolted," "went away"—we won't quarrel over words.

ESTELLE: But you *had* to run away. If you'd stayed they'd have sent you to jail, wouldn't they?

GARCIN: Of course. [*A pause.*] Well, Estelle, am I a coward?

ESTELLE: How can I say? Don't be so unreasonable, darling. I can't put myself in your skin. You must decide that for yourself.

GARCIN [*wearily*]: I can't decide.

ESTELLE: Anyhow, you must remember. You must have had reasons for acting as you did.

GARCIN: I had.

ESTELLE: Well?

GARCIN: But were they the real reasons?

ESTELLE: You've a twisted mind, that's your trouble. Plaguing yourself over such trifles!

GARCIN: I'd thought it all out, and I wanted to make a stand. But was that my real motive?

INEZ: Exactly. That's the question. Was that your real motive? No doubt you argued it out with yourself, you weighed the pros and cons, you found good reasons for what you did. But fear and hatred and all the dirty little instincts one keeps dark—they're motives too. So carry on, Mr. Garcin, and try to be honest with yourself—for once.

GARCIN: Do I need you to tell me that? Day and night I paced my cell, from the window to the door, from the door to the window. I pried into my heart, I sleuthed myself like a detective. By the end of it I felt as if I'd given my whole life to introspection. But always I harked back to the one thing certain—that I had acted as I did, I'd taken that train to the frontier. But why? Why? Finally I thought: My death will settle it. If I face death courageously, I'll prove I am no coward.

INEZ: And how did you face death?

GARCIN: Miserably. Rottenly. [INEZ *laughs.*] Oh, it was only a physical lapse—that might happen to anyone; I'm not ashamed of it. Only everything's been left in suspense forever. [*To* ESTELLE] Come here, Estelle. Look at me. I want to feel someone looking at me while they're talking about me on earth. . . . I like green eyes.

INEZ: Green eyes! Just hark to him! And you, Estelle, do you like cowards?

ESTELLE: If you knew how little I care! Coward or hero, it's all one—provided he kisses well.

GARCIN: There they are, slumped in their chairs, sucking at their cigars. Bored they look. Half-asleep. They're thinking: "Garcin's a coward." But only vaguely, dreamily. One's got to think of something. "That chap Garcin was a coward." That's what they've decided, those dear friends of mine. In six months' time they'll be saying: "Cowardly as that skunk Garcin." You're lucky, you two; no one on earth is giving you another thought. But I—I'm long in dying.

INEZ: What about your wife, Garcin?

GARCIN: Oh, didn't I tell you? She's dead.

INEZ: Dead?

GARCIN: Yes, she died just now. About two months ago.

INEZ: Of grief?

GARCIN: What else should she die of? So all is for the best, you see; the war's over, my wife's dead, and I've carved out my place in history.

[*He gives a choking sob and passes his hand over his face.* ESTELLE *catches his arm.*]

ESTELLE: My poor darling! Look at me. Please look. Touch me. Touch me. [*She takes his hand and puts it on her neck.*] There! Keep your hand there. [GARCIN *makes a fretful movement.*] No, don't move. Why trouble what those men are thinking? They'll die off one by one. Forget them. There's only me, now.

GARCIN: But *they* won't forget *me,* not they! They'll die, but others will come after them to carry on the legend. I've left my fate in their hands.

ESTELLE: You think too much, that's your trouble.

GARCIN: What else is there to do now? I was a man of action once. . . . Oh, if only I could be with them again, for just one day—I'd fling their lie in their teeth. But I'm locked out; they're passing judgment on my life without troubling about me, and they're right, because I'm dead. Dead and done with. [*Laughs.*] A back number.

[*A short pause.*]

ESTELLE [*gently*]: Garcin.

GARCIN: Still there? Now listen! I want you to do me a service. No, don't shrink away. I know it must seem strange to you, having someone asking you for help; you're not used to that. But if you'll make the effort, if you'll only *will* it hard enough, I dare say we can really love each other. Look at it this way. A thousand of them are proclaiming I'm a coward; but what do numbers matter? If there's someone, just one person, to say quite positively I did not run away, that I'm not the sort who runs away, that I'm brave and decent and the rest of it—well, that one person's faith would save me. Will you have that faith in me? Then I shall love you and cherish you for ever. Estelle—will you?

ESTELLE [*laughing*]: Oh, you dear silly man, do you think I could love a coward?

GARCIN: But just now you said—

ESTELLE: I was only teasing you. I like men, my dear, who're real men, with tough skin and strong hands. You haven't a coward's chin, or a coward's mouth, or a coward's voice, or a coward's hair. And it's for your mouth, your hair, your voice, I love you.

GARCIN: Do you mean this? *Really* mean it?

ESTELLE: Shall I swear it?

GARCIN: Then I snap my fingers at them all, those below and those in here. Estelle, we shall climb out of hell. [INEZ *gives a shrill laugh. He breaks off and stares at her.*] What's that?

INEZ [*still laughing*]: But she doesn't mean a word of what she says. How can you be such a simpleton? "Estelle, am I a coward?" As if she cared a damn either way.

ESTELLE: Inez, how dare you? [*To* GARCIN] Don't listen to her. If you want me to have faith in you, you must begin by trusting me.

INEZ: That's right! That's right! Trust away! She wants a man—that far you can trust her—she wants a man's arm round her waist, a man's smell, a man's eyes glowing with desire. And that's all she wants. She'd assure you you were God Almighty if she thought it would give you pleasure.

GARCIN: Estelle, is this true? Answer me. Is it true?

ESTELLE: What do you expect me to say? Don't you realize how maddening it is to have to answer questions one can't make head or tail of? [*She stamps her foot.*] You do make things difficult. . . . Anyhow, I'd love you just the same, even if you were a coward. Isn't that enough?

[*A short pause.*]

GARCIN [*to the two women*]: You disgust me, both of you.

[*He goes towards the door.*]

ESTELLE: What are you up to?

GARCIN: I'm going.

INEZ [*quickly*]: You won't get far. The door is locked.

GARCIN: I'll *make* them open it. [*He presses the bell-push. The bell does not ring.*]

ESTELLE: Please! Please!

INEZ [*to* ESTELLE]: Don't worry, my pet. The bell doesn't work.

GARCIN: I tell you they shall open. [*Drums on the door.*] I can't endure it any longer, I'm through with you both. [ESTELLE *runs to him; he pushes her away.*] Go away. You're even fouler than she. I won't let myself get bogged in your eyes. You're soft and slimy. Ugh! [*Bangs on the door again.*] Like an octopus. Like a quagmire.

ESTELLE: I beg you, oh, I beg you not to leave me. I'll promise not to speak again, I won't trouble you in any way—but don't go. I daren't be left alone with Inez, now she's shown her claws.

GARCIN: Look after yourself. I never asked you to come here.

ESTELLE: Oh, how mean you are! Yes, it's quite true you're a coward.

INEZ [*going up to* ESTELLE]: Well, my little sparrow fallen from the nest, I hope you're satisfied now. You spat in my face—playing up to him, of course—and we had a tiff on his account. But he's going, and a good riddance it will be. We two women will have the place to ourselves.

ESTELLE: You won't gain anything. If that door opens, I'm going, too.

INEZ: Where?

ESTELLE: I don't care where. As far from you as I can. [GARCIN *has been drumming on the door while they talk.*]

GARCIN: Open the door! Open, blast you! I'll endure anything, your red-hot tongs and molten lead, your racks and prongs and garrotes—all your fiendish gadgets, everything that burns and flays and tears—I'll put up with any torture you impose. Anything, anything would be better than this agony of mind, this creeping pain that gnaws and fumbles and caresses one and never hurts quite enough. [*He grips the doorknob and rattles it.*] Now will you open? [*The door flies open with a jerk, and he just avoids falling.*] Ah! [*A long silence.*]

INEZ: Well, Garcin? You're free to go.

GARCIN [*meditatively*]: Now I wonder why that door opened.

INEZ: What are you waiting for? Hurry up and go.

GARCIN: I shall not go.

INEZ: And you, Estelle? [ESTELLE *does not move.* INEZ *bursts out laughing.*] So what? Which shall it be? Which of the three of us will leave? The barrier's down, why are we waiting? . . . But what a situation! It's a scream! We're—inseparables!

[ESTELLE *springs at her from behind.*]

ESTELLE: Inseparables? Garcin, come and lend a hand. Quickly. We'll push her out and slam the door on her. That'll teach her a lesson.

INEZ [*struggling with* ESTELLE]: Estelle! I beg you, let me stay. I won't go, I won't go! Not into the passage.

GARCIN: Let go of her.

ESTELLE: You're crazy. She hates you.

GARCIN: It's because of her I'm staying here. [ESTELLE *releases* INEZ *and stares dumbfoundedly at* GARCIN.]

INEZ: Because of me? [*Pause.*] All right, shut the door. It's ten times hotter here since it opened. [GARCIN *goes to the door and shuts it.*] Because of me, you said?

GARCIN: Yes. *You,* anyhow, know what it means to be a coward.

INEZ: Yes, I know.

GARCIN: And you know what wickedness is, and shame, and fear. There were days when you peered into yourself, into the secret places of your heart, and what you saw there made you faint with horror. And then, next day, you didn't know what to make of it, you couldn't interpret the horror you had glimpsed the day before. Yes, you know what evil costs. And when you say I'm a coward, you know from experience what that means. Is that so?

INEZ: Yes.

GARCIN: So it's you whom I have to convince; you are of my kind. Did you suppose I meant to go? No, I couldn't leave you here, gloating over my defeat, with all those thoughts about me running in your head.

INEZ: Do you really wish to convince me?

GARCIN: That's the one and only thing I wish for now. I can't hear them any longer, you know. Probably that means they're through with me. For good and all. The curtain's down, nothing of me is left on earth—not even the name of coward. So, Inez, we're alone. Only you two remain to give a thought to me. She—she doesn't count. It's you who matter; you who hate me. If you'll have faith in me I'm saved.

INEZ: It won't be easy. Have a look at me. I'm a hard-headed woman.

GARCIN: I'll give you all the time that's needed.

INEZ: Yes, we've lots of time in hand. *All* time.

GARCIN [*putting his hands on her shoulders*]: Listen! Each man has an aim in life, a leading motive; that's so, isn't it? Well, I didn't give a damn for wealth, or for love. I aimed at being a real man. A tough, as they say. I staked everything on the same horse. . . . Can one possibly be a coward when one's deliberately courted danger at every turn? And can one judge a life by a single action?

INEZ: Why not? For thirty years you dreamt you were a hero, and condoned a thousand petty lapses—because a hero, of course, can do no wrong. An easy method, obviously. Then a day came when you were up against it, the red light of real danger—and you took the train to Mexico.

GARCIN: I "dreamt," you say. It was no dream. When I chose the hardest path, I made my choice deliberately. A man is what he wills himself to be.

INEZ: Prove it. Prove it was no dream. It's what one does, and nothing else, that shows the stuff one's made of.

GARCIN: I died too soon. I wasn't allowed time to—to do my deeds.

INEZ: One always dies too soon—or too late. And yet one's whole life is complete at that moment, with a line drawn neatly under it, ready for the summing up. You are—your life, and nothing else.

GARCIN: What a poisonous woman you are! With an answer for everything.

INEZ: Now then! Don't lose heart. It shouldn't be so hard, convincing me. Pull yourself together, man, rake up some arguments. [GARCIN *shrugs his shoulders.*] Ah, wasn't I right when I said you were vulnerable? Now you're going to pay the price, and what a price! You're a coward, Garcin, because I wish it. I wish it—do you hear?—I wish it. And yet, just look at me, see how weak I am, a mere breath on the air, a gaze observing you, a formless thought that thinks you. [*He walks towards her, opening his hands.*] Ah, they're open now, those big hands, those coarse, man's hands! But what do you hope to do? You can't throttle thoughts with hands. So you've no choice, you must convince me, and you're at my mercy.

ESTELLE: Garcin!

GARCIN: What?

ESTELLE: Revenge yourself.

GARCIN: How?

ESTELLE: Kiss me, darling—then you'll hear her squeal.

GARCIN: That's true, Inez. I'm at your mercy, but you're at mine as well.

[*He bends over* ESTELLE. INEZ *gives a little cry.*]

INEZ: Oh, you coward, you weakling, running to women to console you!

ESTELLE: That's right, Inez. Squeal away.

INEZ: What a lovely pair you make! If you could see his big paw splayed out on your back, rucking up your skin and creasing the silk. Be careful, though! He's perspiring, his hand will leave a blue stain on your dress.

ESTELLE: Squeal away, Inez, squeal away! . . . Hug me tight, darling; tighter still—that'll finish her off, and a good thing too!

INEZ: Yes, Garcin, she's right. Carry on with it, press her to you till you feel your bodies melting into each other; a lump of warm, throbbing flesh. . . . Love's a grand solace, isn't it, my friend? Deep and dark as sleep. But I'll see you don't sleep.

ESTELLE: Don't listen to her. Press your lips to my mouth. Oh, I'm yours, yours, yours.

INEZ: Well, what are you waiting for? Do as you're told. What a lovely scene: coward Garcin holding baby-killer Estelle in his manly arms! Make your stakes, everyone. Will coward Garcin kiss the lady, or won't he dare? What's the betting? I'm watching you, everybody's watching, I'm a crowd all by myself. Do you hear the crowd? Do you hear them muttering, Garcin? Mumbling and muttering. "Coward! Coward! Coward! Coward!"—that's what they're saying. . . . It's no use trying to escape, I'll never let you go. What do you hope to get from her silly lips? Forgetfulness? But I shan't forget you, not I! "It's I you must convince." So come to me. I'm waiting. Come along, now. . . . Look how obedient he is, like a well-trained dog who comes when his mistress calls. You can't hold him, and you never will.

GARCIN: Will night never come?

INEZ: Never.

GARCIN: You will always see me?

INEZ: Always.

[GARCIN *moves away from* ESTELLE *and takes some steps across the room. He goes to the bronze ornament.*]

GARCIN: This bronze. [*Strokes it thoughtfully.*] Yes, now's the moment; I'm looking at this thing on the mantelpiece, and I understand that I'm in hell. I tell you, everything's been thought out beforehand. They knew I'd stand at the fireplace stroking this thing of bronze, with all those eyes intent on me. Devouring me. [*He swings round abruptly.*] What? Only two of you? I thought there were more; many more. [*Laughs.*] So this is hell. I'd never have believed it. You remember all we were told about the torture-chambers, the fire and brimstone, the "burning marl." Old wives' tales. There's no need for red-hot pokers. Hell is—other people!

ESTELLE: My darling! Please—

GARCIN [*thrusting her away*]: No, let me be. She is between us. I cannot love you when she's watching.

ESTELLE: Right! In that case, I'll stop her watching. [*She picks up the paper-knife from the table, rushes at* INEZ *and stabs her several times.*]

INEZ [*struggling and laughing*]: But, you crazy creature, what do you think you're doing? You know quite well I'm dead.

ESTELLE: Dead?

[*She drops the knife. A pause.* INEZ *picks up the knife and jabs herself with it regretfully.*]

INEZ: Dead! Dead! Dead! Knives, poison, ropes—all useless. It has happened *already,* do you understand? Once and for all. So here we are, forever. [*Laughs.*]

ESTELLE [*with a peal of laughter*]: Forever. My God, how funny! Forever.

GARCIN [*looks at the two women, and joins in the laughter*]: For ever, and ever, and ever.

[*They slump onto their respective sofas. A long silence. Their laughter dies away and they gaze at each other.*]

GARCIN: Well, well, let's get on with it. . . .

CURTAIN

Basic Existentialist Concepts

Being-with-Others Despite their emphasis on individuality, twentieth-century existentialists rejected the notion of an individualized self existing independently of others. They understood the individual as inescapably linked with others. A human being does not exist statically among others without affecting them or being affected by them. Moreover, when one undertakes practical tasks, one understands the meanings of situations, objects, and events in ways that draw one into a world peopled by others and shaped by them. The individual's activities and understanding do not occur in a self-enclosed space; rather they open into the world—a world shared by others.

Our active engagement with the world is permeated by our relations with others. The things in the world we experience—houses, roads, books, lights, and so on—are designed for human use; others invented them, gave them meanings, and share in using them. We may spend time alone in wild nature, but we do not live in nature without knowing how other people name the things in nature (e.g., "oak tree") or use the things in nature (e.g., berries for food). Thus, we are always implicitly encountering others with whom we share the world. For example, the sidewalk I use is a path designed for others' use as well as my own. I am aware of this whenever I walk on one; I am aware of anonymous others, before and after me, for whom the sidewalk exists as well. (In *No Exit*, the furniture of the room symbolizes this relation to anonymous others encountered in the things of the world.)

When I enter into concrete relations with others in friendship, love, kinship, or mere acquaintance, my self-awareness is reflected in the awareness others have of me. Others can watch me, interpret my behavior, judge me, love me, or hate me; I exist for them. Their feedback about what I do and who I am deprives me of full control over my own self-definition. To exist as a human being is not simply to be with others in the way that we exist with the trees on the surface of the earth, but to exist *for* others. Most of our emotions and many of our decisions register how aware we are that we exist for others: We are happy, nervous, angry, or jealous, usually as a result of our relations with others; we choose many of our actions in view of how others will be affected by them or how others will judge us.

The Look Sartre refined the concept of Being-with-others by analyzing how different our experiences of the world become when we notice that others are looking at us or at the world, too. When we know we are under another's gaze, the ineliminable presence of others in our life becomes a palpable force that pins us down. We become self-conscious because we believe that the other is not only viewing us, but also interpreting what we do and even judging us. We can see the other's eyes cast upon us, but we cannot get behind their eyes, inside their head, to find out what they really think of us.

In *Being and Nothingness* Sartre asks us to imagine two examples of *the Look:* The first occurs when I surreptitiously look through the keyhole of someone's door to spy on them; the second occurs when somebody else suddenly comes up behind me and watches me while I am looking through the keyhole. Sartre's point is that the Look is a kind of power play: The person who can look at another without being looked at in turn is in a position of power over the other.

In Sartre's play *No Exit*, the Look becomes an important dynamic force in the relationships between the three characters. It is the initial source of the judgments they make about one another, and it becomes an instrument of torture that the three characters inflict on one another.

Bad Faith Sartre's concept of bad faith is the concept of self-deception. According to Sartre, most of our lives are spent in bad faith because we can never be fully sincere or even sure about who we are. The paradox of bad faith is stated most boldly in Sartre's famous claim that "I am what I am not, and I am not what I am."

The reason why we cannot be fully sincere or sure about who we are is that we are always in the process of becoming who we are; we are not finished as long as we live. We have the freedom to create ourselves and the freedom to change ourselves at any time. In contrast, nonhuman things lack freedom and simply are what they are; they are unable to become anything else.

In Sartre's claim that "I am what I am not," the phrase "what I am not" refers to what I shall be in the future (though I am not that in the present). Because my existence is freedom, what I shall be in the future, as a result of my own free actions, is as important to who I am as anything I have done in the past. In Sartre's second claim that "I am not what I am," the phrase "what I am" refers to the essence I have already created for myself out of my past actions. But because I am free, I am not merely my essence; I am also existence, the ever forward moving upsurge of my own freedom.

Sartre's characters in *No Exit* are portrayed ambiguously as both dead (they are in hell) and alive (they act in many of the same ways as they did on earth). Although the essence of who they were during their earthly lifetimes has been fixed by their deaths, and although they no longer have the freedom to change any of their past actions on earth, they converse with one another and relate to one another with the kind of freedom that characterizes human existence. Their ambiguous status, as both dead and alive, does not imply that Sartre believes in an afterlife, but it symbolizes Sartre's claim that our essence is constituted by our past actions. Just as death fixes our essence definitively because we can no longer act, so the impossibility of going back to change our past actions fixes them definitively as part of our essence.

Sartre usually uses the notion of bad faith to characterize individuals who are more self-deceived than they should be, even though none of us can escape self-deception entirely. What makes some self-deception so flagrant is an unwillingness to acknowledge either one's own freedom or one's responsibility for one's past actions. Some people are in bad faith because they deny that they are free; they think that they have a certain fixed character and can never change. (Inez, for example, believes that her character is fixed.) Such self-deceived people believe that their essence cannot be modified by their existence.

Others are in bad faith because they deny responsibility for their past actions; they think that their freedom gives them a license to disavow anything they might have done. (Garcin, for example, argues that it is irrelevant that he acted cowardly because if he had lived longer, his future actions would have proved to be courageous.) Self-deceived people of the latter sort believe that their existence creates no essence at all. Both kinds of self-deceived people fail to understand the full truth about who they are—namely, that they are free to change but they are also responsible for what they have already made of themselves.

There are two other forms of bad faith which are generated in our relations with others: crediting others with the ability and responsibility to define me, and completely ignoring what others think of me. These two forms of bad faith are closely related to the concept of the Look and to the inability of others to know me as I know myself. For Sartre, an individual is the sum total of his or her actions. The actions one has already performed can be known by others; others may have even looked at the individual while she was performing them. But the actions the individual would freely choose to perform in the future cannot be known in the same way by others. Their judgment is based upon what the individual has already done and made of herself, but this is only a part of who the individual is. Others' judgment leaves out the future dimension of the individual's freedom, which allows her to transcend whatever she has already done.

If an individual relies too heavily on what others think of her, she falls into bad faith. She overemphasizes her Being-for-others and de-emphasizes her own freedom to interpret her actions and her projects for herself. She resigns herself to being defined by the roles others expect her to play or by the personality traits that others see in her. Her sense of her own identity is placed in the control of others, instead of being counterbalanced by her personal view of herself. (Estelle is the prime example of this form of bad faith.)

If an individual ignores what others think of him and insists upon characterizing himself by his own lights, he falls into a different form of bad faith—the bad faith of denying that he is Being-for-others. Such a person will deny that his past actions, as interpreted by others, matter much, and he will define himself instead as a free spirit, unrestricted by others' views of him. He pretends that his existence is a possession that he, as proprietor, alone manages, rather than a movement out into the world, engaged in relations with others. (Garcin attempts to view himself in this way, but Inez continually reminds him that she defines him in terms of his past actions.)

Questions for Discussion

1. List the various features of the room or the characters' own bodies that relate to visual experience (e.g., the absence of mirrors). How do these features symbolize the nature of the Look?

2. Can others judge an individual's intentions or only his actions?

3. Could one of the three characters exist alone and not fall into bad faith? Why, or why not?

4. Do you agree with Sartre that an individual is the sum total of his or her actions?

5. Do you agree with Sartre that relationships with others are always conflictual?

Chapter 8

Simone de Beauvoir's "The Woman Destroyed"

Introduction: Critique of Women's Dependency

In her literary and autobiographical works, Simone de Beauvoir investigated the various kinds of relations that individuals develop with one another. In almost all cases, her characters were neither loners, as Roquentin was in Sartre's *Nausea,* nor social misfits, as Meursault was in Camus' *The Stranger.* Instead, her characters were integrated within families, circles of friends, or political cadres in which familiarity, cooperation, alliance, and intimacy were not unknown. Yet they also struggled with the emotions and tensions that arise in personal and social relationships, making it clear that even if hell is not other people, conflict certainly is.

Among Beauvoir's most compelling interests was her project to describe and analyze women's lives. In her feminist treatise *The Second Sex,* written in the late 1940s, Beauvoir investigated the features of women's lives that made women different from men. She argued that biological, psychological, or economic causes could not alone account for women's inferior social position. What Beauvoir saw as crucial for the inequality between women and men were oppressive social relations in which women's aspirations and sense of identity were dictated by men. "One is not born a woman, one becomes one," she declared, blaming the social conditioning through which womanhood is constructed, rather than a biologically determined essence of womanhood, for the characteristics that distinguish women from men.

In the short story "The Woman Destroyed," Monique describes her relations with her husband and daughters as central to her sense of herself. A housewife married to a doctor, Monique made family her project in life: She quit school to support her husband through medical school; she was fully absorbed in raising her two daughters to the point of being overbearing; she refused to take a job outside the home with the excuse that she needed to be available at all times to help others. By making herself so dependent on her family for the meaning of her life, Monique created the conditions for her own destruction. But one must ask, as Beauvoir did: Have women like Monique been conditioned by society to become dependent on others for their self-definition?

Beauvoir's "The Woman Destroyed" (Excerpts)[1]

Monday 13 September. Les Salines.

It is an astonishing setting, this rough draft of a town lying deserted here, on the edge of a village and outside the flow of the centuries. I went along one half of the hemicycle and climbed the steps of the central building; for a long while I gazed at the quiet splendor of these structures that were put up for functional purposes and that have never been used for anything at all. They are solid; they are real: yet their abandoned state changes them into a fantastic pretense—of what, one wonders. The warm grass under the autumn sky and the smell of dead leaves told me that I had certainly not left this world; but I had gone back two hundred years into the past. I went to fetch things out of the car: I spread a rug on the ground, cushions, the transistor, and I smoked, listening to Mozart. Behind two or three dusty windows I could make out people moving to and fro—offices no doubt. A truck stopped in front of one of the massive doors; men opened it; they loaded sacks into the back. Nothing else disturbed the silence of that afternoon: I traveled away, a great way off, to the shores of an unknown river; and then when I looked up there I was among these stones, far, far from my own life.

For the most surprising thing about it is my being here, and the cheerfulness of my being here. I had not looked forward to the loneliness of this drive back to Paris at all. Hitherto, if Maurice were not there, the girls were always with me, in all my journeys. I had thought I was going to miss Colette's raptures and Lucienne's demandingness. And here I am with happiness of a forgotten kind given back to me. My freedom makes me twenty years younger. So much so that when I closed the book I began writing just for myself, as I did when I was twenty.

I never part from Maurice with a light heart. The congress is only going to last a week, yet there was a lump in my throat as we drove from Mougins to the Nice airfield. He, too, was moved. When the loudspeaker summoned the travelers for Rome he squeezed me tight. "Don't get killed on the road. Don't get killed in the plane." Before he vanished he turned around to look at me again: there was anxiety in his eyes, and I caught it at once. The takeoff seemed to me dramatic. Four-engined planes rise gently into the air—it is a long drawn-out *au revoir.* This jet left the ground with the violence of a last goodbye.

But presently I began to bubble with happiness. No, my daughters' absence did not sadden me at all—quite the reverse. I could drive as fast or as slowly as I liked, go where I liked, stop when the whim took me. I made up my mind to spend the week wandering about. I get up as soon as it is light. The car is waiting for me in the street or in the courtyard like a faithful animal; it is wet with dew; I wipe its eyes, and full of delight I tear away through the growing sunlight. Beside me there is the white bag with the Michelin maps, the Guide Bleu, some books, a cardigan and my cigarettes—a reticent companion. No one grows impatient if I ask the owner of the little hotel for her recipe for chicken with crayfish.

Dusk is about to fall, but it is still warm. It is one of these heart-touching moments when the world is so well attuned to men that it seems impossible that they should not all be happy.

Tuesday 14 September.

One of the things that really pleased Maurice was the intensity of what he called "my awareness of life." It was revived during this short colloquy with myself. Now that Colette is married and Lucienne is in America I shall have all the time in the world to cultivate it. "You'll

[1] From *The Woman Destroyed* by Simone de Beauvoir, translated by Patrick O'Brien.

be bored. You ought to look for a job," Maurice said to me at Mougins. He went on and on about it. But I do not want one; not for the moment, anyhow. I want to live for myself a little, after all this time. And for us, Maurice and I, to make the most of this double solitude that we have been deprived of for so long. I have plans by the dozen in my mind.

Friday 17 September.

On Tuesday I telephoned Colette: she had flu. She protested when I said I was coming straight back to Paris—Jean-Pierre was looking after her very well. But I was worried, and I got back that same day. I found her in bed, much thinner: she has a fever every evening. When I went into the mountains with her back in August—even then I was anxious about her health. I can't wait for Maurice to examine her, and I should like him to call in Talbot for a consultation. . . .

Wednesday 22 September.

Here is one of the reasons—indeed the main reason—why I have not the least wish to be tied down to a job: I should find it hard to bear if I were not entirely free to help the people who need me. I spend almost all my days at Colette's bedside. Her temperature will not go down. "It's nothing serious," says Maurice. But Talbot wants analyses. Terrifying notions run through my mind. . . .

And I am worried now. Reading is impossible. The only thing that could ease my mind would be talking to Maurice: he will not be here before midnight. Since he came back from Rome he spends his evenings at the laboratory with Talbot and Couturier. He says they are getting near to their goal. I can understand his giving up everything to his research. But this is the first time in my life that I have a serious worry that he does not share.

Saturday 25 September.

The window was black. I had expected it. Before—before what?—when by some extraordinary chance I went out without Maurice there was always a streak of light between the red curtains when I came back. I would run up the two flights of stairs and ring, too impatient to look for my key. This time I went up the stairs without running; I pushed my key into the lock. How empty the apartment was! How empty it is! Of course it is, since there is no one in it. No, that's not it: usually when I come home I find Maurice here, even when he is out. This evening the doors open onto wholly empty rooms. Eleven o'clock. Tomorrow the results of the analyses will be known, and I am afraid. I am afraid, and Maurice is not here. I know. His research must be carried through. Still, I am angry with him. *I need you, and you aren't here!* I feel like writing those words on a piece of paper and leaving it in an obvious place in the hall before I go to bed. Otherwise I shall be bottling it in, as I did yesterday, and as I did the day before that. He always used to be there when I needed him.

I watered the potted plants; I began to tidy the books and I stopped dead. I had been astonished by his lack of interest when I talked to him about arranging this sitting room. I must tell myself the truth: I have always wanted the truth and the reason why I have had it is that I desired it. Well, then. Maurice has changed. He has let himself be eaten up by his profession. He no longer reads. He no longer listens to music. (I used so to love our silence and his attentive face as we listened to Monteverdi or Charlie Parker.) We no longer go out together in or around Paris. It might almost be said we no longer have any real conversation. He is beginning to be like his colleagues who are merely machines for getting on and for making money. I'm being unfair. He doesn't give a damn for money or social success. But ever since he decided, ten years ago, against my wishes, to specialize, gradually (and that was what I had been afraid of) he has grown hard. Even at Mougins this year I thought him remote—intensely eager to get back to the hospital and the laboratory, absent-minded and indeed moody. Come! I might as well tell myself the truth right through to the end. The reason why my heart was so heavy at Nice airfield was those dismal holidays behind us. And the reason why I had so vivid a happiness in the deserted saltworks was that Maurice, hundreds of miles away, was close to me again. (What an odd thing a diary is: the things you omit are more important than those you put in.) Anyone would say he was no longer interested in his private life. How easily he gave up our trip to Alsace last spring! Yet my disappointment grieved him deeply. I said cheerfully, "A cure for leukemia is certainly worth a few sacrifices!" But there was a time when for Maurice medicine meant the relief of men and women made of flesh and blood. . . .I am afraid that now his patients are merely cases for him. Knowing concerns him more than healing. And even in his relations with people close to him he is growing remote, he who was so alive, so cheerful, as young at forty-five as when I first met him. . . .Yes, something has changed, since here I am writing about him, about myself, behind his back. If he had done so, I should have felt betrayed. Each of us used to be able to see entirely into the other.

So we can still; it is my anger that is keeping us apart—he will soon make it die away. He will ask me to be patient a little longer; after spells of furious overwork come the calm, easy days. Last year too he often worked in the evenings. Yes, but then I had Lucienne. And above all there was nothing tormenting me. He knows very well that at present I can neither read nor listen to a record, because I am afraid. I shall not leave a note in the hall, but I shall talk to him. After twenty—twenty-two—years of marriage one relies too much upon silence—it is dangerous. I believe these last years I was too wrapped up in the girls—Colette was so lovable and Lucienne so difficult. Perhaps I was not as free, as available, as Maurice might have wished. He ought to have pointed it out instead of flinging himself into work that now cuts him off from me. We must have it out together.

Midnight. I am in such a hurry to be at one with him again and to stifle the anger that is still rumbling inside me that I keep my eyes fixed on the clock. Its hands do not move: I grow irritated, all on edge. My mental image of Maurice falls to pieces: what sense is there in fighting against illness and suffering if you behave so stupidly toward your own wife? It's indifference. It's hardness of heart. No point in losing one's temper. Stop it. If Colette's analyses are not good, I shall need all my self-control tomorrow. I must try to go to sleep, then.

Sunday 26 September.

So it's happened. It's happened to me.

Monday 27 September.

Yes, here I am! It's happened to me. It is *perfectly usual.* I must convince myself of that and strangle this fury that shattered me all yesterday. Maurice lied to me: yes, that too is perfectly usual. He might have gone on doing so instead of telling me. However late it is, I ought to feel grateful to him for his candor.

In the end I did go to sleep on Saturday. From time to time I stretched out to touch the other bed—its sheet was flat. (I like going to sleep before him when he is working in his consulting room. Through my dreams I hear water running, smell a faint whiff of eau de Cologne; I reach out, his body molds the sheet, and I sink deep down into happiness.) The front door slammed. I called, "Maurice!" It was three in the morning. They had not been working until three: they had been drinking and gossiping. I sat up in bed. "What kind of time is this to come home? Where have you been?"

He sat down in an armchair. He was holding a glass of whiskey in his hand.

"It's three o'clock, I know."

"Colette is ill, I'm racked with anxiety, and you come home at three. You haven't all been working until three?"

"Is Colette worse?"

"She's not better. You don't care! Clearly, when you take the health of all mankind under your wing an ill daughter doesn't amount to much."

"Don't be inimical." He looked at me with a rather saddened gravity, and I melted as I always do melt when he envelops me in that dark, warm light. Gently I asked, "Tell me why you have come home so late."

He made no reply.

"Were you drinking? Playing poker? Did you all go out? Did you forget the time?" He went on being silent, as it were emphatically silent, twirling his glass between his fingers. I flung out nonsensical words to make him lose his temper—to jerk an explanation out of him. "What's the matter? Is there a woman in your life?"

Looking at me steadily he said, "Yes, Monique, there is a woman in my life."

(Everything was blue above our heads and beneath our feet: on the other side of the strait loomed the coast of Africa. He squeezed me against him. "If you were to deceive me I should kill myself." "If you were to deceive me I should have no need to kill myself. I should die of grief." Fifteen years ago. Already? What do fifteen years count? Twice two is four. I love you, I love you alone. Truth cannot be destroyed: time has no effect upon it.)

"Who is it?"

"Noëllie Guérard."

"Noëllie! Why?"

He shrugged. Of course. I knew the answer—pretty, dashing, bitchy, available. The sort of adventure that has no importance and that flatters a man. Did he need flattery?

He smiled at me. "I'm glad you questioned me. I hated lying to you."

"Since when have you been lying to me?"

He scarcely hesitated at all. "I lied to you at Mougins. And since I came back."

That made five weeks. Was he thinking about her at Mougins? "Did you go to bed with her when you stayed in Paris by yourself?"

"Yes."

"Do you see her often?"

"Oh, no! You know very well I am working . . . ."

I asked him to be more exact. Two evenings and one afternoon since he came back: that seems often enough to me.

"Why didn't you tell me right away?"

He looked at me shyly, and with sorrow in his voice he said, "You used to say you would die of grief. . . ."

"One says that."

Suddenly I wanted to cry: I should not die of it—that was the saddest thing about it. We gazed at Africa, a great way off through the blue haze, and the words we uttered were merely words. I lay back. The blow had stunned me. My head went empty with shock. I had to have a pause, a break in time, to understand what had happened to me. "Let's go to sleep," I said.

Anger woke me early. How innocent he looked lying there, with his hair tangled over a forehead that sleep had made young again. (In August, when I was away, she woke up at his side: I can't bring myself to believe it! Why did I go to the mountains with Colette? It was not as though she very much wanted to—I was the one who insisted.) For five weeks he had been lying to me. "This evening we made an important step forward." And he had just come from Noëllie's. I felt like shaking him, insulting him, shrieking. I took myself in hand. I left a note on my pillow: *see you this evening.* I was sure my absence would affect him more than any reproaches: there is no possible reply to absence. I walked through the streets, wherever chance led me, obsessed by the words: *He lied to me.* Mental images pierced me through—Maurice's eyes set on Noëllie, his smile. I dismissed them. He doesn't look at her as he looks at me. I did not want to suffer; I did not suffer; but I choked with bitterness. He lied to me! I had said, "I should die of grief": yes, but he had made me say it. He had been more eager than I in drawing up our pact—no compromise, no deviating. We were driving along the little road to Saint-Bertrand-de-Comminges, and he pressed me: "Shall I always be enough for you?" He blazed up because there was not enough ardor in my reply (but what a reconciliation in our room at the old inn, with the scent of honeysuckle coming in at the window! Twenty years ago—

it was yesterday). He has been enough for me: I have lived only for him. And for a mere whim he has betrayed our vows. I said to myself, I shall insist upon his breaking it off, right away. . . . I went to Colette's apartment; all day long I looked after her, but inside I was boiling. I came home, quite worn out. "I'm going to insist upon his breaking it off." But what does the word insist mean after a whole life of love and understanding? I have never asked anything for myself that I did not also wish for him.

He took me in his arms, looking quite distraught. He had telephoned to Colette's several times and no one had answered (I had jammed the bell, so that she would not be disturbed). He was out of his mind with anxiety.

"But you didn't really imagine I was going to do myself in?"

"There was nothing I didn't imagine."

His anxiety went to my heart, and I listened to him without hostility. Of course he had been wrong to lie, but I had to understand: the first reluctance snowballs—you no longer dare confess because then you would also have to admit to having lied. It is an even more impossible hurdle for people who rate sincerity so very high, as we do. (I admit that: how furiously I should have lied to conceal a falsehood.) I have never made proper allowance for untruth. Lucienne's and Colette's first fibs utterly flabbergasted me. I found it very hard to accept that all children lie to their mothers. Not to me! I am not the kind of mother that is lied to: not a wife that is lied to. Idiotic vanity. All women think they are different; they all think there are some things that will never happen to them; and they are all wrong. . . .

Friday 1 October.

I behaved badly for the first time. During breakfast Maurice told me that from now on, when he goes with Noëllie in the evening, he is going to spend the whole night at her place. It is more seemly for her, just as it is for me, he says. "Since you acquiesce in my having this affair, let me live it decently."

Taking into account the number of evenings he spends at the laboratory and the number of lunches he skips, he is giving Noëllie almost as much time as me. I flared up. He bewildered me with calculations. If the actual number of hours is counted, all right, he is more often with me. But during a great many of them he is working, reading periodicals—or else we are seeing friends. When he is with Noëllie he gives himself entirely up to her.

In the end I gave way. Since I have adopted an understanding, kindly attitude I must stick to it. No head-on collision with him. If I spoil his affair for him distance will make it seem charming—he will regret it. If I let him "live it decently" he will soon get tired of it. That's what Isabelle assures me. I repeat to myself, *Patience.*

Still, I must realize that at Maurice's age an infatuation means a good deal. At Mougins he was thinking of Noëllie, obviously. Now I understand the anxiety in his eyes at the Nice airfield—he was wondering whether I suspected anything. Or was he ashamed of having lied to me? Was it shame rather than anxiety? I can see his face once more, but I cannot make it out properly.

Saturday 2 October. Morning.

They are in their pajamas; they are drinking coffee, smiling at one another. . . .There is an image that hurts me. When you hit against a stone at first you only feel the impact—the pain comes after. Now, with a week's delay, I am beginning to suffer. Before, I was more bewildered—amazed. I rationalized, I thrust aside the pain that is pouring over me this morning—these images. I pace up and down the flat, up and down, and at each step another strikes me. I opened his cupboard. I looked at his pajamas, shirts, drawers, vests; and I began to weep. Another woman stroking his cheek, as soft as this silk, as warmly gentle as this pullover—that I cannot bear.

I was not watchful enough. I thought Maurice was aging, that he was overworking, that I ought to adapt myself to his lack of warmth. He took to thinking of me as a sister, more or less. Noëllie awoke his desires. Whether she has any sexual appetite or not she certainly knows how to conduct herself in bed. He has rediscovered the proud delight of fully satisfying a woman. Going to bed does not mean only going to bed. Between them there is that intimacy that used to belong only to me. When they wake up does he snuggle her against his shoulder, calling her his doe, his honeymouth? Or has he invented other names that he says in the same voice? Or has he found himself another voice? He is shaving, smiling at her, with his eyes darker and more brilliant, his mouth more naked under that mask of white foam. He appeared in the doorway holding a great bunch of red roses in his arms, wrapped in cellophane: does he take her flowers?

My heart is being sawed in two with a very fine-tooth saw. . . .

Tuesday 5 October.

I am spending rather too much time at Colette's, now that she is no longer ill. In spite of her great sweetness I feel that my anxious concern is on the edge of being a nuisance. When one has lived so much for others it is quite hard to turn oneself back again—to live for oneself. I must not plunge into the pitfall of devotion—I know very well that the words *give* and *receive* are interchangeable, and I know very well how much I needed the need my daughters had of me. On that point I have never played false. "You're wonderful," Maurice used to say to me—he used to say it to me so often, on one pretext or another "because giving others pleasure is in the first place a pleasure to you." I would laugh. "Yes, it's a form of selfishness." That tenderness in his eyes—"The most enchanting form there is." . . .

Thursday 7 October.

When all is said and done, what has it profited me, his telling me the truth? He spends whole nights with her now—it suits them splendidly. I wonder. . . . Oh really, it's too obvious. He brought on my questions, provoked them. And I, poor fool, I thought he was just telling me out of fairness. . . .

God, how painful it is, being angry. I thought I should never get over it before he came back. In fact I have no reason for getting myself into such a state. He did not know how to set about it: he used cunning to solve his difficulties—that is not a crime.

Still, I should like to know whether he told me for my sake or for his own ease and comfort. . . .

Sunday 17 October.

. . . That man who is traveling with Noëllie, that man whose face, whose words, I cannot even picture to myself—do not want to picture to myself? The man I love and who loves me? Are they the same one? I can no longer tell. And I do not know whether I am making a mountain out of a molehill or what I take to be a molehill is in fact a mountain.

I sought shelter in our past. I spread out boxfuls of photographs in front of the fire. I found the one with Maurice wearing his armband: how much at one we were that day when we were looking after the wounded FFI near the Quai des Grands Augustins. Here, on the Cap Corse Road, is the gasping old motorcar his mother gave us. I remember that night when we broke down, near Corte. We sat there motionless, overawed by the solitude and silence. I said, "We must try to put it right." "Kiss me first," said Maurice. We held each other tightly, for a long while, and we felt that no cold or weariness or anything on earth could touch us.

It's odd. Does it mean something? All these pictures that rise up in my heart are more than ten years old: Europa Point, the liberation of Paris, our return from Nancy, our housewarming, that breakdown on the Corte Road. I can bring others to mind—our last summers at Mougins, Venice, my fortieth birthday. They don't move me in the same way. Perhaps the more remote memories always seem the loveliest.

I am tired of asking myself questions and not knowing the answers. I am out of my depth. I no longer recognize the apartment. The things in it have the air of imitations of themselves. The massive table in the sitting room—it is hollow. As though both I and the house had been projected into a fourth dimension. If I were to go out it would not astonish me to find myself in a prehistoric forest, or in a city of the year 3000. . . .

Sunday 24 October.

I am beginning to see through Noëllie's little game: she is trying to reduce me to the role of the affectionate, resigned, house-loving wife who is left at home. I do like sitting by the fireside with Maurice; but it vexes me that it should always be she that he takes to concerts and to the theater. On Friday I cried out when he told me that he had been to a private viewing with her.

"But you loathe private viewings!" he replied.

"I love painting, though," I said.

Easy enough to say. Noëllie lends him books—she plays at being the intellectual. All right, so I know less about modern writing and music than she does: but taken all in all I am not less cultured or less intelligent. Maurice told me once that he trusted in my judgement more than anyone else's because it was both "enlightened and naïve." I try to say exactly what I think, what I feel; so does he; and there is nothing that seems more precious to us than this sincerity. I must not let Noëllie dazzle Maurice with her showing off. . . .

Monday 22 November.

No, I must not try to follow Noëllie on to her ground, but fight it out on my own. Maurice used to be touched by all the little things I did for him, and now I am neglecting him. I spent today tidying our wardrobes. I finally put away the summer things, brought the winter clothes out of their mothballs and aired them, and drew up a list. Tomorrow I shall go and buy him the socks, pullovers and pajamas he needs. He also needs two good pairs of shoes; we'll choose them together the next time he has a free moment. Well-filled cupboards with everything in its place are a great comfort to one. Plenty: security. . . . The heaps of delicate handkerchiefs and stockings and lingerie gave me the feeling that the future could not possibly let me down. . . .

Friday 26 November.

When I am with Maurice I cannot prevent myself from feeling I am in front of a judge. He thinks things about me that he does not tell me: it makes my head swim. I used to see myself so clearly through his eyes. Indeed I saw myself only through his eyes—too flattering a picture, perhaps, but one in which I recognized myself. Now I ask myself, *Whom does he see?* Does he think me mean-minded, jealous, blabbing and even disloyal because I make inquiries behind his back? It's unfair. He forgives Noëllie so much—can't he understand my restless curiosity about her? I loathe gossip; and I have stirred it up, but I have plenty of excuse for doing so. He never mentions that business, by the way: he is as kind as can be. But I realize that he no longer talks to me quite without reserve. And sometimes I think I read in his eyes . . . not exactly pity. Shall I say a very faint mockery? . . .

Saturday 27 November.

I must learn to control myself. But it's so foreign to my nature! I always used to be spontaneous and completely open: serene, too. Whereas now my heart is filled with anxiety and bitterness. When he opened a magazine directly after leaving the table, I thought, *He wouldn't do that at Noëllie's.* And I couldn't help it—I burst out, "You wouldn't do that at Noëllie's!"

His eyes flashed. "I just wanted to glance at an article," he said evenly. "Don't bristle like that over trifles."

"It's not my fault. Everything makes me bristle."

There was a silence. At the table I told him about how I had spent the day, and now I could not find anything to say. He made an effort. "Have you finished Wilde's *Letters*?"

"No. I didn't go on."

"You said they were interesting—"

"If only you knew how unspeakably dreary I find Wilde, and how little I feel like talking to you about him!" I went to fetch a record out of the shelves. "Would you like me to put on the cantata you bought?"

"All right."

I did not listen for long; sobs rose in my throat; the music was now merely a refuge. We no longer had anything to say to one another, haunted as we were by this affair that he did not want to discuss.

"Why are you crying?" he asked, in a long-suffering voice.

"Because you're bored when you're with me. Because we can't talk to one another anymore. Because you have built a wall between us."

"It's you who built it: you never stop going over and over your grievances."

I irritate him a little more every day. I don't mean to. And yet there is a part of me that does. When he seems too cheerful and unconcerned I say to myself, *This is too easy.* And then any excuse is good enough for me to destroy his peace of mind. . . .

Sunday 6 December.

When this happens to other people it seems to be a limited, bounded event, easy to ring around and to overcome. And then you find yourself absolutely alone, in a hallucinating experience that your imagination had not even begun to approach.

I am afraid of not sleeping and I am afraid of sleeping, on the nights that Maurice spends with Noëllie. That empty bed next to mine, these flat, cold sheets. . . . I take sleeping pills, but in vain: for I dream. Often in my dreams I faint with distress. I lie there under Maurice's gaze, paralyzed, with the whole world's anguish on my face. I expect him to rush toward me. He glances indifferently in my direction and walks off. I woke up and it was still night—I could feel the weight of the darkness; I was in a corridor; I hurried down it, and it grew narrower and narrower; I could scarcely breathe. Presently I should have to crawl and I should stay wedged there until I died. I screamed. And I began calling him more quietly, weeping as I did so. Every night I call him: not him—the other one, the one who loved me. And I wonder whether I should not prefer it if he were dead. I used to tell myself that death was the only irremediable misfortune and that if he were to leave me I should get over it. Death was dreadful because it was possible; a break was bearable because I could not imagine it. But now in fact I tell myself that if he were dead I should at least know whom I had lost and who I was myself. I no longer know anything. The whole of my past life has collapsed behind me, as the land does in those earthquakes where the ground consumes and destroys itself—is swallowed up behind you as you flee. There is no going back. The house has vanished, and the village and the whole of the valley. Even if you survive there is nothing left, not even what had been your living space on earth.

I am so destroyed by the morning that if the daily woman did not come at ten o'clock I should stay in bed every day until past noon, as I do on Sundays: or even all day long, when Maurice does not come back to lunch. Mme. Dormoy senses that something is wrong. Taking away the breakfast tray, she says reproachfully, "You haven't eaten anything!"

She presses me, and sometimes for the sake of peace I swallow a square of toast. But the mouthfuls won't go down.

Why doesn't he love me anymore? The question is why did he love me in the first place. One never asks oneself. Even if one is neither vain nor self-obsessed, it is so extraordinary to be oneself—exactly oneself and no one else—and so unique, that it seems natural that one should also be unique for someone else. He loved me, that's all. And for ever, since I should always be me. (And I have been astonished at this blindness, in other women. Strange that one can only understand one's own case by the help of other people's experience—experience that is not the same as mine, and that doesn't help.)

Stupid things fleeting through one's head. A film I saw when I was a child. A wife going to see her husband's mistress. "For you it's only fun. But I love him!" And the mistress is moved, and she sends the wife to take her place at the nocturnal rendezvous. In the darkness the husband takes her for the other one, and in the morning he comes back to her, looking shamefaced. It was an old silent film that the studio put on for laughs, but that stirred me a great deal. I can still see the wife's long dress, and her bandeaux.

Talk to Noëllie? But it's not just fun for her: it's a major undertaking. She would tell me that she loved him too; and certainly she's very fond of all that he can give a woman nowadays. For my part I loved him when he was twenty-three—an uncertain future—difficulties. I loved him with no security; and I gave up the idea of a career for myself. Anyhow I regret nothing. . . .

Saturday 12.

. . . I am torturing myself. What is the general opinion of me? Quite objectively, who am I? Am I less intelligent than I suppose? As for that, it is the kind of question it is no use asking anybody: no one would like to reply that I was a fool. And how can one tell? Everybody thinks he is intelligent, even the people I find stupid. That is why a woman is always more affected by compliments about her looks than by those about her mind—for she has inner certainties about her mind, those which everybody has and which therefore prove nothing. To know your limits you have to be able to go beyond them: in other words, you have to be able to jump right over your own shadow. I always understand what I hear and what I read: but perhaps I grasp it all too quickly, for want of being able to understand the full wealth and complexity of an idea. Is it my shortcomings that prevent me from seeing Noëllie's superiority? . . .

Wednesday 16.

I watch the drops of water running down the windowpane—a moment ago the rain was beating upon it. They don't go down straight: they are like little creatures that for mysterious reasons of their own slant off to the right or the left, slipping between other motionless drops, stopping and then starting again as though they were in quest of something. It seems to me that I no longer have anything whatever to do. I always used to be busy. Now everything—knitting, cooking, reading, putting on a record—everything seems pointless. Maurice's love gave every moment of my life a meaning. Now it is hollow. Everything is hollow—things are empty: time is empty. And so am I. . . .

3 February.

I ought not to ask questions. They are holds that I reach out to him and that he grasps at once. I asked Maurice, "Is it true what Noëllie says, that you have made up your mind to live with her?"

"She certainly can't be saying that, since it is not true." He hesitated. "What I should like—I have not spoken of it to her: you are the one it concerns—is to live by myself for a certain time. There is a tension between us that would vanish if—just for the time being, of course—we were to give up living together."

"You want to leave me?"

"No, of course not. We should see just as much of one another."

"I can't bear it."

I screamed. He took me by the shoulders. "Stop! Stop!" he said gently. "It was just a thought in the air. If you find it so very disagreeable I will abandon it."

Noëllie wants him to leave me; she is pressing him; she is making scenes: I'm sure of it. It is her pushing him on. I shall not give way.

6 February: then with no date.

What useless energy you need for even the simplest things, when all liking for life is gone! In the evening I get the teapot, the cup, and the saucepan ready; I put each thing in its place so that life may start in the morning with the least possible effort. And even so it is almost more than I can bring myself to do, creeping out of my bed, starting the day. I get the daily woman to come in the afternoon so that I can stay in bed as long as I like in the morning. Sometimes I get up just as Maurice is coming home to lunch at one o'clock. . . . Maurice frowns when he sees me at one o'clock in a dressing gown and with my hair undone. He thinks I am putting on a desperation act for his benefit. Or at least that I am not making the necessary effort "to live the situation decently." He too tells me over and over again, "You ought to see a psychiatrist."

I go on bleeding. If only my life could run out of me without my having to make the slightest effort!

There must exist a truth in all this. I ought to take the plane for New York and ask Lucienne the truth. She does not love me: she will tell me. Then I should wipe out all that is bad, all that does me harm: I should put everything between Maurice and me back in its place.

Yesterday evening when Maurice came home I was sitting in the living room, in the darkness, wearing my dressing gown. It was Sunday; I had got up in the middle of the afternoon: I had eaten a slice of ham and drunk some cognac. And then I had stayed sitting there, following the thoughts that went around and around in my head. Before he came in I took some tranquilizers and went back to sit in the armchair, without even thinking of turning on the light.

"What are you doing? Why don't you turn on the light?"

"Why should I?"

He scolded me, affectionately, but with irritation behind his kindness. Why don't I see my friends? Why haven't I been to the cinema? He told me the names of five films worth seeing. It's impossible. There was a time when I could go to the cinema and even to the theater all by myself. For I was not alone. His presence was there in me and all around me. Now when I am by myself I say to myself, *I am alone*. And I am afraid.

"You can't go on like this," he said.

"Like what?"

"Not eating, not dressing, shutting yourself up in this apartment."

"Why not?"

"You'll get ill. Or go off your head. As for me, I can't help you because I'm part of it. But I beg you, do see a psychiatrist."

I said no. He pressed me and pressed me. In the end he grew impatient. "How do you expect to get out of it? You do nothing to help."

"Get out of what?"

"Out of this depression. Anyone would say you were sinking deeper into it on purpose."

He shut himself up in his study. He thinks I am trying to blackmail him with misery, so as to frighten him and prevent him from leaving me. Maybe he's right. Do I know what I am? Perhaps a kind of leech that feeds on the life of others—on Maurice's, on our daughters', on the life of all those lame ducks I claimed to be helping. An egoist who will not let go: I drink, I let myself slide, I make myself ill with the unadmitted intention of softening his heart. Completely phony through and through, rotten to the bone, playacting, exploiting his pity. I ought to tell him to go and live with Noëllie, to be happy without me. I can't bring myself to do so.

In a dream the other night I had on a sky-blue dress and the sky was blue.

Those smiles, looks, words—they cannot have vanished. They float here in the air of this apartment. As for the words, I often hear them. In my ear a voice says, very distinctly, "Darling; sweetheart, my sweetheart. . . ." As for the looks and the smiles, I ought to catch them as they pass and clap them suddenly onto Maurice's face, and then everything would be the same as before.

I still go on bleeding. I am afraid.

"When one is so low, any movement must be upwards," says Marie Lambert. What foolishness! You can always go lower, and lower still, and still lower. There is no bottom. She says that to get rid of me. She is sick of me. They are all sick of me. Tragedies are all right for a while: you are concerned, you are curious, you feel good. And then it gets repetitive, it doesn't advance, it grows dreadfully boring: it is so very boring, even for me. Isabelle, Diana, Colette, Marie Lambert—they are all fed to the teeth; and Maurice . . .

There was once a man who lost his shadow. I forget what happened to him, but it was dreadful. As for me, I've lost my own image. I did not look at it often but it was there, in the background, just as Maurice had drawn it for me. A straightforward, genuine, "authentic" woman, without mean-mindedness, uncompromising, but at the same time understanding, indulgent, sensitive, deeply feeling, intensely aware of things and of people, passionately devoted to those she loved and creating happiness for them. A fine life, serene, full, "harmonious." It is dark: I cannot see myself anymore. And what do the others see? Maybe something hideous.

There are plottings that go on behind my back. Between Colette and her father, Isabelle and Marie Lambert, Isabelle and Maurice.

20 February.

I have ended up by yielding to them. I was afraid of my blood, and the way it flowed away from me. Afraid of the silence. I had taken to telephoning Isabelle three times a day and Colette in the middle of the night. And now I am paying someone to listen to me: it's killingly funny.

He urged me to take up this diary again. I see the gimmick perfectly well—he is trying to give me back an interest in myself, to reconstruct my identity for me. But the only thing that counts is Maurice. My self, what does that amount to? I have never paid much attention to it. I was safe, because he loved me. If he does not love me anymore. . . . It is only the transition that haunts my mind—how have I deserved it that he should no longer love me? Or have I not deserved it, and is he a swine—a swine that should be punished, and his accomplice with him? Dr. Marquet sets about it at the other end—my father, my mother, my father's death: he wants to make me talk about myself, and I only want to talk to him about Maurice and Noëllie. Still, I did ask him whether he thought me intelligent. Yes, undoubtedly; but intelligence is not a quality with an independent existence: when I go on and on pursuing my obsessions, my intelligence is no longer available to me.

Maurice treats me with that mixture of tactfulness and muffled irritation that one puts on for invalids. He is patient, so patient that I feel like shrieking; and indeed I do sometimes. Go mad. That would be a good way out. But Maurice assures me there is no danger of it—my structure is too sound. Even with drink and drugs I have never pushed myself very far off the middle line. It is a way out that is closed to me. . . .

26 February.

I have obeyed the psychiatrist; I have accepted a job. I go to the periodicals room in the Bibliothéque Nationale and I comb through the back numbers of medical magazines for a fellow who is writing on the history of medicine. I can't see how this can do anything toward solving my problems. When I have written up two or three index cards I don't get the least satisfaction out of it. . . .

8 March.

The psychiatrist has put the last touches to my demoralization. I no longer have any strength; I no longer attempt to struggle. Maurice is looking for a furnished apartment—he has several in view. This time I did not even protest. Yet our conversation was appalling. Without any anger, totally reduced, empty, I said to him, "It would have been better if you had told me at the end of the holidays, or even at Mougins, that you had made up your mind to leave me."

"To begin with I am not leaving you."

"That's quibbling."

"And then again I had not made up my mind about anything."

A mist floated in front of my eyes. "Do you mean you have been putting me on trial these six months and that I have wrecked my chances? That is atrocious."

"Not at all. It is me I was thinking about. I hoped I should manage somehow with Noëllie and you. And I'm going off my head. I can't even work anymore."

"It's Noëllie who insists on your leaving."

"She can't bear the situation any more than you can."

"If I had stood it better, would you have stayed?"

"But you couldn't. Even your kindness and your silence tore my heart out."

"You're leaving me because the pity you feel for me makes you suffer too much?"

"Oh, I beg you to understand me!" he said in an imploring voice.

"I understand," I said. . . .

24 March.

There. Colette and Jean-Pierre were waiting for me. I had dinner at their apartment. They brought me here. The window was dark: it always will be dark. We climbed the stairs. . . . I would not let Colette stay and sleep here: I just have to get used to it. I sat down at the table. I am sitting there now. And I look at those two doors—Maurice's study, our bedroom. Closed. A closed door: something that is watching behind it. It will not open if I do not stir. Do not stir: ever. Stop the flow of time and of life.

But I know that I shall move. The door will open slowly, and I shall see what there is behind the door. It is the future. The door to the future will open. Slowly. Unrelentingly. I am on the threshold. There is only this door and what is watching behind it. I am afraid. And I cannot call to anyone for help.

I am afraid.

Basic Existentialist Concepts

Woman as Other In *The Ethics of Ambiguity*, Beauvoir compared the situation of women in many parts of the world to the condition of slavery, with the argument that a large number of women can only exercise their freedom within preestablished boundaries that were set up "before them, without them." Even women in modern Western democracies do not fully use their freedom because they consent to the unequal situation in which they find themselves.

For Beauvoir, the cause of women's failure to be truly free and equal to men is a complex social dynamic by which women are defined as Other, while men define themselves as the One. Beauvoir expounds this theory in *The Second Sex*, adapting an idea from the nineteenth-century philosopher F. G. W. Hegel, who argued that individuals form a sense of their own identity through conflict with another person. In Beauvoir's theory, men form a sense of their own identity by contrasting themselves with women; men regard themselves as central and thus assume the position of the One in the bipolar relation. Men regard women as Other, or essentially different from themselves.

In Beauvoir's theory, it is important that, in the relationship between men and women, there is no reciprocity between One and Other. The inequality in power results in men always having the central status of the One and women always having the ancillary status of the Other. Women cannot become the One and define men as their Other, because men occupy and defend the central position of being the One; men do not allow women to define themselves as the One, with men being the Other in turn. Moreover, most women acquiesce in this male-dominated dynamic of self-definition; women come to believe that their identity is as men have defined it.

This rather abstract theory can be understood in more concrete terms by reflecting on the many ways in which men have expressed their opinions about themselves and about women. Down through the centuries, men have created myths, artwork, religious doctrines, philosophical and scientific theories, and political institutions that portray themselves as central and women as secondary to culture. "Mankind" is defined as "humankind" ; what characterizes men is taken to be what is human. Women are not portrayed in male-created myth, art, theory, and institutions in ways that women think about themselves. When someone can express his view about himself and about somebody else, while the other person is not allowed to express her view either about herself or about him, then the first person is the One, and the second person is always the Other.

Questions for Discussion

1. Monique describes her feelings of freedom at the beginning of the story when she drives back to Paris alone. Are her feelings of freedom as significant as the freedom one exercises in choosing a profession and working on a project that extends throughout one's life?

2. Is Monique in bad faith? If so, explain the nature of Monique's bad faith.

3. Do women care more for others than for themselves? Is caring for others part of women's sense of self-identity?

4. When a woman becomes dependent on her husband or children, is she responsible for her dependency?

5. Is it possible for women *not* to see themselves through men's eyes? Is it possible for women *not* to acquiesce in being defined as Other?

Chapter 9

Richard Wright's "The Man Who Lived Underground"

Introduction: Black Activism and Existentialism

Richard Wright (1908–1960) wrote about the conflict between the individual and society long before he encountered existentialism. An African-American author who knew racism and economic oppression firsthand, Wright drew from his own experiences in the Deep South and Depression-era Chicago for his novel *Native Son* and his autobiography, *Black Boy.* The alienation and despair expressed in these early works were not philosophical conclusions based on existentialist theory, but Wright's own indictment of American society destroying itself through racism, industrialization, and materialism.

Wright flirted briefly with communism in the 1930s and spoke out strongly against racism. Because of his political activism, the FBI monitored his activities, and a Southern Senator denounced his work on the floor of the U.S. Senate. He turned to existentialism when he moved to France in 1947. He read the works of Husserl and Heidegger, discussed existentialism with his friends Sartre and Beauvoir, and helped Sartre and Camus found the political group *Rassemblement Démocratique Révolutionnaire.* During his remaining years in France, he continued to be artistically and politically active, developing close relationships with African intellectuals and meeting many of the world's great political leaders.

In the short story "The Man Who Lived Underground," Wright creates a variation on the theme of Dostoyevsky's underground man. The main character, Fred Daniels, is a solitary rebel, who is alienated not only from racist, white society, which has falsely accused him of a crime, but also from the black community, which is enervated by religion. Although he attempts to live on his own apart from society, he cannot pull away from it completely. Hidden in society's subterranean regions, he observes its materialism and violence.

Wright's "The Man Who Lived Underground"[1]

I've got to hide, he told himself. His chest heaved as he waited, crouching in a dark corner of the vestibule. He was tired of running and dodging. Either he had to find a place to hide, or he had to surrender. A police car swished by through the rain, its siren rising sharply. They're looking for me all over . . . He crept to the door and squinted through the fogged plate glass. He stiffened as the siren rose and died in the distance. Yes, he had to hide, but where? He gritted his teeth. Then a sudden movement in the street caught his attention. A throng of tiny columns of water snaked into the air from the perforations of a manhole cover. The columns stopped abruptly, as though the perforations had become clogged; a gray spout of sewer water jutted up from underground and lifted the circular metal cover, juggled it for a moment, then let it fall with a clang.

He hatched a tentative plan: he would wait until the siren sounded far off, then he would go out. He smoked and waited, tense. At last the siren gave him his signal; it wailed, dying, going away from him. He stepped to the sidewalk, then paused and looked curiously at the open manhole, half expecting the cover to leap up again. He went to the center of the street and stooped and peered into the hole, but could see nothing. Water rustled in the black depths.

He started with terror; the siren sounded so near that he had the idea that he had been dreaming and had awakened to find the car upon him. He dropped instinctively to his knees and his hands grasped the rim of the manhole. The siren seemed to hoot directly above him and with a wild gasp of exertion he snatched the cover far enough off to admit his body. He swung his legs over the opening and lowered himself into watery darkness. He hung for an eternal moment to the rim by his finger tips, then he felt rough metal prongs and at once he knew that sewer workmen used these ridges to lower themselves into manholes. Fist over fist, he let his body sink until he could feel no more prongs. He swayed in dank space; the siren seemed to howl at the very rim of the manhole. He dropped and was washed violently into an ocean of warm, leaping water. His head was battered against a wall and he wondered if this were death. Frenziedly his fingers clawed and sank into a crevice. He steadied himself and measured the strength of the current with his own muscular tension. He stood slowly in water that dashed past his knees with fearful velocity.

He heard a prolonged scream of brakes and the siren broke off. Oh, God! They had found him! Looming above his head in the rain a white face hovered over the hole. "How did this damn thing get off?" he heard a policeman ask. He saw the steel cover move slowly until the hole looked like a quarter moon turned black. "Give me a hand here," someone called. The cover clanged into place, muffling the sights and sounds of the upper world. Knee-deep in the pulsing current, he breathed with aching chest, filling his lungs with the hot stench of yeasty rot.

From the perforations of the manhole cover, delicate lances of hazy violet sifted down and wove a mottled pattern upon the surface of the streaking current. His lips parted as a car swept past along the wet pavement overhead, its heavy rumble soon dying out, like the hum of a plane speeding through a dense cloud. He had never thought that cars could sound like that; everything seemed strange and unreal under here. He stood in darkness for a long time, knee-deep in rustling water, musing.

The odor of rot had become so general that he no longer smelled it. He got his cigarettes, but discovered that his matches were wet. He

[1] "The Man Who Lived Underground" from *Eight Men* by Richard Wright.

searched and found a dry folder in the pocket of his shirt and managed to strike one; it flared weirdly in the wet gloom, glowing greenishly, turning red, orange, then yellow. He lit a crumpled cigarette; then, by the flickering light of the match, he looked for support so that he would not have to keep his muscles flexed against the pouring water. His pupils narrowed and he saw to either side of him two steaming walls that rose and curved inward some six feet above his head to form a dripping,mouse-colored dome. The bottom of the sewer was a sloping V-trough. To the left, the sewer vanished in ashen fog. To the right was a steep down-curve into which water plunged.

He saw now that had he not regained his feet in time, he would have been swept to death, or had he entered any other manhole he would have probably drowned. Above the rush of the current he heard sharper juttings of water; tiny streams were spewing into the sewer from smaller conduits. The match died; he struck another and saw a mass of debris sweep past him and clog the throat of the down-curve. At once the water began rising rapidly. Could he climb out before he drowned? A long hiss sounded and the debris was sucked from sight; the current lowered. He understood now what had made the water toss the manhole cover; the down-curve had become temporarily obstructed and the perforations had become clogged.

He was in danger; he might slide into a down-curve; he might wander with a lighted match into a pocket of gas and blow himself up; or he might contract some horrible disease . . . Though he wanted to leave, an irrational impulse held him rooted. To the left, the convex ceiling swooped to a height of less than five feet. With cigarette slanting from pursed lips, he waded with taut muscles, his feet sloshing over the slimy bottom, his shoes sinking into spongy slop, the slate-colored water cracking in creamy foam against his knees. Pressing his flat left palm against the lowered ceiling, he struck another match and saw a metal pole nestling in a niche of the wall. Yes, some sewer workman had left it. He reached for it, then jerked his head away as a whisper of scurrying life whisked past and was still. He held the match close and saw a huge rat, wet with slime, blinking beady eyes and baring tiny fangs. The light blinded the rat and the frizzled head moved aimlessly. He grabbed the pole and let it fly against the rat's soft body; there was shrill piping and the grizzly body splashed into the dun-colored water and was snatched out of sight, spinning in the scuttling stream.

He swallowed and pushed on, following the curve of the misty cavern, sounding the water with the pole. By the faint light of another manhole cover he saw, amid loose wet brick, a hole with walls of damp earth leading into blackness. Gingerly he poked the pole into it; it was hollow and went beyond the length of the pole. He shoved the pole before him, hoisted himself upward, got to his hands and knees, and crawled. After a few yards he paused, struck to wonderment by the silence; it seemed that he had traveled a million miles away from the world. As he inched forward again he could sense the bottom of the dirt tunnel becoming dry and lowering slightly. Slowly he rose and to his astonishment he stood erect. He could not hear the rustling of the water now and he felt confoundingly alone, yet lured by the darkness and silence.

He crept a long way, then stopped, curious, afraid. He put his right foot forward and it dangled in space; he drew back in fear. He thrust the pole outward and it swung in emptiness. He trembled, imagining the earth crumbling and burying him alive. He scratched a match and saw that the dirt floor sheered away steeply and widened into a sort of cave some five feet below him. An old sewer, he muttered. He cocked his head, hearing a feathery cadence which he could not identify. The match ceased to burn.

Using the pole as a kind of ladder, he slid down and stood in darkness. The air was a little fresher and he could still hear vague noises.

Where was he? He felt suddenly that someone was standing near him and he turned sharply, but there was only darkness. He poked cautiously and felt a brick wall; he followed it and the strange sounds grew louder. He ought to get out of here. This was crazy. He could not remain here for any length of time; there was no food and no place to sleep. But the faint sounds tantalized him; they were strange but familiar. Was it a motor? A baby crying? Music? A siren? He groped on, and the sounds came so clearly that he could feel the pitch and timbre of human voices. Yes, singing! That was it! He listened with open mouth. It was a church service. Enchanted, he groped toward the waves of melody.

Jesus, take me to your home above
And fold me in the bosom of Thy love. . .

The singing was on the other side of a brick wall. Excited, he wanted to watch the service without being seen. Whose church was it? He knew most of the churches in this area above ground, but the singing sounded too strange and detached for him to guess. He looked to the left, to the right, down to the black dirt, then upward and was startled to see a bright sliver of light slicing the darkness like the blade of a razor. He struck one of his two remaining matches and saw rusty pipes running along an old concrete ceiling. Photographically he located the exact position of the pipes in his mind. The match flame sank and he sprang upward; his hands clutched a pipe. He swung his legs and tossed his body onto the bed of pipes and they creaked, swaying up and down; he thought that the tier was about to crash, but nothing happened. He edged to the crevice and saw a segment of black men and women, dressed in white robes, singing, holding tattered songbooks in their black palms. His first impulse was to laugh, but he checked himself.

What was he doing? He was crushed with a sense of guilt. Would God strike him dead for that? The singing swept on and he shook his head, disagreeing in spite of himself. They oughtn't to do that, he thought. But he could think of no reason *why* they should not do it. Just singing with the air of the sewer blowing in on them . . . He felt that he was gazing upon something abysmally obscene, yet he could not bring himself to leave.

After a long time he grew numb and dropped to the dirt. Pain throbbed in his legs and a deeper pain, induced by the sight of those black people groveling and begging for something they could never get, churned in him. A vague conviction made him feel that those people should stand unrepentant and yield no quarter in singing and praying, yet *he* had run away from the police, had pleaded with them to believe in *his* innocence. He shook his head, bewildered.

How long had he been down here? He did not know. This was a new kind of living for him; the intensity of feelings he had experienced when looking at the church people sing made him certain that he had been down here a long time, but his mind told him that the time must have been short. In this darkness the only notion he had of time was when a match flared and measured time by its fleeting light. He groped back through the hole toward the sewer and the waves of song subsided and finally he could not hear them at all. He came to where the earth hole ended and he heard the noise of the current and time lived again for him, measuring the moments by the wash of water.

The rain must have slackened, for the flow of water had lessened and came only to his ankles. Ought he to go up into the streets and take his chances on hiding somewhere else? But they would surely catch him. The mere thought of dodging and running again from the police made him tense. No, he would stay and plot how to elude them. But what could he do down here? He walked forward into the sewer and came to another manhole cover; he stood beneath it, debating. Fine pencils of gold spilled suddenly from the little circles in the manhole cover and trembled on the surface of the current. Yes, street lamps . . . It must be night . . .

He went forward for about a quarter of an hour, wading aimlessly, poking the pole carefully before him. Then he stopped, his eyes fixed and intent. What's that? A strangely familiar image attracted and repelled him. Lit by the yellow stems from another manhole cover was a tiny nude body of a baby snagged by debris and half-submerged in water. Thinking that the baby was alive, he moved impulsively to save it, but his roused feelings told him that it was dead, cold, nothing, the same nothingness he had felt while watching the men and women singing in the church. Water blossomed about the tiny legs, the tiny arms, the tiny head, and rushed onward. The eyes were closed, as though in sleep; the fists were clenched, as though in protest; and the mouth gaped black in a soundless cry.

He straightened and drew in his breath, feeling that he had been staring for all eternity at the ripples of veined water skimming impersonally over the shriveled limbs. He felt as condemned as when the policemen had accused him. Involuntarily he lifted his hand to brush the vision away, but his arm fell listlessly to his side. Then he acted; he closed his eyes and reached forward slowly with the soggy shoe of his right foot and shoved the dead baby from where it had been lodged. He kept his eyes closed, seeing the little body twisting in the current as it floated from sight. He opened his eyes, shivered, placed his knuckles in the sockets, hearing the water speed in the somber shadows.

He tramped on, sensing at times a sudden quickening in the current as he passed some conduit whose waters were swelling the stream that slid by his feet. A few minutes later he was standing under another manhole cover, listening to the faint rumble of noises above ground. Streetcars and trucks, he mused. He looked down and saw a stagnant pool of gray-green sludge; at intervals a balloon pocket rose from the scum, glistening a bluish-purple, and burst. Then another. He turned, shook his head, and tramped back to the dirt cave by the church, his lips quivering.

Back in the cave, he sat and leaned his back against a dirt wall. His body was trembling slightly. Finally his senses quieted and he slept. When he awakened he felt stiff and cold. He had to leave this foul place, but leaving meant facing those policemen who had wrongly accused him. No, he could not go back aboveground. He remembered the beating they had given him and how he had signed his name to a confession, a confession which he had not even read. He had been too tired when they had shouted at him, demanding that he sign his name; he had signed it to end his pain.

He stood and groped about in the darkness. The church singing had stopped. How long had he slept? He did not know. But he felt refreshed and hungry. He doubled his fist nervously, realizing that he could not make a decision. As he walked about he stumbled over an old rusty iron pipe. He picked it up and felt a jagged edge. Yes, there was a brick wall and he could dig into it. What would he find? Smiling, he groped to the brick wall, sat, and began digging idly into damp cement. I can't make any noise, he cautioned himself. As time passed he grew thirsty, but there was no water. He had to kill time or go aboveground. The cement came out of the wall easily; he extracted four bricks and felt a soft draft blowing into his face. He stopped, afraid. What was beyond? He waited a long time and nothing happened; then he began digging again, soundlessly, slowly; he enlarged the hole and crawled through into a dark room and collided with another wall. He felt his way to the right; the wall ended and his fingers toyed in space, like the antennae of an insect.

He fumbled on and his feet struck something hollow, like wood. What's this? He felt with his fingers. Steps . . . He stooped and pulled off his shoes and mounted the stairs and saw a yellow chink of light shining and heard a low voice speaking. He placed his eye to a keyhole and saw the nude waxen figure of a man stretched out upon a white table. The voice, low-pitched and vibrant, mumbled indistinguishable words, neither rising nor falling. He craned his neck and squinted to see the man who was talking, but he could not locate him. Above the naked figure was suspended a huge glass container filled with a blood-red liquid from which a white rubber tube dangled. He crouched closer to the door, and saw the tip end of a black object lined with pink satin. A coffin, he breathed. This is an undertaker's establishment. . . . A fine-spun lace of ice covered his body and he shuddered. A throaty chuckle sounded in the depths of the yellow room.

He turned to leave. Three steps down it occurred to him that a light switch should be nearby; he felt along the wall, found an electric button, pressed it, and a blinding glare smote his pupils so hard that he was sightless, defenseless. His pupils contracted and he wrinkled his nostrils at a peculiar odor. At once he knew that he had been dimly aware of this odor in the darkness, but the light had brought it sharply to his attention. Some kind of stuff they used to embalm, he thought. He went down the steps and saw piles of lumber, coffins, and a long workbench. In one corner was a tool chest. Yes, he could use tools, could tunnel through walls with them. He lifted the lid of the chest and saw nails, a hammer, a crowbar, a screwdriver, a light bulb, and a long length of electric wire. Good! He would lug these back to his cave.

He was about to hoist the chest to his shoulders when he discovered a door behind the furnace. Where did it lead? He tried to open it and found it securely bolted. Using the crowbar so as to make no sound, he pried the door open; it swung on creaking hinges, outward. Fresh air came to his face and he caught the faint roar of faraway sound. Easy now, he told himself. He widened the door and a lump of coal rattled toward him. A coalbin . . . Evidently the door led into another basement. The roaring noise was louder now, but he could not identify it. Where was he? He groped slowly over the coal pile, then ranged in darkness over a gritty floor. The roaring noise seemed to come from above him, then below. His fingers followed a wall until he touched a wooden ridge. A door, he breathed.

The noise died to a low pitch; he felt his skin prickle. It seemed that he was playing a game with an unseen person whose intelligence outstripped his. He put his ear to the flat surface of the door. Yes, voices . . . Was this a prize fight stadium? The sound of the voices came near and sharp, but he could not tell if they were joyous or despairing. He twisted the knob until he heard a soft click and felt the springy weight of the door swinging toward him. He was afraid to open it, yet captured by curiosity and wonder. He jerked the door wide and saw on the far side of the basement a furnace glowing red. Ten feet away was still another door, half ajar. He crossed and peered through the door into an empty, high-ceilinged corridor that terminated in a dark complex of shadow. The belling voices rolled about him and his eagerness mounted. He stepped into the corridor and the voices swelled louder. He crept on and came to a narrow stairway leading circularly upward; there was no question but that he was going to ascend those stairs.

Mounting the spiraled staircase, he heard the voices roll in a steady wave, then leap to crescendo, only to die away, but always remaining audible. Ahead of him glowed red letters: E—X—I—T. At the top of the steps he paused in front of a black curtain that fluttered uncertainly. He parted the folds and looked into a convex depth that gleamed with clusters of shimmering lights. Sprawling below him was a stretch of human faces, tilted upward, chanting, whistling, screaming, laughing. Dangling before the faces, high upon a screen of silver, were jerking shadows. A movie, he said with slow laughter breaking from his lips.

He stood in a box in the reserved section of a movie house and the impulse he had had to tell the people in the church to stop their singing seized him. These people were laughing at their lives, he thought with amazement. They were shouting and yelling at the animated shadows of themselves. His compassion fired his imagination and he stepped out of the box, walked out upon thin air, walked on down to the audience; and, hovering in the air just above them, he stretched out his hand to touch them . . . His tension snapped and he found himself back in the box, looking down into the sea of faces. No; it could not be done; he could not awaken them. He sighed. Yes, these people were children, sleeping in their living, awake in their dying.

He turned away, parted the black curtain, and looked out. He saw no one. He started down the white stone steps and when he reached the bottom he saw a man in trim blue uniform coming toward him. So used had he become to being underground that he thought that he could walk past the man, as though he were a ghost. But the man stopped. And he stopped.

"Looking for the men's room, sir?" the man asked, and, without waiting for an answer, he turned and pointed. "This way, sir. The first door to your right."

He watched the man turn and walk up the steps and go out of sight. Then he laughed. What a funny fellow! He went back to the basement and stood in the red darkness, watching the glowing embers in the furnace. He went to the sink and turned the faucet and the water flowed in a smooth silent stream that looked like a spout of blood. He brushed the mad image from his mind and began to wash his hands leisurely, looking about for the usual bar of soap. He found one and rubbed it in his palms until a rich lather bloomed in his cupped fingers, like a scarlet sponge. He scrubbed and rinsed his hands meticulously, then hunted for a towel; there was none. He shut off the water, pulled off his shirt, dried his hands on it; when he put it on again he was grateful for the cool dampness that came to his skin.

Yes, he was thirsty; he turned on the faucet again, bowled his fingers and when the water bubbled over the brim of his cupped palms, he drank in long, slow swallows. His bladder grew tight; he shut off the water, faced the wall, bent his head, and watched a red stream strike the floor. His nostrils wrinkled against acrid wisps of vapor; though he had tramped in the waters of the sewer, he stepped back from the wall so that his shoes, wet with sewer slime, would not touch his urine.

He heard footsteps and crawled quickly into the coalbin. Lumps rattled noisily. The footsteps came into the basement and stopped. Who was it? Had someone heard him and come down to investigate? He waited, crouching, sweating. For a long time there was silence, then he heard the clang of metal and a brighter glow lit the room. Somebody's tending the furnace, he thought. Footsteps came closer and he stiffened. Looming before him was a white face lined with coal dust, the face of an old man with watery blue eyes. Highlights spotted his gaunt cheekbones, and he held a huge shovel. There was a screechy scrape of metal against stone, and the man lifted a shovelful of coal and went from sight.

The room dimmed momentarily, then a yellow glare came as coal flared at the furnace door. Six times the old man came to the bin and went to the furnace with shovels of coal, but not once did he lift his eyes. Finally he dropped the shovel, mopped his face with a dirty handkerchief, and sighed: "Wheeew!" He turned slowly and trudged out of the basement, his footsteps dying away.

He stood, and lumps of coal clattered down the pile. He stepped from the bin and was startled to see the shadowy outline of an electric bulb hanging above his head. Why had not the old man turned it on? Oh, yes . . . He understood. The old man had worked here for so long that he had no need for light; he had learned a way of seeing in his dark world, like those sightless worms that inch along underground by a sense of touch.

His eyes fell upon a lunch pail and he was afraid to hope that it was full. He picked it up; it was heavy. He opened it. *Sandwiches!* He looked guiltily around; he was alone. He searched farther and found a folder of matches and a half-empty tin of tobacco; he put them eagerly into his pocket and clicked off the light. With the lunch pail under his arm, he went through the door, groped over the pile of coal, and stood again in the lighted basement of the undertaking establishment. I've got to get those tools, he told himself. And turn off that light. He tiptoed back up the steps and switched off the light; the invisible voice still droned on behind the door. He crept down and, seeing with his fingers, opened the lunch pail and tore off a piece of paper bag and brought out the tin and spilled grains of tobacco into the makeshift concave. He rolled it and wet it with spittle, then inserted one end into his mouth and lit it: he sucked smoke that bit his lungs. The nicotine reached his brain, went out along his arms to his finger tips, down to his stomach, and over all the tired nerves of his body.

He carted the tools to the hole he had made in the wall. Would the noise of the falling chest betray him? But he would have to take a chance; he had to have those tools. He lifted the chest and shoved it; it hit the dirt on the other side of the wall with a loud clatter. He waited, listening; nothing happened. Head first, he slithered through and stood in the cave. He grinned, filled with a cunning idea. Yes, he would now go back into the basement of the undertaking establishment and crouch behind the coal pile and dig another hole. Sure! Fumbling, he opened the tool chest and extracted a crowbar, a screwdriver, and a hammer; he fastened them securely about his person.

With another lumpish cigarette in his flexed lips, he crawled back through the hole and over the coal pile and sat, facing the brick wall. He jabbed with the crowbar and the cement sheered away; quicker than he thought, a brick came loose. He worked an hour; the other bricks did not come easily. He sighed, weak from effort. I ought to rest a little, he thought. I'm hungry. He felt his way back to the cave and tumbled along the wall till he came to the tool chest. He sat upon it, opened the lunch pail, and took out two thick sandwiches. He smelled them. Pork chops . . . His mouth watered. He closed his eyes and devoured a sandwich, savoring the smooth rye bread and juicy meat. He ate rapidly, gulping down lumpy mouthfuls that made him long for water. He ate the other sandwich and found an apple and gobbled that up too, sucking the core till the last trace of flavor was drained from it. Then, like a dog, he ground the meat bones with his teeth, enjoying the salty, tangy marrow. He finished and stretched out full length on the ground and went to sleep. . . .

. . . His body was washed by cold water that gradually turned warm and he was buoyed upon a stream and swept out to sea where waves rolled gently and suddenly he found himself walking upon the water how strange and delightful to walk upon the water and he came upon a nude woman holding a nude baby in her arms and the woman was sinking into the water holding the baby above her head and screaming *help* and he ran over the water to the woman and he reached her just before she went down and he took the baby from her hands and stood watching the breaking bubbles where the woman sank and he called *lady* and still no answer yes dive down there and rescue that woman but he could not take this baby with him and he stooped and laid the baby tenderly upon the surface of the water expecting it to sink but it floated and he leaped into the water and held his breath and strained his eyes to see through the gloomy volume of water but there was no woman and he opened his mouth and called *lady* and the water bubbled and his chest ached and his arms were tired but he could not see the woman and he called again *lady lady* and his feet touched sand at the bottom of the sea and his chest felt as though it would burst and he bent his knees and propelled himself upward and water rushed past him and his head bobbed out and he breathed deeply and looked around where was the baby the baby was gone and he rushed over the water looking for the baby calling *where is it* and the empty sky and sea threw back his voice *where is it* and he began to doubt that he could stand upon the water and then he was sinking and as he struggled the water rushed him downward spinning dizzily and he opened his mouth to call for help and water surged into his lungs and he choked . . .

He groaned and leaped erect in the dark, his eyes wide. The images of terror that thronged his brain would not let him sleep. He rose, made sure that the tools were hitched to his belt, and groped his way to the coal pile and found the rectangular gap from which he had taken the bricks. He took out the crowbar and hacked. Then dread paralyzed him. How long had he slept? Was it day or night now? He had to be careful. Someone might hear him if it were day. He hewed softly for hours at the cement, working silently. Faintly quivering in the air above him was the dim sound of yelling voices. Crazy people, he muttered. They're still there in that movie . . .

Having rested, he found the digging much easier. He soon had a dozen bricks out. His spirits rose. He took out another brick and his fingers fluttered in space. Good! What lay ahead of him? Another basement? He made the hole larger, climbed through, walked over an uneven floor and felt a metal surface. He lighted a match and saw that he was standing behind a furnace in a basement; before him, on the far side of the room, was a door. He crossed and opened it; it was full of odds and ends. Daylight spilled from a window above his head.

Then he was aware of a soft, continuous tapping. What was it? A clock? No, it was louder than a clock and more irregular. He placed an old empty box beneath the window, stood upon it, and looked into an areaway. He eased the window up and crawled through; the sound of the tapping came clearly now. He glanced about; he was alone. Then he looked upward at a series of window ledges. The tapping identified itself. That's a typewriter, he said to himself. It seemed to be coming from just above. He grasped the ridges of a rain pipe and lifted himself upward; through a half-inch opening of window he saw a doorknob about three feet away. No, it was not a doorknob; it was a small circular disk made of stainless steel with many fine markings upon it. He held his breath; an eerie white hand, seemingly detached from its arm, touched the metal knob and whirled it, first to the left, then to the right. It's a safe! . . . Suddenly he could see the dial no more; a huge metal door swung slowly toward him and he was looking into a safe filled with green wads of paper money, rows of coins wrapped in brown paper, and glass jars and boxes of various sizes. His heart quickened. Good Lord! The white hand went in and out of the safe, taking wads of bills and cylinders of coins. The hand vanished and he heard the muffled click of the big door as it closed. Only the steel dial was visible now. The typewriter still tapped in his ears, but he could not see it. He blinked, wondering if what he had seen was real. There was more money in that safe than he had seen in all his life.

As he clung to the rain pipe, a daring idea came to him and he pulled the screwdriver from his belt. If the white hand twirled that dial again, he would be able to see how far to left and right it spun and he would have the combination! His blood tingled. I can scratch the numbers right here, he thought. Holding the pipe with one hand, he made the sharp edge of the screwdriver bite into the brick wall. Yes, he could do it. Now, he was set. Now, he had a reason for staying here in the underground. He waited for a long time, but the white hand did not return. Goddamn! Had he been more alert, he could have counted the twirls and he would have had the combination. He got down and stood in the areaway, sunk in reflection.

How could he get into that room? He climbed back into the basement and saw wooden steps leading upward. Was that the room where the safe stood? Fearing that the dial was now being twirled, he clambered through the window, hoisted himself up the rain pipe, and peered; he saw only the naked gleam of the steel dial. He got down and doubled his fists. Well, he would explore the basement. He returned to the basement room and mounted the steps to the door and squinted through the keyhole; all was dark, but the tapping was still somewhere near, still faint and directionless. He pushed the door in; along one wall of a room was a table piled with radios and electrical equipment. A radio shop, he muttered.

Well, he could rig up a radio in his cave. He found a sack, slid the radio into it, and slung it across his back. Closing the door, he went down the steps and stood again in the basement, disappointed. He had not solved the problem of the steel dial and he was irked. He set the radio on the floor and again hoisted himself through the window and up the rain pipe and squinted; the metal door was swinging shut. Goddamn! He's worked the combination again. If I had been patient, I'd have had it! How could he get into that room? He *had* to get into it. He could jimmy the window, but it would be much better if he could get in without any traces. To the right of him, he calculated, should be the basement of the building that held the safe; therefore, if he dug a hole right *here,* he ought to reach his goal.

He began a quiet scraping; it was hard work, for the bricks were not damp. He eventually got one out and lowered it softly to the floor. He had to be careful; perhaps people were beyond this wall. He extracted a second layer of brick and found still another. He gritted his teeth, ready to quit. I'll dig one more, he resolved. When the next brick came out he felt air blowing into his face. He waited to be challenged, but nothing happened.

He enlarged the hole and pulled himself through and stood in quiet darkness. He scratched a match to flame and saw steps; he mounted and peered through a keyhole: Darkness . . . He strained to hear the typewriter, but there was only silence. Maybe the office had closed? He twisted the knob and swung the door in; a frigid blast made him shiver. In the shadows before him were halves and quarters of hogs and lambs and steers hanging from metal hooks on the low ceiling, red meat encased in folds of cold white fat. Fronting him was frost-coated glass from behind which came indistinguishable sounds. The odor of fresh raw meat sickened him and he backed away. A meat market, he whispered.

He ducked his head, suddenly blinded by light. He narrowed his eyes; the red-white rows of meat were drenched in yellow glare. A man wearing a crimson-spotted jacket came in and took down a bloody meat cleaver. He eased the door to, holding it ajar just enough to watch the man, hoping that the darkness in which he stood would keep him from being seen. The man took down a hunk of steer and placed it upon a bloody wooden block and bent forward and whacked with the cleaver. The man's face was hard, square, grim; a jet of mustache smudged his upper lip and a glistening cowlick of hair fell over his left eye. Each time he lifted the cleaver and brought it down upon the meat, he let out a short, deep-chested grunt. After he had cut the meat, he wiped blood off the wooden block with a sticky wad of gunny sack and hung the cleaver upon a hook. His face was proud as he placed the chunk of meat in the crook of his elbow and left.

The door slammed and the light went off, once more he stood in shadow. His tension ebbed. From behind the frosted glass he heard the man's voice: "Forty-eight cents a pound, ma'am." He shuddered, feeling that there was something he had to do. But what? He stared fixedly at the cleaver, then he sneezed and was terrified for fear that the man had heard him. But the door did not open. He took down the cleaver and examined the sharp edge smeared with cold blood. Behind the ice-coated glass a cash register rang with a vibrating, musical tinkle.

Absent-mindedly holding the meat cleaver, he rubbed the glass with his thumb and cleared a spot that enabled him to see into the front of the store. The shop was empty, save for the man who was now putting on his hat and coat. Beyond the front window a wan sun shone in the streets; people passed and now and then a fragment of laughter or the whir of a speeding auto came to him. He peered closer and saw on the right counter of the shop a mosquito netting covering pears, grapes, lemons, oranges, bananas, peaches, and plums. His stomach contracted.

The man clicked out the light and he gritted his teeth muttering, Don't lock the icebox door . . . The man went through the door of the shop and locked it from the outside. Thank God! Now, he would eat some more! He waited, trembling. The sun died and its rays lingered on in the sky, turning the streets to dusk. He opened the door and stepped inside the shop. In reverse letters across the front window was: NICK'S FRUITS AND MEATS. He laughed, picked up a soft ripe yellow pear and bit into it; juice squirted; his mouth ached as his saliva glands reacted to the acid of the fruit. He ate three pears, gobbled six bananas, and made away with several oranges, taking a bit out of their tops and holding them to his lips and squeezing them as he hungrily sucked the juice.

He found a faucet, turned it on, laid the cleaver aside, pursed his lips under the stream until his stomach felt about to burst. He straightened and belched, feeling satisfied for the first time since he had been underground. He sat upon the floor, rolled and lit a cigarette, his bloodshot eyes squinting against the film of drifting smoke. He watched a patch of sky turn red, then purple; night fell and he lit another cigarette, brooding. Some part of him was trying to remember the world he had left, and another part of him did not want to remember it. Sprawling before him in his mind was his wife, Mrs. Wooten for whom he worked, the three policemen who had picked him up . . . He possessed them now more completely than he had ever possessed them when he had lived above ground. How this had come about he could not say, but he had no desire to go back to them. He laughed, crushed the cigarette, and stood up.

He went to the front door and gazed out. Emotionally he hovered between the world aboveground and the world underground. He longed to go out, but sober judgment urged him to remain here. Then impulsively he pried the lock loose with one swift twist of the crowbar; the door swung outward. Through the twilight he saw a white man and a white woman coming toward him. He held himself tense, waiting for them to pass; but they came directly to the door and confronted him.

"I want to buy a pound of grapes," the woman said.

Terrified, he stepped back into the store. The white man stood to one side and the woman entered.

"Give me a pound of dark ones," the woman said.

The white man came slowly forward, blinking his eyes.

"Where's Nick?" the man asked.

"Were you just closing?" the woman asked.

"Yes, ma'am," he mumbled. For a second he did not breathe, then he mumbled again: "Yes, ma'am."

"I'm sorry," the woman said.

The street lamps came on, lighting the store somewhat. Ought he run? But that would raise an alarm. He moved slowly, dreamily, to a counter and lifted up a bunch of grapes and showed them to the woman.

"Fine," the woman said. "But isn't that more than a pound?"

He did not answer. The man was staring at him intently.

"Put them in a bag for me," the woman said, fumbling with her purse.

"Yes, ma'am."

He saw a pile of paper bags under a narrow ledge; he opened one and put the grapes in.

"Thanks," the woman said, taking the bag and placing a dime in his dark palm.

"Where's Nick?" the man asked again. "At supper?"

"Sir? Yes, sir," he breathed.

They left the store and he stood trembling in the doorway. When they were out of sight, he burst out laughing and crying. A trolley car rolled noisily past and he controlled himself quickly. He flung the dime to the pavement with a gesture of contempt and stepped into the warm night air. A few shy stars trembled above him. The look of things was beautiful, yet he felt a lurking threat. He went to an unattended newsstand and looked at a stack of papers. He saw a headline: HUNT NEGRO FOR MURDER.

He felt that someone had slipped up on him from behind and was stripping off his clothes; he looked about wildly, went quickly back into the store, picked up the meat cleaver where he had left it near the sink, then made his way through the icebox to the basement. He stood for a long time, breathing heavily. They know I didn't do anything, he muttered. But how could he prove it? He had signed a confession. Though innocent, he felt guilty, condemned. He struck a match and held it near the steel blade, fascinated and repelled by the dried blotches of blood. Then his fingers gripped the handle of the cleaver with all the strength of his body, he wanted to fling the cleaver from him, but he could not. The match flame wavered and fled; he struggled through the hole and put the cleaver in the sack with the radio. He was determined to keep it, for what purpose he did not know.

He was about to leave when he remembered the safe. Where was it? He wanted to give up, but felt that he ought to make one more try. Opposite the last hole he had dug, he tunneled again, plying the crowbar. Once he was so exhausted that he lay on the concrete floor and panted. Finally he made another hole. He wriggled through and his nostrils filled with the fresh smell of coal. He struck a match; yes, the usual steps led upward. He tiptoed to a door and eased it open. A fair-haired white girl stood in front of a steel cabinet, her blue eyes wide upon him. She turned chalky and gave a high-pitched scream. He bounded down the steps and raced to his hole and clambered through, replacing the bricks with nervous haste. He paused, hearing loud voices.

"What's the matter, Alice?"

"A man . . ."

"What man? Where?"

"A man was at that door . . ."

"Oh, nonsense!"

"He was looking at me through the door!"

"Aw, you're dreaming."

"I *did* see a man!"

The girl was crying now.

"There's nobody here."

Another man's voice sounded.

"What is it, Bob?"

"Alice says she saw a man in here, in that door!"

"Let's take a look."

He waited, poised for flight. Footsteps descended the stairs.

"There's nobody down here."

"The window's locked."

"And there's no door."

"You ought to fire that dame."

"Oh, I don't know. Women are that way."

"She's too hysterical."

The men laughed. Footsteps sounded again on the stairs. A door slammed. He sighed, relieved that he had escaped. But he had not done what he had set out to do; his glimpse of the room had been too brief to determine if the safe was there. He had to know. Boldly he groped through the hole once more; he reached the steps and pulled off his shoes and tip-toed up and peered through the keyhole. His head accidentally touched the door and it swung silently in a fraction of an inch; he saw the girl bent over the cabinet, her back to him. Beyond her was the safe. He crept back down the steps, thinking exultingly: I found it!

Now he had to get the combination. Even if the window in the areaway was locked and bolted, he could gain entrance when the office closed. He scoured through the holes he had dug and stood again in the basement where he had left the radio and the cleaver. Again he crawled out of the window and lifted himself up the rain pipe and peered. The steel dial showed lonely and bright, reflecting the yellow glow of an unseen light. Resigned to a long wait, he sat and leaned against the wall. From far off came the faint sounds of life above-ground; once he looked with a baffled expression at the dark sky. Frequently he rose and climbed the pipe to see the white hand spin the dial, but nothing happened. He bit his lip with impatience. It was not the money that was luring him, but the mere fact that he could get it with impunity. Was the hand now twirling the dial? He rose and looked, but the white hand was not in sight.

Perhaps it would be better to watch continuously? Yes; he clung to the pipe and watched the dial until his eyes thickened with tears. Exhausted, he stood again in the areaway. He heard a door being shut and he clawed up the pipe and looked. He jerked tense as a vague figure passed in front of him. He stared unblinkingly, hugging the pipe with one hand and holding the screwdriver with the other, ready to etch the combination upon the wall. His ears caught: *Dong . . . Dong . . . Dong . . . Dong . . . Dong . . . Dong . . . Dong* . . . Seven o'clock, he whispered. Maybe they were closing now? What kind of a store would be open as late as this? he wondered. Did anyone live in the rear? Was there a night watchman? Perhaps the safe was *already* locked for the night! Goddamn! While he had been eating in that shop, they had locked up everything . . . Then, just as he was about to give up, the white hand touched the dial and turned it once to the right and stopped at six. With quivering fingers, he etched 1—R—6 upon the brick wall with the tip of the screwdriver. The hand twirled the dial twice to the left and stopped at two, and he engraved 2—L—2 upon the wall. The dial was spun four times to the right and stopped at six again; he wrote 4—R—6. The dial rotated three times to the left and was centered straight up and down, he wrote 3—L—0. The door swung open and again he saw the piles of green money and the rows of wrapped coins. I got it, he said grimly.

Then he was stone still, astonished. There were two hands now. A right hand lifted a wad of green bills and deftly slipped it up the sleeve of a left arm. The hands trembled; again the right hand slipped a packet of bills up the left sleeve. He's stealing, he said to himself. He grew indignant, as if the money belonged to him. Though *he* had planned to steal the money, he despised and pitied the man. He felt that his stealing the money and the man's stealing were two entirely different things. He wanted to steal the money merely for the sensation involved in getting it, and he had no intention whatever of spending a penny of it; but he knew that the man who was now stealing it was going to spend it, perhaps for pleasure. The huge steel door closed with a soft click.

Though angry, he was somewhat satisfied. The office would close soon. I'll clean the place out, he mused. He imagined the entire office staff cringing with fear; the police would question everyone for a crime they had not committed, just as they had questioned him. And they would have no idea of how the money had been stolen until they discovered the holes he had tunneled in the walls of the basements. He lowered himself and laughed mischievously, with the abandoned glee of an adolescent.

He flattened himself against the wall as the window above him closed with rasping sound. He looked; somebody was bolting the window securely with a metal screen. That won't help you, he snickered to himself. He clung to the rain pipe until the yellow light in the office went out. He went back into the basement, picked up the sack containing the radio and cleaver, and crawled through the two holes he had dug and groped his way into the basement of the building that held the safe. He moved in slow motion, breathing softly. Be careful now, he told himself. There might be a night watchman . . . In his memory was the combination written in bold white characters as upon a blackboard. Eel-like he squeezed through the last hole and crept up the steps and put his hand on the knob and pushed the door in about three inches. Then his courage ebbed; his imagination wove dangers for him.

Perhaps the night watchman was waiting in there, ready to shoot. He dangled his cap on a forefinger and poked it past the jamb of the door. If anyone fired, they would hit his cap; but nothing happened. He widened the door, holding the crowbar high above his head, ready to beat off an assailant. He stood like that for five minutes; the rumble of a streetcar brought him to himself. He entered the room. Moonlight floated in from a side window. He confronted the safe, then checked himself. Better take a look around first . . . He stepped about and found a closed door. Was the night watchman in there? He opened it and saw a washbowl, a faucet, and a commode. To the left was still another door that opened into a huge dark room that seemed empty; on the far side of that room he made out the shadow of still another door. Nobody's here, he told himself.

He turned back to the safe and fingered the dial; it spun with ease. He laughed and twirled it just for fun. Get to work, he told himself. He turned the dial to the figures he saw on the blackboard of his memory; it was so easy that he felt that the safe had not been locked at all. The heavy door eased loose and he caught hold of the handle and pulled hard, but the door swung open with a slow momentum of its own. Breathless, he gaped at wads of green bills, rows of wrapped coins, curious glass jars full of white pellets, and many oblong green metal boxes. He glanced guiltily over his shoulder; it seemed impossible that someone should not call to him to stop.

They'll be surprised in the morning, he thought. He opened the top of the sack and lifted a wad of compactly tied bills; the money was crisp and new. He admired the smooth, cleancut edges. The fellows in Washington sure know how to make this stuff, he mused. He rubbed the money with his fingers, as though expecting it to reveal hidden qualities. He lifted the wad to his nose and smelled the fresh odor of ink. Just like any other paper, he mumbled. He dropped the wad into the sack and picked up another. Holding the bag, he thought and laughed.

There was in him no sense of possessiveness; he was intrigued with the form and color of the money, with the manifold reactions which he knew that men aboveground held toward it. The sack was one-third full when it occurred to him to examine the denominations of the bills; without realizing it, he had put many wads of one-dollar bills into the sack. Aw, nuts, he said in disgust. Take the big ones . . . He dumped the one-dollar bills onto the floor and swept all the hundred-dollar bills he could find into the sack, then he raked in rolls of coins with crooked fingers.

He walked to a desk upon which sat a typewriter, the same machine which the blond girl had used. He was fascinated by it; never in his life had he used one of them. It was a queer instrument of business, something beyond the rim of his life. Whenever he had been in an office where a girl was typing, he had almost always spoken in whispers. Remembering vaguely what he had seen others do, he inserted a sheet of paper into the machine; it went in lopsided and he did not know how to straighten it. Spelling in a soft diffident voice, he pecked out his name on the keys: *freddaniels.* He looked at it and laughed. He would learn to type correctly one of these days.

Yes, he would take the typewriter too. He lifted the machine and placed it atop the bulk of money in the sack. He did not feel that he was stealing, for the cleaver, the radio, the money, and the typewriter were all on the same level of value, all meant the same thing to him. They were the serious toys of the men who lived in the dead world of sunshine and rain he had left, the world that had condemned him, branded him guilty.

But what kind of a place is this? he wondered. What was in that dark room to his rear? He felt for his matches and found that he had only one left. He leaned the sack against the safe and groped forward into the room, encountering smooth, metallic objects that felt like machines. Baffled, he touched a wall and tried vainly to locate an electric switch. Well, he *had* to strike his last match. He knelt and struck it, cupping the flame near the floor with his palms. The place seemed to be a factory, with benches and tables. There were bulbs with green shades spaced about the tables; he turned on a light and twisted it low so that the glare was limited. He saw a half-filled packet of cigarettes and appropriated it. There were stools at the benches and he concluded that men worked here at some trade. He wandered and found a few half-used folders of matches. If only he could find more cigarettes! But there were none.

But what kind of a place was this? On a bench he saw a pad of paper captioned: PEER'S—MANUFACTURING JEWELERS. His lips formed an "O," then he snapped off the light and ran back to the safe and lifted one of the glass jars and stared at the tiny white pellets. Gingerly he picked up one and found that it was wrapped in tissue paper. He peeled the paper and saw a glittering stone that looked like glass, glinting white and blue sparks. Diamonds, he breathed.

Roughly he tore the paper from the pellets and soon his palm quivered with precious fire. Trembling, he took all four glass jars from the safe and put them into the sack. He grabbed one of the metal boxes, shook it, and heard a tinny rattle. He pried off the lid with the screwdriver. Rings! Hundreds of them . . . Were they worth anything? He scooped up a handful and jets of fire shot fitfully from the stones. These are diamonds too, he said. He pried open another box. Watches! A chorus of soft, metallic ticking filled his ears. For a moment he could not move, then he dumped all the boxes into the sack.

He shut the safe door, then stood looking around, anxious not to overlook anything: Oh! He had seen a door in the room where the machines were. What was in there? More valuables? He re-entered the room, crossed the floor, and stood undecided before the door. He finally caught hold of the knob and pushed the door in; the room beyond was dark. He advanced cautiously inside and ran his fingers along the wall for the usual switch, then he was stark still. *Something had moved in the room!* What was it? Ought he to creep out, taking the rings and diamonds and money? Why risk what he already had? He waited and the ensuing silence gave him confidence to explore further. Dare he strike a match? Would not a match flame make him a good target? He tensed again as he heard a faint sigh; he was now convinced that there was something alive near him, something that lived and breathed. On tiptoe he felt slowly along the wall, hoping that he would not collide with anything. Luck was with him; he found the light switch.

No; don't turn the light on . . . Then suddenly he realized that he did not know in what direction the door was. Goddamn! He had to turn the light on or strike a match. He fingered the switch for a long time, then thought of an idea. He knelt upon the floor, reached his arm up to the switch and flicked the button, hoping that if anyone shot, the bullet would go above his head. The moment the light came on he narrowed his eyes to see quickly. He sucked in his breath and his body gave a violent twitch and was still. In front of him, so close that it made him want to bound up and scream, was a human face.

He was afraid to move lest he touch the man. If the man had opened his eyes at that moment, there was no telling what he might have done. The man—long and rawboned—was stretched out on his back upon a little cot, sleeping in his clothes, his head cushioned by a dirty pillow; his face, clouded by a dark stubble of beard, looked straight up to the ceiling. The man sighed, and he grew tense to defend himself; the man mumbled and turned his face away from the light. I've got to turn off that light, he thought. Just as he was about to rise, he saw a gun and cartridge belt on the floor at the man's side. Yes, he would take the gun and cartridge belt, not to use them, but just to keep them, as one takes a memento from a country fair. He picked them up and was about to click off the light when his eyes fell upon a photograph perched upon a chair near the man's head; it was the picture of a woman, smiling, shown against a background of open fields; at the woman's side were two young children, a boy and a girl. He smiled indulgently; he could send a bullet into that man's brain and time would be over for him . . .

He clicked off the light and crept silently

back into the room where the safe stood; he fastened the cartridge belt about him and adjusted the holster at his right hip. He strutted about the room on tiptoe, lolling his head nonchalantly, then paused, abruptly pulled the gun, and pointed it with grim face toward an imaginary foe. "Boom!" he whispered fiercely. Then he bent forward with silent laughter. That's just like they do it in the movies, he said.

He contemplated his loot for a long time, then got a towel from the washroom and tied the sack securely. When he looked up he was momentarily frightened by his shadow looming on the wall before him. He lifted the sack, dragged it down the basement steps, lugged it across the basement, gasping for breath. After he had struggled through the hole, he clumsily replaced the bricks, then tussled with the sack until he got it to the cave. He stood in the dark, wet with sweat, brooding about the diamonds, the rings, the watches, the money; he remembered the singing in the church, the people yelling in the movie, the dead baby, the nude man stretched out upon the white table . . . He saw these items hovering before his eyes and felt that some dim meaning linked them together, that some magical relationship made them kin. He stared with vacant eyes, convinced that all of these images, with their tongueless reality, were striving to tell him something. . .

Later, seeing with his fingers, he untied the sack and set each item neatly upon the dirt floor. Exploring, he took the bulb, the socket, and the wire out of the tool chest; he was elated to find a double socket at one end of the wire. He crammed the stuff into his pockets and hoisted himself upon the rusty pipes and squinted into the church; it was dim and empty. Somewhere in this wall were live electric wires; but where? He lowered himself, groped and tapped the wall with the butt of the screwdriver, listening vainly for hollow sounds. I'll just take a chance and dig, he said.

For an hour he tried to dislodge a brick, and when he struck a match, he found that he had dug a depth of only an inch! No use in digging here, he sighed. By the flickering light of a match, he looked upward, then lowered his eyes, only to glance up again, startled. Directly above his head, beyond the pipes, was a wealth of electric wiring. I'll be damned, he snickered.

He got an old dull knife from the chest and, seeing again with his fingers, separated the two strands of wire and cut away the insulation. Twice he received a slight shock. He scraped the wiring clean and managed to join the two twin ends, then screwed in the bulb. The sudden illumination blinded him and he shut his lids to kill the pain in his eyeballs. I've got that much done, he thought jubilantly.

He placed the bulb on the dirt floor and the light cast a blatant glare on the bleak clay walls. Next he plugged one end of the wire that dangled from the radio into the light socket and bent down and switched on the button; almost at once there was the harsh sound of static, but no words or music. Why won't it work? he wondered. Had he damaged the mechanism in any way? Maybe it needed grounding? Yes . . . He rummaged in the tool chest and found another length of wire, fastened it to the ground of the radio, and then tied the opposite end to a pipe. Rising and growing distinct, a slow strain of music entranced him with its measured sound. He sat upon the chest, deliriously happy.

Later he searched again in the chest and found a half-gallon can of glue; he opened it and smelled a sharp odor. Then he recalled that he had not even looked at the money. He took a wad of green bills and weighed it in his palm, then broke the seal and held one of the bills up to the light and studied it closely. *The United States of America will pay to the bearer on demand one hundred dollars,* he read in slow speech; then: *This note is legal tender for all debts, public and private.* . . . He broke into a musing laugh, feeling that he was reading of the doings of people who lived on some far-off planet. He turned the bill over and saw on the other side of it a delicately beautiful building gleaming with paint and set amidst green grass. He had no desire whatever to count the money; it was what it stood for—the various currents of life swirling aboveground—that captivated him. Next he opened the rolls of coins and let them slide from their paper wrappings to the ground; the bright, new gleaming pennies and nickels and dimes piled high at his feet, a glowing mound of shimmering copper and silver. He sifted them through his fingers, listening to their tinkle as they struck the conical heap.

Oh, yes! He had forgotten. He would now write his name on the typewriter. He inserted a piece of paper and poised his fingers to write. But what was his name? He stared, trying to remember. He stood and glared about the dirt cave, his name on the tip of his lips. But it would not come to him. Why was he here? Yes, he had been running away from the police. But why? His mind was blank. He bit his lips and sat again, feeling a vague terror. But why worry? He laughed, then pecked slowly: *itwasalonghotday.* He was determined to type the sentence without making any mistakes. How did one make capital letters? He experimented and luckily discovered how to lock the machine for capital letters and then shift it back to lower case. Next he discovered how to make spaces, then he wrote neatly and correctly: *It was a long hot day.* Just why he selected that sentence he did not know; it was merely the ritual of performing the thing that appealed to him. He took the sheet out of the machine and looked around with stiff neck and hard eyes and spoke to an imaginary person:

"Yes, I'll have the contracts ready tomorrow."

He laughed. That's just the way they talk, he said. He grew weary of the game and pushed the machine aside. His eyes fell upon the can of glue, and a mischievous idea bloomed in him, filling him with nervous eagerness. He leaped up and opened the can of glue, then broke the seals on all the wads of money. I'm going to have some wallpaper, he said with a luxurious, physical laugh that made him bend at the knees. He took the towel with which he had tied the sack and balled it into a swab and dipped it into the can of glue and dabbed glue onto the wall; then he pasted one green bill by the side of another. He stepped back and cocked his head. Jesus! That's funny . . . He slapped his thighs and guffawed. He had triumphed over the world aboveground! He was free! If only people could see this! He wanted to run from this cave and yell his discovery to the world.

He swabbed all the dirt walls of the cave and pasted them with green bills; when he had finished the walls blazed with a yellow-green fire. Yes, this room would be his hide-out; between him and the world that had branded him guilty would stand this mocking symbol. He had not stolen the money; he had simply picked it up, just as a man would pick up firewood in a forest. And that was how the world aboveground now seemed to him, a wild forest filled with death.

The walls of money finally palled on him and he looked about for new interests to feed his emotions. The cleaver! He drove a nail into the wall and hung the bloody cleaver upon it. Still another idea welled up. He pried open the metal boxes and lined them side by side on the dirt floor. He grinned at the gold and fire. From one box he lifted up a fistful of ticking gold watches and dangled them by their gleaming chains. He stared with an idle smile, then began to wind them up; he did not attempt to set them at any given hour, for there was no time for him now. He took a fistful of nails and drove them into the papered walls and hung the watches upon them, letting them swing down by their glittering chains, trembling and ticking busily against the backdrop of green with the lemon sheen of the electric light shining upon the metal watch casings, converting the golden disks into blobs of liquid yellow. Hardly had he hung up the last watch than the idea extended itself; he took more nails from the chest and drove them into the green paper and took the boxes of rings and went from nail to nail and hung up the golden bands. The blue and white sparks from the stones filled the cave with brittle laughter, as though enjoying his hilarious secret. People certainly can do some funny things, he said to himself.

He sat upon the tool chest, alternately laughing and shaking his head soberly. Hours later he became conscious of the gun sagging at his hip and he pulled it from the holster. He had seen men fire guns in movies, but somehow his life had never led him into contact with firearms. A desire to feel the sensation others felt in firing came over him. But someone might hear . . . Well, what if they did? They would not know where the shot had come from. Not in their wildest notions would they think that it had come from under the streets! He tightened his fingers on the trigger; there was a deafening report and it seemed that the entire underground had caved in upon his eardrums; and in the same instant there flashed an orange-blue spurt of flame that died quickly but lingered on as a vivid after-image. He smelled the acrid stench of burnt powder filling his lungs and he dropped the gun abruptly.

The intensity of his feelings died and he hung the gun and cartridge belt upon the wall. Next he lifted the jars of diamonds and turned them bottom upward, dumping the white pellets upon the ground. One by one he picked them up and peeled the tissue paper from them and piled them in a neat heap. He wiped his sweaty hands on his trousers, lit a cigarette, and commenced playing another game. He imagined that he was a rich man who lived aboveground in the obscene sunshine and he was strolling through a park of a summer morning, smiling, nodding to his neighbors, sucking an after-breakfast cigar. Many times he crossed the floor of the cave, avoiding the diamonds with his feet, yet subtly gauging his footsteps so that his shoes, wet with sewer slime, would strike the diamonds at some undetermined moment. After twenty minutes of sauntering, his right foot smashed into the heap and diamonds lay scattered in all directions, glinting with a million tiny chuckles of icy laughter. Oh, shucks, he mumbled in mock regret, intrigued by the damage he had wrought. He continued walking, ignoring the brittle fire. He felt that he had a glorious victory locked in his heart.

He stooped and flung the diamonds more evenly over the floor and they showered rich sparks, collaborating with him. He went over the floor and trampled the stones just deeply enough for them to be faintly visible, as though they were set deliberately in the prongs of a thousand rings. A ghostly light bathed the cave. He sat on the chest and frowned. Maybe *any*thing's right, he mumbled. Yes, if the world as men had made it was right, then anything else was right, any act a man took to satisfy himself, murder, theft, torture.

He straightened with a start. What was happening to him? He was drawn to these crazy thoughts, yet they made him feel vaguely guilty. He would stretch out upon the ground, then get up; he would want to crawl again through the holes he had dug, but would restrain himself; he would think of going again up into the streets, but fear would hold him still. He stood in the middle of the cave, surrounded by green walls and a laughing floor, trembling. He was going to do something, but what? Yes, he was afraid of himself, afraid of doing some nameless thing.

To control himself, he turned on the radio. A melancholy piece of music rose. Brooding over the diamonds on the floor was like looking up into a sky full of restless stars; then the illusion turned into its opposite: he was high up in the air looking down at the twinkling lights of a sprawling city. The music ended and a man recited news events. In the same attitude in which he had contemplated the city, so now, as he heard the cultivated tone, he looked down upon land and sea as men fought, as cities were razed, as planes scattered death upon open towns, as long lines of trenches wavered and broke. He heard the names of generals and the names of mountains and the names of countries and the names and numbers of divisions that were in action on different battle fronts. He saw black smoke billowing from the stacks of warships as they neared each other over wastes of water and he heard their huge guns thunder as red-hot shells screamed across the surface of night seas. He saw hundreds of planes wheeling and droning in the sky and heard the clatter of machine guns as they fought each other and he saw planes falling in plumes of smoke and blaze of fire. He saw steel tanks rumbling across fields of ripe wheat to meet other tanks and there was a loud clang of steel as numberless tanks collided. He saw troops with fixed bayonets charging in waves against other troops who held fixed bayonets and men groaned as steel ripped into their bodies and they went down to die . . . The voice of the radio faded and he was staring at the diamonds on the floor at his feet.

He shut off the radio, fighting an irrational compulsion to act. He walked aimlessly about the cave, touching the walls with his finger tips. Suddenly he stood still. *What was the matter with him?* Yes, he knew . . . It was these walls; these crazy walls were filling him with a wild urge to climb out into the dark sunshine aboveground. Quickly he doused the light to banish the shouting walls, then sat again upon the tool chest. Yes, he was trapped. His muscles were flexed taut and sweat ran down his face. He knew now that he could not stay here and he could not go out. He lit a cigarette with shaking fingers; the match flame revealed the green-papered walls with militant distinctness; the purple on the gun barrel glinted like a threat; the meat cleaver brooded with its eloquent splotches of blood; the mound of silver and copper smoldered angrily; the diamonds winked at him from the floor; and the gold watches ticked and trembled, crowning time the king of consciousness, defining the limits of living . . . The match blaze died and he bolted from where he stood and collided brutally with the nails upon the walls. The spell was broken. He shuddered, feeling that, in spite of his fear, sooner or later he would go up into that dead sunshine and somehow say something to somebody about all this.

He sat again upon the tool chest. Fatigue weighed upon his forehead and eyes. Minutes passed and he relaxed. He dozed, but his imagination was alert. He saw himself rising, wading again in the sweeping water of the sewer; he came to a manhole and climbed out and was amazed to discover that he had hoisted himself into a room filled with armed policemen who were watching him intently. He jumped awake in the dark; he had not moved. He sighed, closed his eyes, and slept again; this time his imagination designed a scheme of protection for him. His dreaming made him feel that he was standing in a room watching over his own nude body lying stiff and cold upon a white table. At the far end of the room he saw a crowd of people huddled in a corner, afraid of his body. Though lying dead upon the table, he was standing in some mysterious way at his side, warding off the people, guarding his body, and laughing to himself as he observed the situation. They're scared of me, he thought.

He awakened with a start, leaped to his feet, and stood in the center of the black cave. It was a full minute before he moved again. He hovered between sleeping and waking, unprotected, a prey of wild fears. He could neither see nor hear. One part of him was asleep; his blood coursed slowly and his flesh was numb. On the other hand he was roused to a strange, high pitch of tension. He lifted his fingers to his face, as though about to weep. Gradually his hands lowered and he struck a match, looking about, expecting to see a door through which he could walk to safety; but there was no door, only the green walls and the moving floor. The match flame died and it was dark again.

Five minutes later he was still standing when the thought came to him that he had been asleep. Yes . . . But he was not yet fully awake; he was still queerly blind and dead. How long had he slept? Where was he? Then suddenly he recalled the green-papered walls of the cave and in the same instant he heard loud singing coming from the church beyond the wall. Yes, they woke me up, he muttered. He hoisted himself and lay atop the bed of pipes and brought his face to the narrow slit. Men and women stood here and there between pews. A song ended and a young black girl tossed back her head and closed her eyes and broke plaintively into another hymn:

Glad, glad, glad, oh, so glad
I got Jesus in my soul . . .

Those few words were all she sang, but what her words did not say, her emotions said as she repeated the lines, varying the mood and tempo, making her tone express meanings which her conscious mind did not know. Another woman melted her voice with the girl's, and then an old man's voice merged with that of the two women. Soon the entire congregation was singing:

Glad, glad, glad, oh, so glad
I got Jesus in my soul . . .

They're wrong, he whispered in the lyric darkness. He felt that their search for a happiness they could never find made them feel that they had committed some dreadful offense which they could not remember or understand. He was now in possession of the feeling that had gripped him when he had first come into the underground. It came to him in a series of questions: Why was this sense of guilt so seemingly innate, so easy to come by, to think, to feel, so verily physical? It seemed that when one felt this guilt one was retracing in one's feelings a faint pattern designed long before; it seemed that one was always trying to remember a gigantic shock that had left a haunting impression upon one's body which one could not forget or shake off, but which had been forgotten by the conscious mind, creating in one's life a state of eternal anxiety.

He had to tear himself away from this; he got down from the pipes. His nerves were so taut that he seemed to feel his brain pushing through his skull. He felt that he had to do something, but he could not figure out what it was. Yet he knew that if he stood here until he made up his mind, he would never move. He crawled through the hole he had made in the brick wall and the exertion afforded him respite from tension. When he entered the basement of the radio store, he stopped in fear, hearing loud voices.

"Come on, boy! Tell us what you did with the radio!"

"Mister, I didn't steal the radio! I swear!"

He heard a dull thumping sound and he imagined a boy being struck violently.

"Please, mister!"

"Did you take it to a pawn shop?"

"No, sir! I didn't steal the radio! I got a radio at home," the boy's voice pleaded hysterically. "Go to my home and look!"

There came to his ears the sound of another blow. It was so funny that he had to clap his hand over his mouth to keep from laughing out loud. They're beating some poor boy, he whispered to himself, shaking his head. He felt a sort of distant pity for the boy and wondered if he ought to bring back the radio and leave it in the basement. No. Perhaps it was a good thing that they were beating the boy; perhaps the beating would bring to the boy's attention, for the first time in his life, the secret of his existence, the guilt that he could never get rid of.

Smiling, he scampered over a coal pile and stood again in the basement of the building where he had stolen the money and jewelry. He lifted himself into the areaway, climbed the rain pipe, and squinted through a two-inch opening of window. The guilty familiarity of what he saw made his muscles tighten. Framed before him in a bright tableau of daylight was the night watchman sitting upon the edge of a chair, stripped to the waist, his head sagging forward, his eyes red and puffy. The watchman's face and shoulders were stippled with red and black welts. Back of the watchman stood the safe, the steel door wide open, showing the empty vault. Yes, they think he did it, he mused.

Footsteps sounded in the room and a man in a blue suit passed in front of him, then another, then still another. Policemen, he breathed. Yes, they were trying to make the watchman confess, just as they had once made him confess to a crime he had not done. He stared into the room, trying to recall something. Oh . . . Those were the same policemen who had beaten him, had made him sign that paper when he had been too tired and sick to care. Now, they were doing the same thing to the watchman. His heart pounded as he saw one of the policemen shake a finger into the watchman's face.

"Why don't you admit it's an inside job, Thompson?" the policeman said

"I've told you all I know," the watchman mumbled through swollen lips.

"But nobody was here but you!" the policeman shouted.

"I was sleeping," the watchman said. "It was wrong, but I was sleeping all that night!"

"Stop telling us that lie!"

"It's the truth!"

"When did you get the combination?"

"I don't know how to open the safe," the watchman said.

He clung to the rain pipe, tense; he wanted to laugh, but he controlled himself. He felt a great sense of power; yes, he could go back to the cave, rip the money off the walls, pick up the diamonds and rings, and bring them here and write a note, telling them where to look for their foolish toys. No . . . What good would that do? It was not worth the effort. The watchman was guilty; although he was not guilty of the crime of which he had been accused, he was guilty, had always been guilty. The only thing that worried him was that the man who had been really stealing was not being accused. But he consoled himself: they'll catch him sometime during his life.

He saw one of the policemen slap the watchman across the mouth.

"Come clean, you bastard!"

"I've told you all I know," the watchman mumbled like a child.

One of the police went to the rear of the watchman's chair and jerked it from under him; the watchman pitched forward upon his face.

"Get up!" a policeman said.

Trembling, the watchman pulled himself up and sat limply again in the chair.

"Now, are you going to talk?"

"I've told you all I know," the watchman gasped.

"Where did you hide the stuff?"

"I didn't take it!"

"Thompson, your brains are in your feet," one of the policemen said. "We're going to string you up and get them back into your skull."

He watched the policemen clamp handcuffs on the watchman's wrists and ankles; then they lifted the watchman and swung him upside-down and hoisted his feet to the edge of a door. The watchman hung, head down, his eyes bulging. They're crazy, he whispered to himself as he clung to the ridges of the pipe.

"You going to talk?" a policeman shouted into the watchman's ear.

He heard the watchman groan.

"We'll let you hang there till you talk, see?"

He saw the watchman close his eyes.

"Let's take 'im down. He passed out," a policeman said.

He grinned as he watched them take the body down and dump it carelessly upon the floor. The policeman took off the handcuffs.

"Let 'im come to. Let's get a smoke," a policeman said.

The three policemen left the scope of his vision. A door slammed. He had an impulse to yell to the watchman that he could escape through the hole in the basement and live with him in the cave. But he wouldn't understand, he told himself. After a moment he saw the watchman rise and stand, swaying from weakness. He stumbled across the room to a desk, opened a drawer, and took out a gun. He's going to kill himself, he thought, intent, eager, detached, yearning to see the end of the man's actions. As the watchman stared vaguely about he lifted the gun to his temple; he stood like that for some minutes, biting his lips until a line of blood etched its way down a corner of his chin. No, he oughtn't do that, he said to himself in a mood of pity.

"Don't!" he half whispered and half yelled.

The watchman looked wildly about; he had

heard him. But it did not help; there was a loud report and the watchman's head jerked violently and he fell like a log and lay prone, the gun clattering over the floor.

The three policemen came running into the room with drawn guns. One of the policemen knelt and rolled the watchman's body over and stared at a ragged, scarlet hole in the temple.

"Our hunch was right," the kneeling policeman said. "He was guilty, all right."

"Well, this ends the case," another policeman said.

"He knew he was licked," the third one said with grim satisfaction.

He eased down the rain pipe, crawled back through the holes he had made, and went back into his cave. A fever burned in his bones. He had to act, yet he was afraid. His eyes stared in the darkness as though propped open by invisible hands, as though they had become lidless. His muscles were rigid and he stood for what seemed to him a thousand years.

When he moved again his actions were informed with precision, his muscular system reinforced from a reservoir of energy. He crawled through the hole of earth, dropped into gray sewer current, and sloshed ahead. When his right foot went forward at a street intersection, he fell backward and shot down into water. In a spasm of terror his right hand grabbed the concrete ledge of a down-curve and he felt the streaking water tugging violently at his body. The current reached his neck and for a moment he was still. He knew that if he moved clumsily he would be sucked under. He held onto the ledge with both hands and slowly pulled himself up. He sighed, standing once more in the sweeping water, thankful that he had missed death.

He waded on through sludge, moving with care, until he came to a web of light sifting down from a manhole cover. He saw steel hooks running up the side of the sewer wall; he caught hold and lifted himself and put his shoulder to the cover and moved it an inch. A crash of sound came to him as he looked into a hot glare of sunshine through which blurred shapes moved. Fear scalded him and he dropped back into the pallid current and stood paralyzed in the shadows. A heavy car rumbled past overhead, jarring the pavement, warning him to stay in his world of dark light, knocking the cover back into place with an imperious clang.

He did not know how much fear he felt, for fear claimed him completely; yet it was not a fear of the police or of people, but a cold dread at the thought of the actions he knew he would perform if he went out into that cruel sunshine. His mind said no; his body said yes; and his mind could not understand his feelings. A low whine broke from him and he was in the act of uncoiling. He climbed upward and heard the faint honking of auto horns. Like a frantic cat clutching a rag, he clung to the steel prongs and heaved his shoulder against the cover and pushed it off halfway. For a split second his eyes were drowned in the terror of yellow light and he was in a deeper darkness than he had ever known in the underground.

Partly out of the hole, he blinked, regaining enough sight to make out meaningful forms. An odd thing was happening. No one was rushing forward to challenge him. He had imagined the moment of his emergence as a desperate tussle with men who wanted to cart him off to be killed; instead, life froze about him as the traffic stopped. He pushed the cover aside, stood, swaying in a world so fragile that he expected it to collapse and drop him into some deep void. But nobody seemed to pay him heed. The cars were now swerving to shun him and the gaping hole.

"Why in hell don't you put up a red light, dummy?" a raucous voice yelled.

He understood; they thought that he was a sewer workman. He walked toward the sidewalk, weaving unsteadily through the moving traffic.

"Look where you're going, nigger!"

"That's right! Stay there and get killed!"

"You blind, you bastard?"

"Go home and sleep your drunk off!"

A policeman stood at the curb, looking in

the opposite direction. When he passed the policeman, he feared that he would be grabbed, but nothing happened. Where was he? Was this real? He wanted to look about to get his bearings, but felt that something awful would happen to him if he did. He wandered into a spacious doorway of a store that sold men's clothing and saw his reflection in a long mirror: his cheekbones protruded from a hairy black face; his greasy cap was perched askew upon his head and his eyes were red and glassy. His shirt and trousers were caked with mud and hung loosely. His hands were gummed with a black stickiness. He threw back his head and laughed so loudly that passers-by stopped and stared.

He ambled on down the sidewalk, not having the merest notion of where he was going. Yet, sleeping within him, was the drive to go somewhere and say something to somebody. Half an hour later his ears caught the sound of spirited singing.

The Lamb, the Lamb, the Lamb
I hear thy voice a-calling
The Lamb, the Lamb, the Lamb
I feel thy grace a-falling

A church! He exclaimed. He broke into a run and came to brick steps leading downward to a subbasement. This is it! The church into which he had peered. Yes, he was going in and tell them. What? He did not know; but, once face to face with them, he would think of what to say. Must be Sunday, he mused. He ran down the steps and jerked the door open; the church was crowded and a deluge of song swept over him.

The Lamb, the Lamb, the Lamb
Tell me again your story
The Lamb, the Lamb, the Lamb
Flood my soul with your glory

He stared at the singing faces with a trembling smile.

"Say!" he shouted.

Many turned to look at him, but the song rolled on. His arm was jerked violently.

"I'm sorry, Brother, but you can't do that in here," a man said.

"But, mister!"

"You can't act rowdy in God's house," the man said.

"He's filthy," another man said.

"But I want to tell 'em," he said loudly.

"He stinks," someone muttered.

The song had stopped, but at once another one began.

Oh, wondrous sight upon the cross
Vision sweet and divine
Oh, wondrous sight upon the cross
Full of such love sublime

He attempted to twist away, but other hands grabbed him and rushed him into the doorway.

"Let me alone!" he screamed, struggling.

"Get out!"

"He's drunk," somebody said. "He ought to be ashamed!"

"He acts crazy!"

He felt that he was failing and he grew frantic.

"But, mister, let me tell—"

"Get away from this door, or I'll call the police!"

He stared, his trembling smile fading in a sense of wonderment.

"The police," he repeated vacantly.

"Now, get!"

He was pushed toward the brick steps and the door banged shut. The waves of song came.

Oh, wondrous sight, wondrous sight
Lift my heavy heart above
Oh, wondrous sight, wondrous sight
Fill my weary soul with love

He was smiling again now. Yes, the police . . . That was it! Why had he not thought of it before? The idea had been deep down in him, and only now did it assume supreme importance. He looked up and saw a street sign: COURT STREET—HARTSDALE AVENUE. He turned and walked northward, his mind filled with the image of the police station. Yes, that was where they had beaten him, accused him, and had made him sign a confession of his guilt. He would go there and clear up everything, make a statement. What statement? He did not know. He was the statement, and since it was all so clear to him, surely he would be able to make it clear to others.

He came to the corner of Hartsdale Avenue and turned westward. Yeah, there's the station . . . A policeman came down the steps and walked past him without a glance. He mounted the stone steps and went through the door, paused; he was in a hallway where several policemen were standing, talking, smoking. One turned to him.

"What do you want, boy?"

He looked at the policeman and laughed.

"What in hell are you laughing about?" the policeman asked.

He stopped laughing and stared. His whole being was full of what he wanted to say to them, but he could not say it.

"Are you looking for the Desk Sergeant?"

"Yes, sir," he said quickly; then: "Oh, no, sir."

"Well, make up your mind, now."

Four policemen grouped themselves around him.

"I'm looking for the men," he said.

"What men?"

Peculiarly, at that moment he could not remember the names of the policemen; he recalled their beating him, the confession he had signed, and how he had run away from them. He saw the cave next to the church, the money on the walls, the guns, the rings, the cleaver, the watches, and the diamonds on the floor.

"They brought me here," he began.

"When?"

His mind flew back over the blur of the time lived in the underground blackness. He had no idea of how much time had elapsed, but the intensity of what had happened to him told him that it could not have transpired in a short space of time, yet his mind told him that time must have been brief.

"It was a long time ago." He spoke like a child relating a dimly remembered dream. "It was a long time," he repeated, following the promptings of his emotions. "They beat me . . . I was scared. I ran away."

A policeman raised a finger to his temple and made a derisive circle.

"Nuts," the policeman said.

"Do you know what place this is, boy?"

"Yes, sir. The police station," he answered sturdily, almost proudly.

"Well, who do you want to see?"

"The men," he said again, feeling that surely they knew the men. "You know the men," he said in a hurt tone.

"What's your name?"

He opened his lips to answer and no words came. He had forgotten. But what did it matter if he had? It was not important.

"Where do you live?"

Where did he live? It had been so long ago since he had lived up here in this strange world that he felt it was foolish even to try to remember. Then for a moment the old mood that had dominated him in the underground surged back. He leaned forward and spoke eagerly.

"They said I killed the woman."

"What woman?" a policeman asked.

"And I signed a paper that said I was guilty," he went on, ignoring their questions. "Then I ran off . . ."

"Did you run off from an institution?"

"No, sir," he said, blinking and shaking his head. "I came from under the ground. I pushed off the manhole cover and climbed out . . ."

"All right, now," a policeman said, placing an arm about his shoulder. "We'll send you to the psycho and you'll be taken care of."

"Maybe he's a Fifth Columnist!" a policeman shouted.

There was laughter and, despite his anxiety, he joined in. But the laughter lasted so long that it irked him.

"I got to find those men," he protested mildly.

"Say, boy, what have you been drinking?"

"Water," he said. "I got some water in a basement."

"Were the men you ran away from dressed in white, boy?"

"No, sir," he said brightly. "They were men like you."

An elderly policeman caught hold of his arm.

"Try and think hard. Where did they pick you up?"

He knitted his brows in an effort to remember, but he was blank inside. The policeman stood before him demanding logical answers and he could no longer think with his mind; he thought with his feelings and no words came.

"I was guilty," he said. "Oh, no, sir. I wasn't then, I mean, mister!"

"Aw, talk sense. Now, where did they pick you up?"

He felt challenged and his mind began reconstructing events in reverse; his feelings ranged back over the long hours and he saw the cave, the sewer, the bloody room where it was said that a woman had been killed.

"Oh, yes, sir," he said, smiling. "I was coming from Mrs. Wooten's."

"Who is she?"

"I work for her."

"Where does she live?"

"Next door to Mrs. Peabody, the woman who was killed."

The policeman were very quiet now, looking at him intently.

"What do you know about Mrs. Peabody's death, boy?"

"Nothing, sir. But they said I killed her. But it doesn't make any difference. I'm guilty!"

"What are you talking about, boy?"

His smile faded and he was possessed with memories of the underground; he saw the cave next to the church and his lips moved to speak. But how could he say it? The distance between what he felt and what these men meant was vast. Something told him, as he stood there looking into their faces, that he would never be able to tell them, that they would never believe him even if he told them.

"All the people I saw was guilty," he began slowly.

"Aw, nuts," a policeman muttered.

"Say," another policeman said, "that Peabody woman was killed over on Winewood. That's Number Ten's beat."

"Where's Number Ten?" a policeman asked.

"Upstairs in the swing room," someone answered.

"Take this boy up, Sam," a policeman ordered.

"O.K. Come along, boy."

An elderly policeman caught hold of his arm and led him up a flight of wooden stairs, down a long hall, and to a door.

"Squad Ten!" the policeman called through the door.

"What?" a gruff voice answered.

"Someone to see you!"

"About what?"

The old policeman pushed the door in and then shoved him into the room.

He stared, his lips open, his heart barely beating. Before him were the three policemen who had picked him up and had beaten him to extract the confession. They were seated about a small table, playing cards. The air was blue with smoke and sunshine poured through a high window, lighting up fantastic smoke shapes. He saw one of the policemen look up; the policeman's face was tired and a cigarette drooped limply from one corner of his mouth and both of his fat, puffy eyes were squinting and his hands gripped his cards.

"Lawson!" the man exclaimed.

The moment the man's name sounded he remembered the names of all of them: Lawson, Murphy, and Johnson. How simple it was. He waited, smiling, wondering how they would react when they knew he had come back.

"Looking for me?" the man who had been called Lawson mumbled, sorting his cards. "For what?"

So far only Murphy, the red-headed one, had recognized him.

"Don't you-all remember me?" he blurted, running to the table.

All three of the policemen were looking at

him now. Lawson, who seemed the leader, jumped to his feet.

"Where in hell have you been?"

"Do you know 'im, Lawson?" the old policeman asked.

"Huh?" Lawson frowned. "Oh, yes. I'll handle 'im." The old policeman left the room and Lawson crossed to the door and turned the key in the lock. "Come here, boy," he ordered in a cold tone.

He did not move; he looked from face to face. Yes, he would tell them about his cave.

"He looks batty to me," Johnson said, the one who had not spoken before.

"Why in hell did you come back here?" Lawson said.

"I—I just didn't want to run away no more," he said. "I'm all right, now." He paused; the men's attitude puzzled him.

"You've been hiding, huh?" Lawson asked in a tone that denoted that he had not heard his previous words. "You told us you were sick, and when we left you in the room, you jumped out of the window and ran away."

Panic filled him. Yes, they were indifferent to what he would say! They were waiting for him to speak and they would laugh at him. He had to rescue himself from this bog; he had to force the reality of himself upon them.

"Mister, I took a sackful of money and pasted it on the walls . . ." he began.

"I'll be damned," Lawson said.

"Listen," said Murphy, "let me tell you something for your own good. We don't want you, see? You're free, free as air. Now go home and forget it. It was all a mistake. We caught the guy who did the Peabody job. He wasn't colored at all. He was an Eyetalian."

"Shut up!" Lawson yelled. "Have you no sense!"

"But I want to tell 'im," Murphy said.

"We can't let this crazy fool go," Lawson exploded. "He acts nuts, but this may be a stunt . . ."

"I was down in the basement," he began in a childlike tone, as though repeating a lesson learned by heart; "and I went into a movie . . ." His voice failed. He was getting ahead of his story. First, he ought to tell them about the singing in the church, but what words could he use? He looked at them appealingly. "I went into a shop and took a sackful of money and diamonds and watches and rings . . . I didn't steal 'em, I'll give 'em all back. I just took 'em to play with . . ." He paused, stunned by their disbelieving eyes.

Lawson lit a cigarette and looked at him coldly.

"What did you do with the money?" he asked in a quiet, waiting voice.

"I pasted the hundred-dollar bills on the walls."

"What walls?" Lawson asked.

"The walls of the dirt room," he said, smiling, "the room next to the church. I hung up the rings and the watches and I stamped the diamonds into the dirt . . ." He saw that they were not understanding what he was saying. He grew frantic to make them believe, his voice tumbled on eagerly. "I saw a dead baby and a dead man . . ."

"Aw, you're nuts," Lawson snarled, shoving him into a chair.

"But, mister . . ."

"Johnson, where's the paper he signed?" Lawson asked.

"What paper?"

"The confession, fool!"

Johnson pulled out his billfold and extracted a crumpled piece of paper.

"Yes, sir, mister," he said, stretching forth his hand. "That's the paper I signed . . ."

Lawson slapped him and he would have toppled had his chair not struck a wall behind him. Lawson scratched a match and held the paper over the flame; the confession burned down to Lawson's fingertips.

He stared, thunderstruck; the sun of the underground was fleeting and the terrible darkness of the day stood before him. They did not believe him, but he *had* to make them believe him!

"But, mister . . ."

"It's going to be all right, boy," Lawson said

with a quiet, soothing laugh. "I've burned your confession, see? You didn't sign anything." Lawson came close to him with the black ashes cupped in his palm. "You don't remember a thing about this, do you?"

"Don't you-all be scared of me," he pleaded, sensing their uneasiness. "I'll sign another paper, if you want me to. I'll show you the cave."

"What's your game, boy?" Lawson asked suddenly.

"What are you trying to find out?" Johnson asked.

"Who sent you here?" Murphy demanded.

"Nobody sent me, mister," he said. "I just want to show you the room . . ."

"Aw, he's plumb bats," Murphy said. "Let's ship 'im to the psycho."

"No," Lawson said. "He's playing a game and I wish to God I knew what it was."

There flashed through his mind a definite way to make them believe him; he rose from the chair with nervous excitement.

"Mister, I saw the night watchman blow his brains out because you accused him of stealing," he told them. "But he didn't steal the money and diamonds. I took 'em."

Tigerishly Lawson grabbed his collar and lifted him bodily.

"Who told you about that?"

"Don't get excited, Lawson," Johnson said. "He read about it in the papers."

Lawson flung him away.

"He couldn't have," Lawson said, pulling papers from his pocket. "I haven't turned in the reports yet."

"Then how *did* he find out?" Murphy asked.

"Let's get out of here," Lawson said with quick resolution. "Listen, boy, we're going to take you to a nice, quiet place, see?"

"Yes, sir," he said. "And I'll show you the underground."

"Goddamn," Lawson muttered, fastening the gun at his hip. He narrowed his eyes at Johnson and Murphy. "Listen," he spoke just above a whisper, "say nothing about this, you hear?"

"O.K.," Johnson said.

"Sure," Murphy said.

Lawson unlocked the door and Johnson and Murphy led him down the stairs. The hallway was crowded with policemen.

"What have you got there, Lawson?"

"What did he do, Lawson?"

"He's psycho, ain't he, Lawson?"

Lawson did not answer; Johnson and Murphy led him to the car parked at the curb, pushed him into the back seat. Lawson got behind the steering wheel and the car rolled forward.

"What's up, Lawson?" Murphy asked.

"Listen," Lawson began slowly, "we tell the papers that he spilled about the Peabody job, then he escapes. The Wop is caught and we tell the papers that we steered them wrong to trap the real guy, see? Now this dope shows up and acts nuts. If we let him go, he'll squeal that we framed him, see?"

"I'm all right, mister," he said, feeling Murphy's and Johnson's arm locked rigidly into his. "I'm guilty . . . I'll show you everything in the underground. I laughed and laughed . . ."

"Shut that fool up!" Lawson ordered.

Johnson tapped him across the head with a blackjack and he fell back against the seat cushion, dazed.

"Yes, sir," he mumbled. "I'm all right."

The car sped along Hartsdale Avenue, then swung onto Pine Street and rolled to State Street, then turned south. It slowed to a stop, turned in the middle of a block, and headed north again.

"You're going around in circles, Lawson," Murphy said.

Lawson did not answer; he was hunched over the steering wheel. Finally he pulled the car to a stop at a curb.

"Say, boy, tell us the truth," Lawson asked quietly. "Where did you hide?"

"I didn't hide, mister."

The three policemen were staring at him now; he felt that for the first time they were willing to understand him.

"Then what happened?"

"Mister, when I looked through all of those holes and saw how people were living, I loved 'em . . ."

"Cut out that crazy talk!" Lawson snapped. "Who sent you back here?"

"Nobody, mister."

"Maybe he's talking straight," Johnson ventured.

"All right," Lawson said. "Nobody hid you. Now, tell us *where* you hid."

"I went underground . . ."

"What goddamn underground do you keep talking about?"

"I just went . . ." He paused and looked into the street, then pointed to a manhole cover. "I went down in there and stayed."

"In the *sewer*?"

"Yes, sir."

The policemen burst into a sudden laugh and ended quickly. Lawson swung the car around and drove to Woodside Avenue; he brought the car to a stop in front of a tall apartment building.

"What're we going to do, Lawson?" Murphy asked.

"I'm taking him up to my place," Lawson said. "We've got to wait until night. There's nothing we can do now."

They took him out of the car and led him into a vestibule.

"Take the steps," Lawson muttered.

They led him up four flights of stairs and into the living room of a small apartment. Johnson and Murphy let go of his arms and he stood uncertainly in the middle of the room.

"Now, listen, boy," Lawson began, "forget those wild lies you've been telling us. Where did you hide?"

"I just went underground, like I told you."

The room rocked with laughter. Lawson went to a cabinet and got a bottle of whiskey; he placed glasses for Johnson and Murphy. The three of them drank.

He felt that he could not explain himself to them. He tried to muster all the sprawling images that floated in him; the images stood out sharply in his mind, but he could not make them have the meaning for others that they had for him. He felt so helpless that he began to cry.

"He's nuts, all right," Johnson said. "All nuts cry like that."

Murphy crossed the room and slapped him. "Stop that raving!"

A sense of excitement flooded him; he ran to Murphy and grabbed his arm.

"Let me show you the cave," he said. "Come on, and you'll see!"

Before he knew it a sharp blow had clipped him on the chin; darkness covered his eyes. He dimly felt himself being lifted and laid out on the sofa. He heard low voices and struggled to rise, but hard hands held him down. His brain was clearing now. He pulled to a sitting posture and stared with glazed eyes. It had grown dark. How long had he been out?

"Say, boy," Lawson said soothingly, "will you show us the underground?"

His eyes shone and his heart swelled with gratitude. Lawson believed him! He rose, glad; he grabbed Lawson's arm, making the policeman spill whiskey from the glass to his shirt.

"Take it easy, goddammit," Lawson said.

"Yes, sir."

"O.K. We'll take you down. But you'd better be telling us the truth, you hear?"

He clapped his hands in wild joy.

"I'll show you everything!"

He had triumphed at last! He would now do what he had felt was compelling him all along. At last he would be free of his burden.

"Take 'im down," Lawson ordered.

They led him down to the vestibule; when he reached the sidewalk he saw that it was night and a fine rain was falling.

"It's just like when I went down," he told them.

"What?" Lawson asked.

"The rain," he said, sweeping his arm in a wide arc. "It was raining when I went down. The rain made the water rise and lift the cover off."

"Cut it out," Lawson snapped.

They did not believe him now, but they would. A mood of high selflessness throbbed in him. He could barely contain his rising spirits. They would see what he had seen; they would feel what he had felt. He would lead them through all the holes he had dug and . . . He wanted to make a hymn, prance about in physical ecstasy, throw his arm about the policemen in fellowship.

"Get into the car," Lawson ordered.

He climbed in and Johnson and Murphy sat at either side of him; Lawson slid behind the steering wheel and started the motor.

"Now, tell us where to go," Lawson said.

"It's right around the corner from where the lady was killed," he said.

The car rolled slowly and he closed his eyes, remembering the song he had heard in the church, the song that had wrought him to such a high pitch of terror and pity. He sang softly, lolling his head:

Glad, glad, glad, oh, so glad
I got Jesus in my soul . . .

"Mister," he said, stopping his song, "you ought to see how funny the rings look on the wall." He giggled. "I fired a pistol, too. Just once, to see how it felt."

"What do you suppose he's suffering from?" Johnson asked.

"Delusions of grandeur, maybe," Murphy said.

"Maybe it's because he lives in a white man's world," Lawson said.

"Say, boy, what did you eat down there?" Murphy asked, prodding Johnson anticipatorily with his elbow.

"Pears, oranges, bananas, and pork chops," he said.

The car filled with laughter.

"You didn't eat any watermelon?" Lawson asked, smiling.

"No, sir," he answered calmly. "I didn't see any."

The three policemen roared harder and louder.

"Boy, you're sure some case," Murphy said, shaking his head in wonder.

The car pulled to a curb.

"All right, boy," Lawson said. "Tell us where to go."

He peered through the rain and saw where he had gone down. The streets, save for a few dim lamps glowing softly through the rain, were dark and empty.

"Right there, mister," he said, pointing.

"Come on; let's take a look," Lawson said.

"Well, suppose he did hide down there," Johnson said, "what is that supposed to prove?"

"I don't believe he hid down there," Murphy said.

"It won't hurt to look," Lawson said. "Leave things to me."

Lawson got out of the car and looked up and down the street.

He was eager to show them the cave now. If he could show them what he had seen, then they would feel what he had felt and they in turn would show it to others and those others would feel as they had felt, and soon everybody would be governed by the same impulse of pity.

"Take 'im out," Lawson ordered.

Johnson and Murphy opened the door and pushed him out; he stood trembling in the rain, smiling. Again Lawson looked up and down the street; no one was in sight. The rain came down hard, slanting like black wires across the wind-swept air.

"All right," Lawson said. "Show us."

He walked to the center of the street, stopped and inserted a finger in one of the tiny holes of the cover and tugged, but he was too weak to budge it.

"Did you really go down in there, boy?" Lawson asked; there was a doubt in his voice.

"Yes, sir. Just a minute. I'll show you."

"Help 'im get that damn thing off," Lawson said.

Johnson stepped forward and lifted the cover; it clanged against the wet pavement. The hole gaped round and black.

"I went down in there," he announced with pride.

Lawson gazed at him for a long time without speaking, then he reached his right hand to his holster and drew his gun.

"Mister, I got a gun just like that down there," he said, laughing and looking into Lawson's face. "I fired it once then hung it on the wall. I'll show you."

"Show us how you went down," Lawson said quietly.

"I'll go down first, mister, and then you-all can come after me, hear?" he spoke like a little boy playing a game.

"Sure, sure," Lawson said soothingly. "Go ahead. We'll come."

He looked brightly at the policemen; he was bursting with happiness. He bent down and placed his hands on the rim of the hole and sat on the edge, his feet dangling into watery darkness. He heard the familiar drone of the gray current. He lowered his body and hung for a moment by his fingers, then he went downward on the steel prongs, hand over hand, until he reached the last rung. He dropped and his feet hit the water and he felt the stiff current trying to suck him away. He balanced himself quickly and looked back upward at the policemen.

"Come on, you-all!" he yelled, casting his voice above the rustling at his feet.

The vague forms that towered above him in the rain did not move. He laughed, feeling that they doubted him. But, once they saw the things he had done, they would never doubt again.

"Come on! The cave isn't far!" he yelled. "But be careful when your feet hit the water, because the current's pretty rough down here!"

Lawson still held the gun. Murphy and Johnson looked at Lawson quizzically.

"What are we going to do, Lawson?" Murphy asked.

"We are not going to follow that crazy nigger down into that sewer, are we?" Johnson asked.

"Come on, you-all!" he begged in a shout.

He saw Lawson raise the gun and point it directly at him. Lawson's face twitched, as though he were hesitating.

Then there was a thunderous report and a streak of fire ripped through his chest. He was hurled into the water, flat on his back. He looked in amazement at the blurred white faces looming above him. They shot me, he said to himself. The water flowed past him, blossoming in foam about his arms, his legs, and his head. His jaw sagged and his mouth gaped soundless. A vast pain gripped his head and gradually squeezed out consciousness. As from a great distance he heard hollow voices.

"What did you shoot him for, Lawson?"

"I had to."

"Why?"

"You've got to shoot his kind. They'd wreck things."

As though in a deep dream, he heard a metallic clank; they had replaced the manhole cover, shutting out forever the sound of wind and rain. From overhead came the muffled roar of a powerful motor and the swish of a speeding car. He felt the strong tide pushing him slowly into the middle of the sewer, turning him about. For a split second there hovered before his eyes the glittering cave, the shouting walls, and the laughing floor . . . Then his mouth was full of thick, bitter water. The current spun him around. He sighed and closed his eyes, a whirling object rushing alone in the darkness, veering, tossing, lost in the heart of the earth.

Basic Existentialist Concepts

Insider–Outsider In his novel *The Outsider*, Wright takes up the existentialist concept of alienation and develops it with a more complex, political meaning. For Wright, alienation is not merely distance from society, but also entrapment within the very heart of society. Wright places his alienated African-American characters in the middle of society so that they are Insiders–Outsiders. They are Insiders because they are integral to the functioning of society; they are part of the underclass that serves the economic needs of society, yet they lack the economic benefits or political freedom of the white, upper classes. African-Americans are also Outsiders because they do not share the values or moral beliefs of society; without commitment to the status quo, they are ready to use their freedom in acts that are viewed as criminal in white society's eyes.

The main character in "The Man Who Lived Underground" is such an Insider–Outsider. He lives unseen within the very center of society. His observations are those of an Insider, who knows the workings of capitalist society well. Yet he is also an Outsider who, because of racial injustice, is not an equal participant in society and thus does not adhere to society's values. His alienation is political, economic, and moral.

Questions for Discussion

1. Do individuals who want to be free have to hide themselves from society?

2. What are Wright's views on religion?

3. From the underground, Fred Daniels observes a church, an undertaker's establishment, a movie theater, a butcher's store, and a jeweler's office. What do these particular places symbolize about American society?

4. What is the relation between racial injustice and the actions of the police?

5. Are all African-Americans Insiders and Outsiders in society?

Part Three

Existentialist Views on Religion

10 *Friedrich Nietzsche's* Thus Spoke Zarathustra

11 *Søren Kierkegaard's* Fear and Trembling

12 *Fyodor Dostoyevsky's* "*The Grand Inquisitor*"

13 *Franz Kafka's* "*Before the Law*"

Chapter 10

Friedrich Nietzsche's Thus Spoke Zarathustra

Introduction: Critique of Morality

Friedrich Nietzsche (1844–1900) called himself an *immoralist;* in his many writings, he disputed the existence of universal moral values, denounced the religious underpinnings of morality, and reflected on the widely varying views on morality held in different cultures. Always controversial, his published legacy incurred an even worse reputation after his death when it was manipulated by his anti-Semitic sister and appropriated by the Nazis for their own purposes. Nietzsche himself was neither an anti-Semite nor a racist, but his attacks against the Judeo-Christian tradition were so caustic that many misread him and denounced him as a proto-Nazi.

Nietzsche's ideas are disturbing because they challenge some of our most comforting assumptions. Drawing out the consequences of atheism, Nietzsche proclaims the death of God as a world-shattering event because it means that some of our most basic philosophical and ethical beliefs have no foundation. No God's-eye view of the world exists to identify objective truth; no divine law specifies what is good and what is evil. Yet Nietzsche does not believe that the nonexistence of God means that everything lacks meaning and value. Instead, he insists that the meaning of human life lies in a liberating undertaking of self-transcendence and the creation of one's own values; the meaning of human life is the *Superman.*

In *Thus Spoke Zarathustra,* Nietzsche uses the concept of the Superman (or Overman) as a symbol for the transformation that must take place in us in order to overcome traditional, religiously based morality and to forge a human life that is healthy, vigorous, and creative. The Superman is neither a master race nor the next step in Darwinian evolution. Instead, it is the lifetime goal of self-creation—and rarely attained by any individual. But to create oneself as one's own work of art, to furnish oneself with one's own values, one's own good and evil, to assume command over oneself—these are the virtues of the Superman that Nietzsche prods us to aim for, and even if we cannot attain them, we shall make our lives meaningful if we strive for them.

Nietzsche's *Thus Spoke Zarathustra* (Excerpts)[1]

Zarathustra's Prologue

1

When Zarathustra was thirty years old, he left his home and the lake of his home and went into the mountains. Here he had the enjoyment of his spirit and his solitude and he did not weary of it for ten years. But at last his heart turned—and one morning he rose with the dawn, stepped before the sun, and spoke to it thus:

Great star! What would your happiness be, if you had not those for whom you shine!

You have come up here to my cave for ten years: you would have grown weary of your light and of this journey, without me, my eagle and my serpent.

But we waited for you every morning, took from you your superfluity and blessed you for it.

Behold! I am weary of my wisdom, like a bee that has gathered too much honey; I need hands outstretched to take it.

I should like to give it away and distribute it, until the wise among men have again become happy in their folly and the poor happy in their wealth.

To that end, I must descend into the depths: as you do at evening, when you go behind the sea and bring light to the underworld too, superabundant star!

Like you I must *go down*—as men, to whom I want to descend, call it.

So bless me then, tranquil eye, that can behold without envy even an excessive happiness!

Bless the cup that wants to overflow, that the waters may flow golden from him and bear the reflection of your joy over all the world!

Behold! This cup wants to be empty again, and Zarathustra wants to be man again.

Thus began Zarathustra's down-going.

2

Zarathustra went down the mountain alone, and no one met him. But when he entered the forest, an old man, who had left his holy hut to look for roots in the forest, suddenly stood before him. And the old man spoke thus to Zarathustra:

"This wanderer is no stranger to me: he passed by here many years ago. He was called Zarathustra; but he has changed.

"Then you carried your ashes to the mountains: will you today carry your fire into the valleys? Do you not fear an incendiary's punishment?

"Yes, I recognize Zarathustra. His eyes are clear, and no disgust lurks about his mouth. Does he not go along like a dancer?

"How changed Zarathustra is! Zarathustra has become—a child, an awakened-one: what do you want now with the sleepers?

"You lived in solitude as in the sea, and the sea bore you. Alas, do you want to go ashore? Alas, do you want again to drag your body yourself?"

Zarathustra answered: "I love mankind."

"Why," said the saint, "did I go into the forest and the desert? Was it not because I loved mankind all too much?"

"Now I love God: mankind I do not love. Man is too imperfect a thing for me. Love of mankind would destroy me."

Zarathustra answered: "What did I say of love? I am bringing mankind a gift."

"Give them nothing," said the saint. "Rather take something off them and bear it with them—that will please them best; if only it be pleasing to you!"

"And if you want to give to them, give no more than an alms, and let them beg for that!"

"No," answered Zarathustra, "I give no alms. I am not poor enough for that."

The saint laughed at Zarathustra, and spoke thus: "See to it that they accept your treasures!

[1] From Friedrich Nietzsche: *Thus Spoke Zarathustra: A Book for Everyone and No One*, translated by R. J. Hollingdale.

They are mistrustful of hermits, and do not believe that we come to give.

"Our steps ring too lonely through their streets. And when at night they hear in their beds a man going by long before the sun has risen, they probably ask themselves: Where is that thief going?

"Do not go to men, but stay in the forest! Go rather to the animals! Why will you not be as I am—bear among bears, a bird among birds?"

"And what does the saint do in the forest?" asked Zarathustra.

The saint answered: "I make songs and sing them, and when I make songs, I laugh, weep, and mutter: thus I praise God.

"With singing, weeping, laughing, and muttering I praise the God who is my God. But what do you bring us as a gift?"

When Zarathustra heard these words, he saluted the saint and said: "What should I have to give you! But let me go quickly, that I may take nothing from you!" And thus they parted from one another, the old man and Zarathustra, laughing as two boys laugh.

But when Zarathustra was alone, he spoke thus to his heart: "Could it be possible! This old saint has not yet heard in his forest that *God is dead!*"

3

When Zarathustra arrived at the nearest of the towns lying against the forest, he found in that very place many people assembled in the market square: for it had been announced that a tight-rope walker would be appearing. And Zarathustra spoke thus to the people:

I teach you the Superman. Man is something that should be overcome. What have you done to overcome him?

All creatures hitherto have created something beyond themselves: and do you want to be the ebb of this great tide, and return to the animals rather than overcome man?

What is the ape to men? A laughing-stock or a painful embarrassment. And just so shall man be to the Superman: a laughing-stock or a painful embarrassment.

You have made your way from worm to man, and much in you is still worm. Once you were apes, and even now man is more of an ape than any ape.

But he who is wisest among you, he also is only a discord and hybrid of plant and of ghost. But do I bid you become ghosts or plants?

Behold, I teach you the Superman.

The Superman is the meaning of the earth. Let your will say: The Superman *shall be* the meaning of the earth!

I entreat you, my brothers, *remain true to the earth,* and do not believe those who speak to you of superterrestial hopes! They are poisoners, whether they know it or not.

They are despisers of life, atrophying and self-poisoned men, of whom the earth is weary: so let them be gone!

Once blasphemy against God was the greatest blasphemy, but God died, and thereupon these blasphemers died too. To blaspheme the earth is now the most dreadful offence, and to esteem the bowels of the Inscrutable more highly than the meaning of the earth.

Once the soul looked contemptuously upon the body: and then this contempt was the supreme good—the soul wanted the body lean, monstrous, famished. So the soul thought to escape from the body and from the earth.

Oh, this soul was itself lean, monstrous, and famished: and cruelty was the delight of this soul!

But tell me, my brothers: What does your body say about your soul? Is your soul not poverty and dirt and a miserable ease?

In truth, man is a polluted river. One must be a sea, to receive a polluted river and not be defiled.

Behold, I teach you the Superman: he is this sea, in him your great contempt can go under.

What is the greatest thing you can experience? It is the hour of the great contempt. The hour in which even your happiness grows loathsome to you, and your reason and your virtue also.

The hour when you say: "What good is my happiness? It is poverty and dirt and a miserable ease. But my happiness should justify existence itself!"

The hour when you say: "What good is my reason? Does it long for knowledge as the lion for its food? It is poverty and dirt and a miserable ease!"

The hour when you say: "What good is my virtue? It has not yet driven me mad! How tired I am of my good and my evil! It is all poverty and dirt and a miserable ease!"

The hour when you say: "What good is my justice? I do not see that I am fire and hot coals. But the just man is fire and hot coals!"

The hour when you say: "What good is my pity? Is not pity the cross upon which he who loves man is nailed? But my pity is no crucifixion!"

Have you ever spoken thus? Have you ever cried thus? Ah, that I had heard you crying thus!

It is not your sin, but your moderation that cries to heaven, your very meanness in sinning cries to heaven!

Where is the lightning to lick you with its tongue? Where is the madness, with which you should be cleansed?

Behold, I teach you the Superman: he is this lightning, he is this madness!

. . . Zarathustra looked at the people and marvelled. Then he spoke thus:

Man is a rope, fastened between animal and Superman—a rope over an abyss.

A dangerous going-across, a dangerous wayfaring, a dangerous looking-back, a dangerous shuddering and staying-still.

What is great in man is that he is a bridge and not a goal . . .

Zarathustra's Discourses

Of the Three Metamorphoses

I name you three metamorphoses of the spirit: how the spirit shall become a camel, and the camel a lion, and the lion at last a child.

There are many heavy things for the spirit, for the strong, weight-bearing spirit in which dwell respect and awe: its strength longs for the heavy, for the heaviest.

What is heavy? thus asks the weight-bearing spirit, thus it kneels down like the camel and wants to be well laden.

What is the heaviest thing, you heroes? so asks the weight-bearing spirit, that I may take it upon me and rejoice in my strength.

Is it not this: to debase yourself in order to injure your pride? To let your folly shine out in order to mock your wisdom?

Or is it this: to desert our cause when it is celebrating its victory? To climb high mountains in order to tempt the tempter?

Or is it this: to feed upon the acorns and grass of knowledge and for the sake of truth to suffer hunger of the soul?

Or is it this: to be sick and to send away comforters and make friends with the deaf, who never hear what you ask?

Or is it this: to wade into dirty water when it is the water of truth, and not to disdain cold frogs and hot toads?

Or is it this: to love those who despise us and to offer our hand to the ghost when it wants to frighten us?

The weight-bearing spirit takes upon itself all these heaviest things: like a camel hurrying laden into the desert, thus it hurries into its desert.

But in the loneliest desert the second metamorphosis occurs: the spirit here becomes a lion; it wants to capture freedom and be lord in its own desert.

It seeks here its ultimate lord: it will be an enemy to him and to its ultimate God, it will struggle for victory with the great dragon.

What is the great dragon which the spirit no longer wants to call lord and God? The great dragon is called "Thou shalt." But the spirit of the lion says "I will!"

"Thou shalt" lies in its path, sparkling with gold, a scale-covered beast, and on every scale glitters golden "Thou shalt."

Values of a thousand years glitter on the scales, and thus speaks the mightiest of all dragons: "All the values of things—glitter on me.

"All values have already been created, and all created values—are in me. Truly, there shall be no more 'I will'! Thus speaks the dragon.

My brothers, why is the lion needed in the spirit? Why does the beast of burden, that renounces and is reverent, not suffice?

To create new values—even the lion is incapable of that: but to create itself freedom for new creation—that the might of the lion can do.

To create freedom for itself and a sacred No even to duty: the lion is needed for that, my brothers.

To seize the right to new values—that is the most terrible proceeding for a weight-bearing and reverential spirit. Truly, to this spirit it is a theft and a work for an animal of prey.

Once it loved this "Thou shalt" as its holiest thing: now it has to find illusion and caprice even in the holiest, that it may steal freedom from its love: the lion is needed for this theft.

But tell me, my brothers, what can the child do that even the lion cannot? Why must the preying lion still become a child?

The child is innocence and forgetfulness, a new beginning, a sport, a self-propelling wheel, a first motion, a sacred Yes.

Yes, a sacred Yes is needed, my brothers, for the sport of creation: the spirit now wills *its own* will, the spirit sundered from the world now wins *its own* world.

I have named you three metamorphoses of the spirit: how the spirit became a camel, and the camel a lion, and the lion at last a child.

Thus spoke Zarathustra. And at that time he was living in the town called The Pied Cow.

Of the Despisers of the Body

I wish to speak to the despisers of the body. Let them not learn differently nor teach differently, but only bid farewell to their own bodies—and so become dumb.

"I am body and soul"—so speaks the child. And why should one not speak like children?

But the awakened, the enlightened man says: I am body entirely, and nothing beside; and soul is only a word for something in the body.

The body is a great intelligence, a multiplicity with one sense, a war and a peace, and herd and a herdsman.

Your little intelligence, my brother, which you call "spirit," is also an instrument of your body, a little instrument and toy of your great intelligence.

You say "I" and you are proud of this word. But greater than this—although you will not believe in it—is your body and its great intelligence, which does not say "I" but performs "I."

What the sense feels, what the spirit perceives, is never an end in itself. But sense and spirit would like to persuade you that they are the end of all things: they are as vain as that.

Sense and spirit are instruments and toys: behind them still lies the Self. The Self seeks with the eyes of the sense, it lives too with the ears of the spirit.

The Self is always listening and seeking: it compares, subdues, conquers, destroys. It rules and is also the Ego's ruler.

Behind your thoughts and feelings, my brother, stands a mighty commander, an unknown sage—he is called Self. He lives in your body, he is your body.

There is more reason in your body than in your best wisdom. And who knows for what purpose your body requires precisely your best wisdom?

Your Self laughs at your Ego and its proud leapings. "What are these leapings and flights of thought to me?" it says to itself. "A by-way to my goal. I am the Ego's leading-string and I prompt its conceptions."

The Self says to the Ego: "Feel pain!" Thereupon it suffers and gives thought to how to end its suffering—and it is *meant* to think for just that purpose.

The Self says to the Ego: "Feel joy!" Thereupon it rejoices and gives thought how it may often rejoice—and it is *meant* to think for just that purpose.

I want to say a word to the despisers of the body. It is their esteem that produces this disesteem. What is it that created esteem and disesteem and value and will?

The creative Self created for itself esteem and disesteem, it created for itself joy and sorrow. The creative body created spirit for itself, as a hand of its will.

Even in your folly and contempt, you despisers of the body, you serve your Self. I tell you: your Self itself wants to die and turn away from life.

Your Self can no longer perform that act which it most desires to perform: to create beyond itself. That is what it most wishes to do, that is its whole ardour.

But now it has grown too late for that: so your Self wants to perish, you despisers of the body.

Your Self wants to perish, and that is why you have become despisers of the body! For no longer are you able to create beyond yourselves.

And therefore you are not angry with life and with the earth. An unconscious envy lies in the sidelong glance of your contempt.

I do not go your way, you despisers of the body! You are not bridges to the Superman!

Thus spoke Zarathustra.

Of the Thousand and One Goals

Zarathustra has seen many lands and many peoples: thus he has discovered the good and evil of many peoples. Zarathustra has found no greater power on earth than good and evil.

No people could live without evaluating; but if it wishes to maintain itself it must not evaluate as its neighbour evaluates.

Much that seemed good to one people seemed shame and disgrace to another: thus I found. I found much that was called evil in one place was in another decked with purple honours.

One neighbour never understood another: his soul was always amazed at his neighbour's madness and wickedness.

A table of values hangs over every people. Behold, it is the table of its overcomings; behold, it is the voice of its will to power.

What it accounts hard it calls praiseworthy; what it accounts indispensable and hard it calls good; and that which relieves the greatest need, the rare, the hardest of all—it glorifies as holy.

Whatever causes it to rule and conquer and glitter, to the dread and envy of its neighbour, that it accounts the sublimest, the paramount, the evaluation and the meaning of all things.

Truly, my brother, if you only knew a people's need and land and sky and neighbour, you could surely divine the law of its overcomings, and why it is upon this ladder that it mounts towards its hope.

"You should always be the first and outrival all others: your jealous soul should love no one, except your friend"—this precept made the soul of a Greek tremble: in following it he followed his path to greatness.

"To speak the truth and to know well how to handle bow and arrow"—this seemed both estimable and hard to that people from whom I got my name—a name which is both estimable and hard to me.

"To honour father and mother and to do their will even from the roots of the soul": another people hung this table of overcoming over itself and became mighty and eternal with it.

"To practise loyalty and for the sake of loyalty to risk honour and blood even in evil and dangerous causes": another people mastered itself with such teaching, and thus mastering itself it became pregnant and heavy with great hopes.

Truly, men have given themselves all their good and evil. Truly, they did not take it, they did not find it, it did not descend to them as a voice from heaven.

Man first implanted values into things to maintain himself—he created the meaning of things, a human meaning! Therefore he calls himself: "Man," that is: the evaluator.

Evaluation is creation: hear it, you creative men! Valuating is itself the value and jewel of all valued things.

Only through evaluation is there value: and without evaluation the nut of existence would be hollow. Hear it, you creative men!

A change in values—that means a change in the creators of values. He who has to be a creator always has to destroy.

Peoples were the creators at first; only later were individuals creators. Indeed, the individual himself is still the latest creation.

Once the peoples hung a table of values over themselves. The love that wants to rule and the love that wants to obey created together such tables as these.

Joy in the herd is older than joy in the Ego: and as long as the good conscience is called herd, only the bad conscience says: I.

Truly, the cunning, loveless Ego, that seeks its advantage in the advantage of many—that is not the origin of the herd, but the herd's destruction.

It has always been creators and loving men who created good and evil. Fire of love and fire of anger glow in the names of all virtues.

Zarathustra has seen many lands and many peoples: Zarathustra has found no greater power on earth than the works of these loving men: these works are named "good" and "evil."

Truly, the power of this praising and blaming is a monster. Tell me, who will subdue it for me, brothers? Tell me, who will fasten fetters upon the thousand necks of this beast?

Hitherto there have been a thousand goals, for there have been a thousand peoples. Only fetters are still lacking for these thousand necks, the one goal is still lacking.

Yet tell me, my brothers: if a goal for humanity is still lacking, is there not still lacking—humanity itself?

Thus spoke Zarathustra.

Of the Way of the Creator

My brother, do you want to go apart and be alone? Do you want to seek the way to yourself? Pause just a moment and listen to me.

"He who seeks may easily get lost himself. It is a crime to go apart and be alone"—thus speaks the herd.

The voice of the herd will still ring within you. And when you say: "We have no longer the same conscience, you and I," it will be a lament and a grief.

For see, it is still this same conscience that causes your grief: and the last glimmer of this conscience still glows in your affliction.

But you want to go the way of your affliction, which is the way to yourself? If so, show me your strength for it and your right to it!

Are you a new strength and a new right? A first motion? A self-propelling wheel? Can you also compel stars to revolve about you?

Alas, there is so much lusting for eminence! There is so much convulsion of the ambitious! Show me that you are not one of the lustful or the ambitious!

Alas, there are so many great ideas that do no more than a bellows: they inflate and make emptier.

Do you call yourself free? I want to hear your ruling idea, and not that you have escaped from a yoke.

Are you such a man as *ought* to escape a yoke? There are many who threw off their final worth when they threw off their bondage.

Free from what? Zarathustra does not care about that! But your eye should clearly tell me: free *for* what?

Can you furnish yourself with your own good and evil and hang up your own will above yourself as a law? Can you be judge of yourself and avenger of your law? . . .

Of the Bestowing Virtue

When Zarathustra had taken leave of the town to which his heart was attached and which was called "The Pied Cow" there followed him many who called themselves his disciples and escorted him. Thus they came to a cross-road: there Zarathustra told them that from then on he wanted to go alone: for he was a friend of going-alone. But his disciples handed him in farewell a staff, upon the golden haft of which a serpent was coiled about a sun. Zarathustra was delighted with the staff and leaned upon it; then he spoke thus to his disciples:

Tell me: how did gold come to have the highest value? Because it is uncommon and useless and shining and mellow in lustre; it always bestows itself.

Only as an image of the highest virtue did gold come to have the highest value. Gold-like gleams the glance of the giver. Gold-lustre makes peace between moon and sun.

The highest virtue is uncommon and useless, it is shining and mellow in lustre: the highest virtue is a bestowing virtue.

Truly, I divine you well, my disciples, you aspire to the bestowing virtue, as I do. What could you have in common with cats and wolves?

You thirst to become sacrifices and gifts yourselves; and that is why you thirst to heap up all riches in your soul.

Your soul aspires insatiably after treasures and jewels, because your virtue is insatiable in wanting to give.

You compel all things to come to you and into you, that they may flow back from your fountain as gifts of your love.

Truly, such a bestowing love must become a thief of all values; but I call this selfishness healthy and holy.

There is another selfishness, an all-too-poor, a hungry selfishness that always wants to steal, that selfishness of the sick, the sick selfishness.

It looks with the eye of a thief upon all lustrous things; with the greed of hunger it measures him who has plenty to eat; and it is always skulking about the table of the givers.

Sickness speaks from such craving, and hidden degeneration; the thieving greed of this longing speaks of a sick body.

Tell me, my brothers: what do we account bad and the worst of all? Is it not *degeneration?*—And we always suspect degeneration where the bestowing soul is lacking.

Our way is upward, from the species across to the superspecies. But the degenerate mind which says "All for me" is a horror to us. . . .

Stay loyal to the earth, my brothers, with the power of your virtue! May your bestowing love and your knowledge serve towards the meaning of the earth! Thus I beg and entreat you.

Do not let it fly away from the things of earth and beat with its wings against the eternal walls! Alas, there has always been much virtue that has flown away!

Lead, as I do, the flown-away virtue back to earth—yes, back to body and life: that it may give the earth its meaning, a human meaning . . .

I now go away alone, my disciples! You too now go away and be alone! So I will have it.

Truly, I advise you: go away from me and guard yourselves against Zarathustra! And better still: be ashamed of him! Perhaps he has deceived you.

The man of knowledge must be able not only to love his enemies but also to hate his friends.

One repays a teacher badly if one remains only a pupil. And why, then, should you not pluck at my laurels?

You respect me; but how if one day your respect should tumble? Take care that a falling statue does not strike you dead!

You say you believe in Zarathustra? But of what importance is Zarathustra? You are my believers: but of what importance are all believers?

You had not yet sought yourselves when you found me. Thus do all believers; therefore all belief is of so little account.

Now I bid you lose me and find yourselves; and only when you have all denied me will I return to you.

Truly, with other eyes, my brothers, I shall then seek my lost ones; with another love I shall then love you.

And once more you shall have become my friends and children of one hope: and then I will be with you a third time, that I may celebrate the great noontide with you.

And this is the great noontide: it is when man stands at the middle of his course between animal and Superman and celebrates his journey to the evening as his highest hope: for it is the journey to a new morning.

Then man, going under, will bless himself; for he will be going over to Superman; and the sun of his knowledge will stand at noontide.

"All gods are dead: now we want the Superman to live"—let this be our last will one day at the great noontide!

Thus spoke Zarathustra.

On the Blissful Islands

The figs are falling from the trees, they are fine and sweet; and as they fall their red skins split. I am a north wind to ripe figs.

Thus, like figs, do these teachings fall to you, my friends: now drink their juice and eat their sweet flesh! It is autumn all around and clear sky and afternoon.

Behold, what abundance is around us! And it is fine to gaze out upon distant seas from the midst of superfluity.

Once you said "God" when you gazed upon distant seas; but now I have taught you to say "Superman."

God is a supposition; but I want your supposing to reach no further than your creating will.

Could you *create* a god?—So be silent about all gods! But you could surely create the Superman.

Perhaps not you yourselves, my brothers! But you could transform yourselves into forefathers and ancestors of the Superman: and let this be your finest creating!

God is a supposition: but I want your supposing to be bounded by conceivability.

Could you *conceive* a god?—But may the will to truth mean this to you: that everything shall be transformed into the humanly-conceivable, the humanly-evident, the humanly-palpable! You should follow your own sense to the end!

And you yourselves should create what you have hitherto called the World: the World should be formed in your image by your reason, your will, and your love! And truly, it will be to your happiness, you enlightened men!

And how should you endure life without this hope, you enlightened men? Neither in the incomprehensible nor in the irrational can you be at home.

But to reveal my heart entirely to you, friends: *if* there were gods, how could I endure not to be a god! *Therefore* there are no gods.

I, indeed, drew that conclusion; but now it draws me.

God is a supposition: but who could imbibe all the anguish of this supposition without dying? Shall the creator be robbed of his faith and the eagle of his soaring into the heights?

God is a thought that makes all that is straight crooked and all that stands giddy. What? Would time be gone and all that is transitory only a lie?

To think this is giddiness and vertigo to the human frame, and vomiting to the stomach: truly, I call it the giddy sickness to suppose such a thing.

I call it evil and misanthropic, all this teaching about the one and the perfect and the unmoved and the sufficient and the intransitory.

All that is intransitory—that is but an image! And the poets lie too much.

But the best images and parables should speak of time and becoming: they should be a eulogy and a justification of all transitoriness.

Creation—that is the great redemption from suffering, and life's easement. But that the creator may exist, that itself requires suffering and much transformation.

Yes, there must be much bitter dying in your life, you creators! Thus you are advocates and justifiers of all transitoriness.

For the creator himself to be the child newborn he must also be willing to be the mother and endure the mother's pain.

Truly, I have gone my way through a hundred souls and through a hundred cradles and birth-pangs. I have taken many departures, I know the heart-breaking last hours.

But my creative will, my destiny, wants it so. Or, to speak more honestly: my will wants precisely such a destiny.

All *feeling* suffers in me and is in prison: but my *willing* always comes to me as my liberator and bringer of joy.

Willing liberates: that is the true doctrine of will and freedom—thus Zarathustra teaches you.

No more to will and no more to evaluate and no more to create! ah, that this great lassitude may ever stay far from me!

In knowing and understanding, too, I feel only my will's delight in begetting and becoming; and if there be innocence in my knowledge it is because will to begetting is in it.

This will lured me away from God and gods; for what would there be to create if gods—existed!

But again and again it drives me to mankind, my ardent, creative will; thus it drives the hammer to the stone.

Ah, you men, I see an image sleeping in the stone, the image of my visions! Ah, that it must sleep in the hardest, ugliest stone!

Now my hammer rages fiercely against its prison. Fragments fly from the stone: what is that to me?

I will complete it: for a shadow came to me—the most silent, the lightest of all things once came to me!

The beauty of the Superman came to me as a shadow. Ah, my brothers! What are the gods to me now!

Thus spoke Zarathustra.

Of Self-Overcoming

What urges you on and arouses your ardour, you wisest of men, do you call it "will to truth"?

Will to the conceivability of all being: that is what *I* call your will!

You first want to *make* all being conceivable: for, with a healthy mistrust, you doubt whether it is in fact conceivable.

But it must bend and accommodate itself to you! Thus will your will have it. It must become smooth and subject to the mind as the mind's mirror and reflection.

That is your entire will, you wisest men; it is a will to power; and that is so even when you talk of good and evil and of the assessment of values.

You want to create the world before which you can kneel: this is your ultimate hope and intoxication.

The ignorant, to be sure, the people—they are like a river down which a boat swims: and in the boat, solemn and disguised, sit the assessments of value.

You put your will and your values upon the river of becoming; what the people believe to be good and evil betrays to me an ancient will to power.

It was you, wisest men, who put such passengers in this boat and gave them splendour and proud names—you and your ruling will!

Now the river bears your boat along: it has to bear it. It is of small account if the breaking wave foams and angrily opposes its keel!

It is not the river that is your danger and the end of your good and evil, you wisest men, it is that will itself, the will to power, the unexhausted, procreating life-will.

But that you may understand my teaching about good and evil, I shall relate to you my teaching about life and about the nature of all living creatures.

I have followed the living creature, I have followed the greatest and the smallest paths, that I might understand its nature.

I caught its glance in a hundredfold mirror when its mouth was closed, that its eye might speak to me. And its eye did speak to me.

But wherever I found living creatures, there too I heard the language of obedience. All living creatures are obeying creatures.

And this is the second thing: he who cannot obey himself will be commanded. That is the nature of living creatures.

But this is the third thing I heard: that commanding is more difficult than obeying. And not only because the commander bears the burden of all who obey, and that this burden can easily crush him.

In all commanding there appeared to me to be an experiment and a risk: and the living creature always risks himself when he commands.

Yes, even when he commands himself: then also must he make amends for his commanding. He must become judge and avenger and victim of his own law.

How has this come about? thus I asked myself. What persuades the living creature to obey and to command and to practise obedience even in commanding?

Listen now to my teaching, you wisest men! Test in earnest whether I have crept into the heart of life itself and down to the roots of its heart!

Where I found a living creature, there I found will to power; and even in the will of the servant I found the will to be master.

The will of the weaker persuades it to serve the stronger; its will wants to be master over those weaker still: this delight alone it is unwilling to forgo.

And as the lesser surrenders to the greater, that it may have delight and power over the least of all, so the greatest, too, surrenders and for the sake of power stakes—life.

The devotion of the greatest is to encounter risk and danger and play dice for death.

And where sacrifice and service and loving glances are, there too is will to be master. There the weaker steals by secret paths into the castle and even into the heart of the more powerful—and steals the power.

And life itself told me this secret: "Behold," it said, "I am that *which must overcome itself again and again.*

"To be sure, you call it will to procreate or impulse towards a goal, towards the higher, more distant, more manifold: but all this is one and one secret.

"I would rather perish than renounce this one thing; and truly, where there is perishing and the falling of leaves, behold, there life sacrifices itself—for the sake of power!

"That I have to be struggle and becoming and goal and conflict of goals: ah, he who divines my will surely divines, too, along what *crooked* path it has to go!

"Whatever I create and however much I love it—soon I have to oppose it and my love: thus will my will have it.

"And you too, enlightened man, are only a path and a footstep of my will: truly, my will to power walks with the feet of your will to truth!

"He who shot the doctrine of 'will to existence' at truth certainly did not hit the truth: this will—does not exist!

"For what does not exist cannot will; but that which is in existence, how could it still want to come into existence?

"Only where life is, there is also will: not will to life, but—so I teach you—will to power!

"The living creature values many things higher than life itself; yet out of this evaluation itself speaks—the will to power!"

Thus life once taught me: and with this teaching do I solve the riddle of your hearts, you wisest men.

Truly, I say to you: Unchanging good and evil does not exist! From out of themselves they must overcome themselves again and again.

You exert power with your values and doctrines of good and evil, you assessors of values; and this is your hidden love and the glittering, trembling, and overflowing of your souls.

But a mightier power and a new overcoming grow from out your values: egg and egg-shell break against them.

And he who has to be a creator in good and evil, truly, has first to be a destroyer and break values.

Thus the greatest evil belongs with the greatest good: this, however, is the creative good.

Let us *speak* of this, you wisest men, even if it is a bad thing. To be silent is worse; all suppressed truths become poisonous.

And let everything that can break upon our truths—break! There is many a house still to build!

Thus spoke Zarathustra.

Basic Existentialist Concepts

The Herd Under various labels—"the crowd," "the public," "the they"—the concept of the *herd* has been a central, negative concept in existential theory. Generally, it signifies a life that is the opposite of authenticity. Instead of being a life in which an individual acknowledges and uses his freedom, the life of the herd is a mass-produced life of conformity. When we live our lives as part of the herd, we do not develop our own beliefs or create our own values, but simply adopt the prevailing beliefs and values of society. This conformity results in a lack of creativity, courage, and inwardness in matters that are of the utmost importance to each individual. Living as part of the herd, a person exists in a mediocre way, adhering to a leveled-down set of beliefs and values that the majority can live by without much effort.

Nietzsche's censure of the herd escalated into antidemocratic views and scathing attacks against Christian morality. He believed that we are not all born equal, that political systems that promote equality erode human creativity and genius, and that the emphasis on humility, pity, and meekness in Christianity corrodes what is healthiest in humankind.

The Superman Nietzsche's idiosyncratic concept of the *Superman* (also translated as the Overman) is an ideal toward which he thinks we should be striving—humankind's most important task. He describes humanity as a tightrope strung between the animal and the Superman, thus proposing that the meaning of human existence does not lie in itself but in what lies beyond itself. The Superman is what we can become if we overcome ourselves, conquering the inner animal nature—especially the herd nature—and compelling our most powerful drives to obey our own command.

The Superman is a self-creator who gives herself values to live by and asserts her will to power. Nietzsche believes that the Superman is possible to achieve but not inevitable. Becoming the Superman requires all of the creativity and risk taking we are capable of, even all of the rule-breaking rebelliousness that society labels as evil. In Nietzsche's metaphor of the three metamorphoses, the Superman is the child who succeeds the camel and the lion—the child who will start fresh, creating her own values unhindered by traditional morality.

Will to Power With this concept, Nietzsche defines life in all of its facets. Not merely the will to survive or even to procreate, but the will to power is the quintessence of life. It is the drive to increase and accumulate power—the power to overcome others and to overcome oneself. At its most active, the will to power generates enhanced vitality, strength, and well-being; it is a basic principle of growth and self-transformation.

Because he believes that life is will to power, Nietzsche criticizes philosophical, religious, and moral theories that object to the pursuit of power by individuals. He also opposes theories that recommend detachment from the body and the five senses so as to achieve a nonearthly, heavenly existence. Life here on earth, with its rich terrain that inspires joy, singing, and dancing, is the only life we shall know. To live it openly as will to power—as Nietzsche believes it is in reality—is the best human life.

Transvaluation of Values Nietzsche argues that moral values are not objective or universal; they arise from the human activity of evaluating. In the past, most people adopted the values prevailing in their culture instead of evaluating for themselves. Because values are human inventions, nothing stops an individual from creating his or her own values except the social pressure of conforming to the herd. Nietzsche's recommendation that we each furnish ourselves with our own good and evil is a call to arms for those who are willing to overturn traditional morality and exert their will to power over themselves by creating their own values.

Turning values around—the *transvaluation of values*—occurs when there is a change in the creators of values. What was once bad becomes good, what was once good becomes bad, because the values are assessed anew; creators of values replace the old values with new ones. Historically, such changes most often occur when rulers of a society are overthrown and superseded by new rulers, because rulers wield the power to create the guiding values for their society. For example, in ancient Greece and Rome, aristocratic warrior elites were supplanted by priestly castes who espoused Judeo-Christian values after an uprising of the enslaved masses. Today, the transvaluation of values may occur individually if individuals break from the herd and become creators of their own values.

The transvaluation of values always includes destruction as well as creation; the rampages of the lion must precede the free play of the child. According to Nietzsche, those who have been the most powerful creators of values have been branded as evil in their own time because their newly invented "good" was not the "good" already prevailing in their societies. But these new creators of values also have been the greatest benefactors of humankind: Once their new values caught on, their power extended over the lives of many others, long after their own deaths.

Questions for Discussion

1. Why does Zarathustra announce the death of God before introducing the possibility of the Superman?

2. Does the meaning of human life lie in what we are or in what we strive for? Is the Superman the meaning of human life?

3. How does Nietzsche's theory of the body differ from the views on the body held in most world religions?

4. Why do the tables of values obeyed by different peoples make it possible for them to achieve greatness?

5. Can modern individuals create their own values?

Chapter 11

Søren Kierkegaard's Fear and Trembling

Introduction: Critique of Organized Religion

Søren Kierkegaard (1813–1855) shaped twentieth-century existentialism by initiating its focus on the individual, subjectivity and freedom. As a religious thinker, he pressed Christians and believers of other faiths to recognize how difficult true faith is, yet also how important faith is to being human. For Kierkegaard, all other human endeavors—be they profane, rational or ethical, could not capture or express the fundamental meaning of human life. Only faith could combine the finite and the infinite, the temporal and the eternal, and thus only faith could confirm what each individual truly is.

Kierkegaard not only investigated different ways in which people live their religion, but also produced scathing attacks on organized religion. He analyzed the stages or movements that an individual goes through in coming to faith, bringing out the most illogical and intimidating facets of a religious process that he could honor but never claim to have accomplished himself. His model for this religious process was Abraham, the father of faith. His opponent was Christendom, a system of beliefs offered to the crowd without any demand that each individual establish his own relationship with God.

Kierkegaard proposed that each individual undertake the ultimate risk of "a leap of faith"—an irrational, unsupported, life-defining decision to believe in God passionately, with every ounce of one's being. Such a leap is performed in inwardness, not in a manner that would be observable to others. Such a leap requires full acceptance of the absurd paradoxes of religion. Those who are able to make such a leap are knights of faith, like Abraham. Those who are not able to make the leap live in despair, trying either to escape from the recognition that they are both earthly and eternal, or to exert their own will as though it would suffice for establishing a relationship to God. The following selection from Kierkegaard's *Fear and Trembling* opens his discussion of what it takes to become a knight of faith. It describes the three stages or movements of faith: the movement of concentrating all one's aspirations into one thing (Abraham regarding Isaac as the fulfillment of God's promise); the movement of infinite resignation, by which one gives up that which one treasures most (Abraham being willing to sacrifice Isaac); and the movement of true faith, by which one fully believes what is impossible or absurd (Abraham being confident that he will get Isaac back). The selection also includes alternative scenarios that depict what might have happened had Abraham lacked true faith.

Søren Kierkegaard's *Fear and Trembling* (Excerpts)[1]

Exordium

Once upon a time there was a man who as a child had heard that beautiful story of how God tempted Abraham and of how Abraham withstood the temptation, kept the faith, and, contrary to expectation, got a son a second time. When he grew older, he read the same story with even greater admiration, for life had fractured what had been united in the pious simplicity of the child. The older he became, the more often his thoughts turned to that story; his enthusiasm for it became greater and greater, and yet he could understand the story less and less. Finally, he forgot everything else because of it; his soul had but one wish, to see Abraham, but one longing, to have witnessed that event. His craving was not to see the beautiful regions of the East, not the earthly glory of the promised land, not that God-fearing couple whose old age God had blessed, not the venerable figure of the aged patriarch, not the vigorous adolescence God bestowed upon Isaac—the same thing could just as well have occurred on a barren heath. His craving was to go along on the three-day journey when Abraham rode with sorrow before him and Isaac beside him. His wish was to be present in that hour when Abraham raised his eyes and saw Mount Moriah in the distance, the hour when he left the asses behind and went up the mountain alone with Isaac—for what occupied him was not the beautiful tapestry of imagination but the shudder of the idea.

That man was not a thinker. He did not feel any need to go beyond faith; he thought that it must be supremely glorious to be remembered as its father, an enviable destiny to possess it, even if no one knew it.

That man was not an exegetical scholar. He did not know Hebrew; if he had known Hebrew, he perhaps would easily have understood the story and Abraham.

I.

"And God tempted Abraham and said to him, take Isaac, your only son, whom you love, and go to the land of Moriah and offer him there as a burnt offering on a mountain that I shall show you."

It was early in the morning when Abraham arose, had the asses saddled, and left his tent, taking Isaac with him, but Sarah watched them from the window as they went down the valley—until she could see them no longer. They rode in silence for three days. On the morning of the fourth day, Abraham said not a word but raised his eyes and saw Mount Moriah in the distance. He left the young servants behind and, taking Isaac's hand, went up the mountain alone. But Abraham said to himself, "I will not hide from Isaac where this walk is taking him." He stood still, he laid his hand on Isaac's head in blessing, and Isaac kneeled to receive it. And Abraham's face epitomized fatherliness; his gaze was gentle, his words admonishing. But Isaac could not understand him, his soul could not be uplifted; he clasped Abraham's knees, he pleaded at his feet, he begged for his young life, for his beautiful hopes; he called to mind the joy in Abraham's house, he called to mind the sorrow and the solitude. Then Abraham lifted the boy up and walked on, holding his hand, and his words were full of comfort and admonition. But Isaac could

[1] From Søren Kierkegaard's *Fear and Trembling*, translated by Howard V. Hong and Edna H. Hong, volume 6 in the *Collected Works of Kierkegaard*.

not understand him. Abraham climbed Mount Moriah, but Isaac could not understand him. Then Abraham turned away from him for a moment, but when Isaac saw Abraham's face again, it had changed: his gaze was wild, his whole being was sheer terror. He seized Isaac by the chest, threw him to the ground, and said, "Stupid boy, do you think I am your father? I am an idolater. Do you think it is God's command? No, it is my desire." Then Isaac trembled and cried out in his anguish: "God in heaven, have mercy on me, God of Abraham, have mercy on me; if I have no father on earth, then you be my father!" But Abraham said softly to himself, "Lord God in heaven, I thank you; it is better that he believes me a monster than that he should lose faith in you."

When the child is to be weaned, the mother blackens her breast. It would be hard to have the breast look inviting when the child must not have it. So the child believes that the breast has changed, but the mother—she is still the same, her gaze is tender and loving as ever. How fortunate the one who did not need more terrible means to wean the child!

II.

It was early in the morning when Abraham arose: he embraced Sarah, the bride of his old age, and Sarah kissed Isaac, who took away her disgrace, Isaac her pride, her hope for all the generations to come. They rode along the road in silence, and Abraham stared continuously and fixedly at the ground until the fourth day, when he looked up and saw Mount Moriah far away, but once again he turned his eyes toward the ground. Silently he arranged the firewood and bound Isaac; silently he drew the knife—then he saw the ram that God had selected. This he sacrificed and went home.—From that day henceforth, Abraham was old; he could not forget that God had ordered him to do this. Isaac flourished as before, but Abraham's eyes were darkened, and he saw joy no more.

When the child has grown big and is to be weaned, the mother virginally conceals her breast, and then the child no longer has a mother. How fortunate the child who has not lost his mother in some other way!

III.

It was early in the morning when Abraham arose: he kissed Sarah, the young mother, and Sarah kissed Isaac, her delight, her joy forever. And Abraham rode thoughtfully down the road; he thought of Hagar and the son, whom he drove out into the desert. He climbed Mount Moriah, he drew the knife.

It was a quiet evening when Abraham rode out alone, and he rode to Mount Moriah; he threw himself down on his face, he prayed God to forgive him his sin, that he had been willing to sacrifice Isaac, that the father had forgotten his duty to his son. He often rode out his lonesome road, but he found no peace. He could not comprehend that it was a sin that he had been willing to sacrifice to God the best that he had, the possession for which he himself would have gladly died many times; and if it was a sin, if he had not loved Isaac in this manner, he could not understand that it could be forgiven, for what more terrible sin was there?

When the child is to be weaned, the mother, too, is not without sorrow, because she and the child are more and more to be separated, because the child who first lay under her heart and later rested upon her breast will never again be so close. So they grieve together the brief sorrow. How fortunate the one who kept the child so close and did not need to grieve any more!

IV.

It was early in the morning, and everything in Abraham's house was ready for the journey. He took leave of Sarah, and Eliezer, the faithful servant, accompanied him along the road until he turned back again. They rode along in harmony, Abraham and Isaac, until they came to Mount Moriah. Abraham made everything ready for the sacrifice, calmly and gently, but when he turned away and drew the knife, Isaac saw that Abraham's left hand was clenched in despair, that a shudder went through his whole body—but Abraham drew the knife.

Then they returned home again, and Sarah hurried to meet them, but Isaac had lost the faith. Not a word is ever said of this in the world, and Isaac never talked to anyone about what he had seen, and Abraham did not suspect that anyone had seen it.

When the child is to be weaned, the mother has stronger sustenance at hand so that the child does not perish. How fortunate the one who has this stronger sustenance at hand.

Thus and in many similar ways did the man of whom we speak ponder this event. Every time he returned from a pilgrimage to Mount Moriah, he sank down wearily, folded his hands, and said, "No one was as great as Abraham. Who is able to understand him?"

Eulogy on Abraham

If a human being did not have an eternal consciousness, if underlying everything there were only a wild, fermenting power that writhing in dark passions produced everything, be it significant or insignificant, if a vast, never appeased emptiness hid beneath everything, what would life be then but despair? If such were the situation, if there were not sacred bond that knit humankind together, if one generation emerged after another like forest foliage, if one generation succeeded another like the singing of birds in the forest, if a generation passed through the world as a ship through the sea, as wind through the desert, an unthinking and unproductive performance, if an eternal oblivion, perpetually hungry, lurked for its prey and there were no power strong enough to wrench that away from it—how empty and devoid of consolation life would be! But precisely for that reason it is not so, and just as God created man and woman, so he created the hero and the poet or orator. The poet or orator can do nothing that the hero does; he can only admire, love, and delight in him. Yet he, too, is happy—no less than that one is, for the hero is, so to speak, his better nature, with which he is enamored—yet happy that the other is not himself, that his love can be admiration. He is recollection's genius. He can do nothing but bring to mind what has been done, can do nothing but admire what has been done; he takes nothing of his own but is zealous for what has been entrusted. He follows his heart's desire, but when he has found the object of his search, he roams about to every man's door with his song and speech so that all may admire the hero as he does, may be proud of the hero as he is. This is his occupation, but his humble task; this is his faithful service in the house of the hero. If he remains true to his love in this way, if he contends night and day against the craftiness of oblivion, which wants to trick him out of his hero, then he has fulfilled his task, then he is gathered together with the hero, who has loved him just as faithfully, for the poet is, so to speak, the hero's better nature, powerless, to be sure, just as a memory is, but also transfigured just as a memory is. Therefore, no one who was great will be forgotten, and even though it takes time, even though a cloud of misunderstanding takes away the hero, his lover will nevertheless come, and the longer the passage of time, the more faithfully he adheres to him.

No! No one who was great in the world will be forgotten, but everyone was great in his own way, and everyone in proportion to the greatness of that which *he loved*. He who loved himself became great by virtue of himself, and he who loved other men became great by his devotedness, but he who loved God became the greatest of all. Everyone shall be remembered, but everyone became great in proportion to his *expectancy*. One became great by expecting the possible, another by expecting the eternal; but he who expected the impossible became the greatest of all. Everyone shall be remembered, but everyone was great wholly in proportion to the magnitude of that with which he *struggled*. For he who struggled with the world became great by conquering the world, and he who struggled with himself became great by conquering himself, but he who struggled with God became the greatest of all. Thus did they struggle in the world, man against man, one against thousands, but he who struggled with God was the greatest of all. Thus did they struggle on earth: there was one who conquered everything by his power, and there was one who conquered God by his powerlessness. There was one who relied upon himself and gained everything; there was one who in the security of his own strength sacrificed everything; but the one who believed God was the greatest of all. There was one who was great by virtue of his power, and one who was great by virtue of his wisdom, and one who was great by virtue of his hope, and one who was great by virtue of his love, but Abraham was the greatest of all, great by that power whose strength is powerlessness, great by that wisdom whose secret is foolishness, great by that hope whose form is madness, great by the love that is hatred to oneself.

By faith Abraham emigrated from the land of his fathers and became an alien in the promised land. He left one thing behind, took one thing along: he left behind his worldly understanding, and he took along his faith. Otherwise he certainly would not have emigrated but surely would have considered it unreasonable. By faith he was an alien in the promised land, and there was nothing that reminded him of what he cherished, but everything by its newness tempted his soul to sorrowful longing. And yet he was God's chosen one in whom the Lord was well pleased! As a matter of fact, if he had been an exile, banished from God's grace, he could have better understood it—but now it was as if he and his faith were being mocked. There was also in the world one who lived in exile from the native land he loved. He is not forgotten, nor are his dirges of lamentation when he sorrowfully sought and found what was lost. There is no dirge by Abraham. It is human to lament, human to weep with one who weeps, but it is greater to have faith, more blessed to contemplate the man of faith.

By faith Abraham received the promise that in his seed all the generations of the earth would be blessed. Time passed, the possibility was there, Abraham had faith; time passed, it became unreasonable, Abraham had faith. There was one in the world who also had an expectancy. Time passed, evening drew near; he was not so contemptible as to forget his expectancy, and therefore he will not be forgotten, either. Then he sorrowed, and his sorrow did not disappoint him as life had done, it did everything it could for him; in the sweetness of his sorrow he possessed his disappointed expectancy. It is human to sorrow, human to sorrow with sorrowing, but it is greater to have faith, more blessed to contemplate the man of faith. We have no dirge of sorrow by Abraham. As time passed, he did not gloomily count the days; he did not look suspiciously at Sarah, wondering if she was not getting old; he did not stop the course of the sun so she would not become old and along with her his expectancy; he did not soothingly sing his mournful lay for Sarah. Abraham became old, Sarah the object of mockery in the land, and yet he was God's chosen one and heir to the promise that in his seed all the generations of the earth would be blessed. Would it not have been better, after all, if he were not God's chosen? What does it mean to be God's chosen? Is it to be denied in youth one's youthful desire in order to have it fulfilled with great difficulty in one's old age? But Abraham believed and held to the promise. If Abraham had wavered, he would have given it up. He would have said to God, "So maybe it is not your will that this should be; then I will give up my wish. It was my one and only wish, it was my blessedness. My soul is open and sincere; I am hiding no secret resentment because you denied me this." He would not have been forgotten, he would have saved many by his example, but he still would not have become the father of faith, for it is great to give up one's desire, but it is greater to hold fast to it after having given it up; it is great to lay hold of the eternal, but it is greater to hold fast to the temporal after having given it up.

Then came the fullness of time. If Abraham had not had faith, then Sarah would surely have died of sorrow, and Abraham, dulled by grief, would not have understood the fulfillment but would have smiled at it as at a youthful dream. But Abraham had faith, and therefore he was young, for he who always hopes for the best grows old and is deceived by life, and he who is always prepared for the worst grows old prematurely, but he who has faith—he preserves an eternal youth. So let us praise and honor that story! For Sarah, although well advanced in years, was young enough to desire the pleasure of motherhood, and Abraham with his gray hairs was young enough to wish to be a father. Outwardly, the wonder of it is that it happened according to their expectancy; in the more profound sense, the wonder of faith is that Abraham and Sarah were young enough to desire and that faith had preserved their desire and thereby their youth. He accepted the fulfillment of the promise, he accepted it in faith, and it happened according to the promise and according to his faith. Moses struck the rock with his staff, but he did not have faith.

So there was joy in Abraham's house when Sarah stood as bride on their golden wedding day.

But it was not to remain that way; once again Abraham was to be tried. He had fought with that crafty power that devises all things, with that vigilant enemy who never dozes, with that old man who outlives everything—he had fought with time and kept his faith. Now all the frightfulness of the struggle was concentrated in one moment. "And God tempted Abraham and said to him, take Isaac, your only son, whom you love, and go to the land of Moriah and offer him as a burnt offering on a mountain that I shall show you."

So everything was lost, even more appallingly than if it had never happened! So the Lord was only mocking Abraham! He wondrously made the preposterous come true; now he wanted to see it annihilated. This was indeed a piece of folly, but Abraham did not laugh at it as Sarah did when the promise was announced. All was lost! Seventy years of trusting expectancy, the brief joy over the fulfillment of faith. Who is this who seizes the staff from the old man, who is this who demands that he himself shall break it! Who is this who makes a man's gray hairs disconsolate, who is this who demands that he himself shall do it! Is there no sympathy for this venerable old man, none for the innocent child? And yet Abraham was God's chosen one, and it was the Lord who imposed the ordeal. Now everything would be lost! All the glorious remembrance of his posterity, the promise in Abraham's seed—it was nothing but a whim, a fleeting thought that the Lord had had and that Abraham was now supposed to obliterate. That glorious treasure, which was just as old as the faith in Abraham's heart and many, many years older than Isaac, the fruit of Abraham's life, sanctified by prayer, matured in battle, the blessing on Abraham's lips—this fruit was now to be torn off prematurely and rendered meaningless, for what meaning would it have if Isaac should be sacrificed! That sad but nevertheless blessed hour when Abraham was to take leave of everything he held dear, when he once more would raise his venerable head, when his face would shine as the Lord's, when he would concentrate all his soul upon a blessing that would be so powerful it would bless Isaac all his days—this hour was not to come! For Abraham would indeed take leave of Isaac, but in such a way that he himself would remain behind; death would separate them, but in such a way that Isaac would become its booty. The old man would not, rejoicing in death, lay his hand in blessing on Isaac, but, weary of life, he would lay a violent hand upon Isaac. And it was God who tested him! Woe to the messenger who brought such news to Abraham! Who would have dared to be the emissary of this sorrow? But it was God who tested Abraham.

Yet Abraham had faith, and had faith for this life. In fact, if his faith had been only for a life to come, he certainly would have more readily discarded everything in order to rush out of a world to which he did not belong. But Abraham's faith was not of this sort, if there is such a faith at all, for actually it is not faith but the most remote possibility of faith that faintly sees its object on the most distant horizon but is separated from it by a chasmal abyss in which doubt plays its tricks. But Abraham had faith specifically for this life—faith that he would grow old in this country, be honored among the people, blessed by posterity, and unforgettable in Isaac, the most precious thing in his life, whom he embraced with a love that is inadequately described by saying he faithfully fulfilled the father's duty to love the son, which is indeed stated in the command: the son, whom you love. Jacob had twelve sons, one of whom he loved; Abraham had but one, whom he loved.

But Abraham had faith and did not doubt; he believed the preposterous. If Abraham had doubted, then he would have done something else, something great and glorious, for how could Abraham do anything else but what is great and glorious! He would have gone to Mount Moriah, he would have split the firewood, lit the fire, drawn the knife. He would have cried out to God, "Reject not this sacrifice; it is not the best that I have, that I know very well, for what is an old man compared with the child of promise, but it is the best I can give you. Let Isaac never find this out so that he may take comfort in his youth." He would have thrust the knife into his own breast. He would have been admired in the world, and his name would never be forgotten; but it is one thing to be admired and another to become a guiding start that saves the anguished.

But Abraham had faith. He did not pray for himself, trying to influence the Lord; it was only when righteous punishment fell upon Sodom and Gomorrah that Abraham came forward with his prayers.

We read in sacred scripture: "And God tempted Abraham and said: Abraham, Abraham, where are you? But Abraham answered: Here am I." You to whom these words are addressed, was this the case with you? When in the far distance you saw overwhelming vicissitudes approaching, did you not say to the mountains, "Hide me," and to the hills, "Fall on me"? Or, if you were stronger, did your feet nevertheless not drag along the way, did they not long, so to speak, for the old trails? And when your name was called, did you answer, perhaps answer softly, in a whisper? Not so with Abraham. Cheerfully, freely, confidently, loudly he answered: Here am I. We read on: "And Abraham arose early in the morning." He hurried as if to a celebration, and early in the morning he was at the appointed place on Mount Moriah. He said nothing to Sarah, nothing to Eliezer—who, after all, could understand him, for did not the nature of the temptation extract from him the pledge of silence? "He split the firewood, he bound Isaac, he lit the fire, he drew the knife." My listener! Many a father has thought himself deprived of every hope for the future when he lost his child, the dearest thing in the world to him; nevertheless, no one was the child of promise in the sense in which Isaac was that to Abraham. Many a father has lost his child, but then it was God, the unchangeable, inscrutable will of the Almighty, it was his hand that took it. Not so with Abraham! A harder test was reserved for him, and Isaac's fate was placed, along with the knife, in Abraham's hand. And there he stood, the old man with his solitary hope. But he did not doubt, he did not look in anguish to the left and to the right, he did not challenge heaven with his prayers. He knew it was God the Almighty who was testing him; he knew it was the hardest sacrifice that could be demanded of him; but he knew also that no sacrifice is too severe when God demands it—and he drew the knife.

Who strengthened Abraham's arm, who braced up his right arm so that it did not sink down powerless! Anyone who looks upon this scene is paralyzed. Who strengthened Abraham's soul lest everything go black for him and he see neither Isaac nor the ram! Anyone who looks upon this scene is paralyzed or blinded, and still more rarely does anyone tell what happened as it deserves to be told. We know it all—it was only an ordeal.

If Abraham had doubted as he stood there on Mount Moriah, if irresolute he had looked around, if he had happened to spot the ram before drawing the knife, if God had allowed him to sacrifice it instead of Isaac—then he would have gone home, everything would have been the same, he would have had Sarah, he would have kept Isaac, and yet how changed! For his return would have been a flight, his deliverance an accident, his reward disgrace, his future perhaps perdition. Then he would have witnessed neither to his faith nor to God's grace but would have witnessed to how appalling it is to go to Mount Moriah. Then Abraham would not be forgotten, nor would Mount Moriah. Then it would not be mentioned in the way Ararat, where the ark landed, is mentioned, but it would be called a place of terror, for it was here that Abraham doubted.

Venerable Father Abraham! When you went home from Mount Moriah, you did not need a eulogy to comfort you for what was lost, for you gained everything and kept Isaac—was it not so? The Lord did not take him away from you again, but you sat happily together at the dinner table in your tent, as you do in the next world for all eternity. Venerable Father Abraham! Centuries have passed since those days, but you have no need of a late lover to snatch your memory from the power of oblivion, for every language calls you to mind—and yet you reward your lover more gloriously than anyone else. In the life to come you make him eternally happy in your bosom; here in this life you captivate his eyes and his heart with the wonder of your act. Venerable Father Abraham! Second Father of the race! You who were the first to feel and to bear witness to that prodigious passion that disdains the terrifying battle with the raging elements and the forces of creation in order to contend with God, you who were the first to know that supreme passion, the holy, pure, and humble expression for the divine madness that was admired by the pagans—forgive the one who aspired to speak your praise if he has not done it properly. He spoke humbly, as his heart demanded; he spoke briefly, as is seemly. But he will never forget that you needed 100 years to get the son of your old age against all expectancy, that you had to draw the knife before you kept Isaac; he will never forget that in 130 years you got no further than faith.

Problemata

Preliminary Expectoration

From the external and visible world there comes an old adage: "Only one who works gets bread." Oddly enough, the adage does not fit the world in which it is most at home, for imperfection is the fundamental law of the external world, and here it happens again and again that he who does not work does get bread, and he who sleeps gets it even more abundantly than he who works. In the external world, everything belongs to the possessor. It is subject to the law of indifference, and the spirit of the ring obeys the one who has the ring, whether he is an Aladdin or a Noureddin, and he who has the wealth of the world has it regardless of how he got it.

It is different in the world of spirit. Here an eternal divine order prevails. Here it does not rain on both the just and the unjust; here the sun does not shine on both good and evil. Here it holds true that only the one who works gets bread, that only the one who was in anxiety finds rest, that only the one who descends into the lower world rescues the beloved, that only the one who draws the knife gets Isaac.

. . .

. . . I am not unfamiliar with what the world has admired as great and magnanimous. My soul feels its kinship with it and in all humility is certain that the cause for which the hero strives is also my cause, and when I consider it, I cry out to myself: *jam tua res agitur* [now your cause is at stake]. I *think* myself *into* the hero; I cannot think myself into Abraham; when I reach that eminence, I sink down, for what is offered me is a paradox. I by no means conclude that faith is something inferior but rather that it is the highest, also that it is dishonest of philosophy to give something else in its place and to disparage faith. Philosophy cannot and must not give faith, but it must understand itself and know what it offers and take nothing away, least of all trick men out of something by pretending that it is nothing. I am not unfamiliar with the hardships and dangers of life. I fear them not and approach them confidently. I am not unfamiliar with the terrifying. My memory is a faithful spouse, and my imagination, unlike myself, is a busy little maid who sits all day at her work and in the evening can coax me so charmingly that I have to look at it, even though it is not always landscapes or flowers or . . . pastoral idylls that she paints. I have seen the terrifying face to face, and I do not flee from it in horror, but I know very well that even though I advance toward it courageously, my courage is still not the courage of faith and is not something to be compared with it. I cannot make the movement of faith, I cannot shut my eyes and plunge confidently into the absurd; it is for me an impossibility, but I do not praise myself for that. I am convinced that God is love; for me this thought has a primal lyrical validity. When it is present to me, I am unspeakably happy; when it is absent, I long for it more vehemently than the lover for the object of his love. But I do not have faith; this courage I lack. To me God's love, in both the direct and the converse sense, is incommensurable with the whole of actuality. Knowing that, I am not so cowardly that I whimper and complain, but neither am I so perfidious as to deny that faith is something far higher. I can bear to live in my own fashion, I am happy and satisfied, but my joy is not the joy of faith, and by comparison with that, it is unhappy. I do not trouble God with my little troubles, details do not concern me; I gaze only at my love and keep its virgin flame pure and clear. Faith is convinced that God is concerned about the smallest things. I am satisfied with a left-handed marriage in this life; faith is humbled enough to insist on the right hand, for I do not deny that this is humility and will never deny it.

I wonder if anyone in my generation is able to make the movements of faith? If I am not mistaken, my generation is rather inclined to be proud of doing what it probably does not even believe me capable of—that is, the imperfect. My soul balks at doing what is so often done—talking inhumanly about the great, as if a few centuries were an enormous distance. I prefer to speak humanly about it, as if it happened yesterday, and only let the greatness itself be the distance that either elevates or judges. If I (*in the capacity of tragic hero*, for higher I cannot come) had been ordered to take such an extraordinary royal journey as the one to Mount Moriah, I know very well what I would have done. I would not have been cowardly enough to stay at home, nor would I have dragged and drifted along the road or forgotten the knife in order to cause a delay. I am quite sure that I would have been punctual and all prepared—more than likely, I would have arrived too early in order to get it over sooner. But I also know what else I would have done. The moment I mounted the horse, I would have said to myself: Now all is lost, God demands Isaac, I sacrifice him and along with him all my joy—yet God is love and continues to be that for me, for in the world of time God and I cannot talk with each other, we have no language in common. Perhaps someone in our time would be so foolish, so envious of the great, as to want to delude himself and me into believing that if I had actually done this I would have done something even greater than what Abraham did, for my immense resignation would be far more ideal and poetic than Abraham's small-mindedness. But this is utterly false, for my immense resignation would be a substitute for faith. I would not be able to do more than make the infinite movement in order to find myself and again rest in myself. Neither would I have loved Isaac as Abraham loved him. That I was determined to make the movement could prove my courage, humanly speaking—that I loved him with my whole soul is the presupposition without which the whole thing becomes a misdeed—nevertheless I would not love as Abraham loved, for then I would have held back at the very last minute, without, however, arriving too late at Mount

Moriah. Furthermore, by my behavior I would have spoiled the whole story, for if I had gotten Isaac again, I would have been in an awkward position. What was the easiest for Abraham would have been difficult for me—once again to be happy in Isaac!—for he who with all the infinity of his soul, *proprio motu et propriis auspiciis* [of his own accord and on his own responsibility], has made the infinite movement and cannot do more, he keeps Isaac only with pain.

But what did Abraham do? He arrived neither too early nor too late. He mounted the ass, he rode slowly down the road. During all this time he had faith, he had faith that God would not demand Isaac of him, and yet he was willing to sacrifice him if it was demanded. He had faith by virtue of the absurd, for human calculation was out of the question, and it certainly was absurd that God, who required it of him, should in the next moment rescind the requirement. He climbed the mountain, and even in the moment when the knife gleamed he had faith—that God would not require Isaac. No doubt he was surprised at the outcome, but through a double-movement he had attained his first condition, and therefore he received Isaac more joyfully than the first time. Let us go further. We let Isaac actually be sacrificed. Abraham had faith. He did not have faith that he would be blessed in a future life but that he would be blessed here in the world. God could give him a new Isaac, could restore to life the one sacrificed. He had faith by virtue of the absurd, for all human calculation ceased long ago. It is evident that sorrow can make a man mentally ill, and that is hard enough; it is also evident that there is a willpower that can haul to the wind so drastically that it rescues the understanding, even though a person becomes a little odd (and I do not intend to disparage this). But to be able to lose one's understanding and along with it everything finite, for which it is the stockbroker, and then to win the very same finitude again by virtue of the absurd—this appalls me, but that does not make me say it is something inferior, since, on the contrary, it is the one and only marvel. It is commonly supposed that what faith produces is no work of art, that it is a coarse and boorish piece of work, only for the more uncouth natures, but it is far from being that. The dialectic of faith is the finest and the most extraordinary of all; it has an elevation of which I can certainly form a conception, but no more than that. I can make the mighty trampoline leap whereby I cross over into infinity; my back is like a tightrope dancer's, twisted in my childhood, and therefore it is easy for me. One, two, three—I can walk upside down in existence, but I cannot make the next movement, for the marvelous I cannot do—I can only be amazed at it. Indeed, if Abraham, the moment he swung his leg over the ass's back, had said to himself: Now Isaac is lost, I could just as well sacrifice him here at home as ride the long way to Moriah—then I do not need Abraham, whereas now I bow seven times to his name and seventy times to his deed. This he did not do, as I can prove by his really fervent joy on receiving Isaac and by his needing no preparation and no time to rally to finitude and its joy. If it had been otherwise with Abraham, he perhaps would have loved God but would not have had faith, for he who loves God without faith reflects upon himself; he who loves God in faith reflects upon God.

This is the peak on which Abraham stands. The last stage to pass from his view is the stage of infinite resignation. He actually goes further and comes to faith. All those travesties of faith—the wretched, lukewarm lethargy that thinks: There's no urgency, there's no use in grieving beforehand; the despicable hope that says: One just can't know what will happen, it could just possibly be—those travesties are native to the paltriness of life, and infinite resignation has already infinitely disdained them.

Abraham I cannot understand; in a certain sense I can learn nothing from him except to be amazed. If someone deludes himself into thinking he may be moved to have faith by pondering the outcome of that story, he cheats himself and cheats God out of the first movement of faith—he wants to suck worldly wisdom out of the paradox. Someone might succeed, for our generation does not stop with faith, does not stop with the miracle of faith, turning water into wine—it goes further and turns wine into water.

Would it not be best to stop with faith, and is it not shocking that everyone wants to go further? Where will it all end when in our age, as declared in so many ways, one does not want to stop with love? In worldly shrewdness, in petty calculation, in paltriness and meanness, in everything that can make man's divine origin doubtful. Would it not be best to remain standing at faith and for him who stands to see to it that he does not fall, for the movement of faith must continually be made by virtue of the absurd, but yet in such a way, please note, that one does not lose the finite but gains it whole and intact. For my part, I presumably can describe the movements of faith, but I cannot make them. In learning to go through the motions of swimming, one can be suspended from the ceiling in a harness and then presumably describe the movements, but one is not swimming. In the same way I can describe the movements of faith. If I am thrown out into the water, I presumably do swim (for I do not belong to the waders), but I make different movements, the movements of infinity, whereas faith makes the opposite movements: after having made the movements of infinity, it makes the movements of finitude. Fortunate is the person who can make these movements! He does the marvelous, and I shall never weary of admiring him; it makes no difference to me whether it is Abraham or a slave in Abraham's house, whether it is a professor of philosophy or a poor servant girl—I pay attention only to the movements. But I do pay attention to them, and I do not let myself be fooled, either by myself or by anyone else. The knights of the infinite resignation are easily recognizable—their walk is light and bold. But they who carry the treasure of faith are likely to disappoint, for externally they have a striking resemblance to bourgeois philistinism, which infinite resignation, like faith, deeply disdains.

I honestly confess that in my experience I have not found a single authentic instance, although I do not therefore deny that every second person may be such an instance. Meanwhile, I have been looking for it for many years, but in vain. Generally, people travel around the world to see rivers and mountains, new stars, colorful birds, freakish fish, preposterous races of mankind; they indulge in the brutish stupor that gawks at life and thinks it has seen something. That does not occupy me. But if I knew where a knight of faith lived, I would travel on foot to him, for this marvel occupies me absolutely. I would not leave him for a second, I would watch him every minute to see how he made the movements; I would consider myself taken care of for life and would divide my time between watching him and practicing myself, and thus spend all my time in admiring him. As I said before, I have not found anyone like that; meanwhile, I may very well imagine him. Here he is. The acquaintance is made, I am introduced to him. The instant I first lay eyes on him, I set him apart at once; I jump back, clap my hands, and say half aloud, "Good Lord, is this the man, is this really the one—he looks just like a tax collector!" But this is indeed the one. I move a little closer to him, watch his slightest movement to see if it reveals a bit of heterogeneous optical telegraphy from the infinite, a glance, a facial expression, a gesture, a sadness, a smile that would betray the infinite in its heterogeneity with the finite. No! I examine his figure from top to toe to see if there may not be a crack through which the infinite would peek. No! He is solid all the way through. His stance? It is vigorous, belongs entirely to finitude; no spruced-up burgher walking out to Fresberg on a Sunday afternoon treads the earth more solidly. He belongs entirely to the world; no bourgeois philistine could belong to it more. Nothing is detectable of that distant and aristocratic nature by which the knight of the infinite is recognized. He finds pleasure in everything, takes part in everything, and every time one sees him participating in something particular, he does it with an assiduousness that marks the worldly man who is attached to such things. He attends to his job. To see him makes one think of him as a pen-pusher who has lost his soul to Italian bookkeeping, so punctilious is he. Sunday is for him a holiday. He goes to church. No heavenly gaze or any sign of the incommensurable betrays him; if one did not know him, it would be impossible to distinguish him from the rest of the crowd, for at most his hearty and powerful singing of hymns proves that he has good lungs. In the afternoon, he takes a walk to the woods. He enjoys everything he sees, the swarms of people, the new omnibuses, the Sound. Encountering him on Strandveien, one would take him for a mercantile soul enjoying himself. He finds pleasure in this way, for he is not a poet, and I have tried in vain to lure the poetic incommensurability out of him. Toward evening, he goes home, and his gait is as steady as a postman's. On the way, he thinks that his wife surely will have a special hot meal for him when he comes home—for example, roast lamb's head with vegetables. If he meets a kindred soul, he would go on talking all the way to Osterport about this delicacy with a passion befitting a restaurant operator. It so happens he does not have four shillings to his name, and yet he firmly believes that his wife has this delectable meal waiting for him. If she has, to see him eat would be the envy of the elite and an inspiration to the common man, for his appetite is keener than Esau's. His wife does not have it—curiously enough, he is just the same. On the way he passes a building site and meets another man. They converse for a moment; in an instant he erects a building, and he himself has at his disposition everything required. The stranger leaves him thinking that he surely is a capitalist, while my admired knight thinks: Well, if it came right down to it, I could easily get it. He sits at an open window and surveys the neighborhood where he lives: everything that happens—a rat scurrying under a plank across the gutter, children playing—engages him with an equanimity akin to that of a sixteen-year-old girl. And yet he is no genius, for I have sought in vain to spy out the incommensurability of genius in him. In the evening, he smokes his pipe; seeing him, one would swear it was the butcher across the way vegetating in the gloaming. With the freedom from care of a reckless good-for-nothing, he lets things take care of themselves, and yet every moment of his life he buys the opportune time at the highest price, for he does not do even the slightest thing except by virtue of the absurd. And yet, yet—yes, I could be infuriated over it if for no other reason than envy—and yet this man has made and at every moment is making the movement of infinity. He drains the deep sadness of life in infinite resignation, he knows the blessedness of infinity, he has felt the pain of renouncing everything, the most precious thing in the world, and yet the finite tastes just as good to him as to one who never knew anything higher, because his remaining in finitude would have no trace of a timorous, anxious routine, and yet he has this security that makes him delight in it as if finitude were the surest thing of all. And yet, yet the whole earthly figure he presents is a new creation by virtue of the absurd. He resigned everything infinitely, and then he grasped everything again by virtue of the absurd. He is continually making the movement of infinity, but he does it with such precision and assurance that he continually gets finitude out of it, and no one ever suspects anything else. It is supposed to be the most difficult feat for a ballet dancer to leap into a specific posture in such a way that he never once strains for the posture but in the very leap assumes the posture. Perhaps there is no ballet dancer who can do it—but this knight does it. Most people live completely absorbed in worldly joys and sorrows; they are benchwarmers who do not take part in the dance. The knights of infinity are ballet dancers and have elevation. They make the upward movement and come down again, and this, too, is not an unhappy diversion and is not unlovely to see. But every time they come down, they are unable to assume the posture immediately, they waver for a moment, and this wavering shows that they are aliens in the world. It is more or less conspicuous according to their skill, but even the most skillful of these knights cannot hide this wavering. One does not need to see them in the air; one needs only to see them the instant they touch and have touched the earth—and then one recognizes them. But to be able to come down in such a way that instantaneously one seems to stand and to walk, to change the leap into life into walking, absolutely to express the sublime in the pedestrian—only that knight can do it, and this is the one and only marvel.

. . .

Infinite resignation is the last stage before faith, so that anyone who has not made this movement does not have faith, for only in infinite resignation do I become conscious of my eternal validity, and only then can one speak of grasping existence by virtue of faith.

. . .

So I can perceive that it takes strength and energy and spiritual freedom to make the infinite movement of resignation; I can also perceive that it can be done. The next [movement] amazes me, my brain reels, for, after having made the movement of resignation, then by virtue of the absurd to get everything, to get one's desire totally and completely—that is over and beyond human powers, that is a marvel. . . . Every time I want to make this movement, I almost faint; the very same moment I admire absolutely, I am seized with great anxiety. For what is it to tempt God? And yet this is the movement of faith and continues to be that, even though philosophy, so as to confuse the concepts, wants to delude us into thinking it has faith, even though theology is willing to sell it off at a low price.

The act of resignation does not require faith, for what I gain in resignation is my eternal consciousness. This is a purely philosophical movement that I venture to make when it is demanded and can discipline myself to make, because every time some finitude will take power over me, I starve myself into submission until I make the movement, for my eternal consciousness is my love for God, and for me that is the highest of all. The act of resignation does not require faith, but to get the least little bit more than my eternal consciousness requires faith, for this is the paradox. The movements are often confused. It is said that faith is needed in order to renounce everything. Indeed, one hears what is even more curious: a person laments that he has lost his faith, and when a check is made to see where he is on the scale, curiously enough, he has only reached the point where he is to make the infinite movement of resignation. Through resignation I renounce everything. I make this movement all by myself, and if I do not make it, it is because I am too cowardly and soft and devoid of enthusiasm and do not feel the significance of the high dignity assigned to every human being, to be his own censor, which is far more exalted than to be the censor general of the whole Roman republic. This movement I make all by myself, and what I gain thereby is my eternal consciousness in blessed harmony with my love for the eternal being. By faith I do not renounce anything; on the contrary, by faith I receive everything exactly in the sense in which it is said that one who has faith like a mustard seed can move mountains. It takes a purely human courage to renounce the whole temporal realm in order to gain eternity, but this I do gain and in all eternity can never renounce—it is a self-contradiction. But it takes a paradoxical and humble courage to grasp the whole temporal realm now by virtue of the absurd, and this is the courage of faith. By faith Abraham did not renounce Isaac, but by faith Abraham received Isaac.

. . .

Should we, then, not dare to speak about Abraham? I surely think we can. If I were to speak about him, I would first of all describe the pain of the ordeal. To that end, I would, like a leech, suck all the anxiety and distress and torment out of a father's suffering in order to describe what Abraham suffered, although under it all he had faith. I would point out that the journey lasted three days and a good part of the fourth; indeed, these three and a half days could be infinitely longer than the few thousand years that separate me from Abraham. I would point out—and this is my view—that every person may still turn back before he begins such a thing and at any time may repentantly turn back. If one does this, I am not apprehensive; I do not fear arousing a desire in people to be tried as Abraham was. But to sell a cheap edition of Abraham and yet forbid everyone to do likewise is ludicrous.

. . .

Epilogue

Once when the price of spices in Holland fell, the merchants had a few cargoes sunk in the sea in order to jack up the price. This was an excusable, perhaps even necessary, deception. Do we need something similar in the world of the spirit? Are we so sure that we have achieved the highest, so that there is nothing left for us to do except piously to delude ourselves into thinking that we have not come that far, simply in order to have something to occupy our time? Is this the kind of self-deception the present generation needs? Should it be trained in a virtuosity along that line, or is it not, instead, adequately perfected in the art of deceiving itself? Or, rather, does it not need an honest earnestness that fearlessly and incorruptibly points to the tasks, and honest earnestness that lovingly maintains the tasks, that does not disquiet people into wanting to attain the highest too hastily but keeps the tasks young and beautiful and lovely to look at, inviting to all and yet also difficult and inspiring to the noble-minded (for the noble nature is inspired only by the difficult)? Whatever one generation learns from another, no generation learns the essentially human from a previous one. In this respect, each generation begins primitively, has no task other than what each previous generation had, nor does it advance further, insofar as the previous generations did not betray the task and deceive themselves. The essentially human is passion, in which one generation perfectly understands another and understands itself. For example, no generation has learned to love from another, no generation is able to begin at any other point than at the beginning, no later generation has a more abridged task than the previous one, and if someone desires to go further and not stop with loving as the previous generation did, this is foolish and idle talk.

But the highest passion in a person is faith, and here no generation begins at any other point than where the previous one did. Each generation begins all over again; the next generation advances no further than the previous one, that is, if that one was faithful to the task and did not leave it high and dry. That it should be fatiguing is, of course, something that one generation cannot say, for the generation does indeed have the task and has nothing to do with the fact that the previous generation had the same task, unless this particular generation, the individuals in it, presumptuously assumes the place that belongs to the spirit who rules the world and who has the patience not to become weary. If the generation does that, it is wrong, and no wonder, then, that all existence seems wrong to it, for there surely is no one who found existence more wrong than the tailor who, according to the fairy story, came to heaven while alive and contemplated the world from that vantage point. As long as the generation is concerned only about its task, which is the highest, it cannot become weary, for the task is always adequate for a person's lifetime. When children on vacation have already played all the games before twelve o'clock and impatiently ask: Can't somebody think up a new game—does this show that these children are more developed and more advanced than the children in the contemporary or previous generation who make the well-known games last all day long? Or does it show instead that the first children lack what I would call the endearing earnestness belonging to play?

Faith is the highest passion in a person. There perhaps are many in every generation who do not come to faith, but no one goes further. Whether there also are many in our day who do not find it, I do not decide. I dare to refer only to myself, without concealing that he has a long way to go, without therefore wishing to deceive himself or what is great by making a trifle of it, a childhood disease one may wish to get over as soon as possible. But life has tasks enough also for the person who does not come to faith, and if he loves these honestly, his life will not be wasted, even if it is never comparable to the lives of those who perceived and grasped the highest. But the person who has come to faith (whether he is extraordinarily gifted or plain and simple does not matter) does not come to a standstill in faith. Indeed, he would be indignant if anyone said this to him, just as the lover would resent it if someone said that he came to a standstill in love; for, he would answer, I am by no means standing still. I have my whole life in it. Yet he does not go further, does not go on to something else, for when he finds this, then he has another explanation.

"One must go further, one must go further." This urge to go further is an old story in the world. Heraclitus the obscure, who deposited his thoughts in his books and his books in Diana's temple (for his thoughts had been his armor in life, and therefore he hung it in the temple of the goddess), Heraclitus the obscure said: One cannot walk through the same river twice. Heraclitus the obscure had a disciple who did not remain standing there but went further—and added: One cannot do it even once. Poor Heraclitus, to have a disciple like that! By this improvement, the Heraclitean thesis was amended into an Eleatic thesis that denies motion, and yet that disciple wished only to be a disciple of Heraclitus who went further, not back to what Heraclitus had abandoned.

Basic Existentialist Concepts

Despair Kierkegaard calls *despair* the "sickness unto death": It is not a disease from which one could die, but is precisely the agony of not being able to die because of being an eternal self. The individual is in despair over himself, tormented by the inability to get rid of himself. This inability leads to futile efforts on the part of the individual, either to escape from himself or to be who he truly is. The first strategy is the despair of not willing to be oneself; the second is the despair of willing to be oneself. Even the second strategy fails because the individual seeks to be the self that he decides to be, instead of recognizing that he was created by a power outside of himself. The only cure for despair is true faith, by which the individual is spirit, established in relationship to God.

Despair is the common condition of individuals, even those who are unaware that they are in despair. Those who protest the most that they are not in despair but happy and contented with their lives are the ones who are really in the deepest despair, for they are unaware that they are spirit. They think of themselves as merely earth-bound bodies or egoistic selves. As painful as despair is, it is actually more beneficial to be aware of one's despair than to be ignorant of it.

Leap of Faith This movement—the *leap of faith*—makes faith into an actual way of living, not just a profession of beliefs. It cannot be undertaken by groups of people united in faith, only by the individual herself alone. The individual who makes the leap of faith does not rely on rational proofs for God's existence or on religious dogma. Instead, she leaves behind all reasons for believing in order to plunge into the absurd paradoxes of religion; she believes what is impossible and, by her belief, she becomes fully related to God.

Kierkegaard believed that it was extremely rare for an individual to make the leap of faith. He deeply desired to make this movement himself but did not think he was able to make it. He credited Abraham with making this leap but did not understand how Abraham did it.

The individual who succeeds in making the leap of faith is called the "knight of faith." Unrecognizable to others, hidden perhaps in the most mundane personalities walking among us, the knights of faith live on earth as spirit, and not just as combinations of mind and body. They personify the synthesis of the temporal and the eternal.

Teleological Suspension of the Ethical One paradox of faith is that the believer must obey God's command, even if it means violating God's commands. In the case of Abraham, he obeyed God's command to kill Isaac even though this violated God's own commandment "Thou shalt not kill." For Kierkegaard, the problem is not merely one of conflicting moral laws, but of faith that requires the individual to be a particular, free from the restraints of any universal law.

Ethical laws are meant to have universal validity; that is, they are meant to be obeyed by all people in all times and all places. The Ten Commandments are examples of universal moral laws. A tragic hero is someone who makes a decision that carries out one universally valid moral law while violating another. In contrast, a knight of faith suspends the ethical laws, not because these laws are wrong or inapplicable or conflicting, but because there is a higher goal (*telos*) to be achieved: the establishment of oneself in full, unquestioning relationship to God. Ethical laws can be suspended only if one is commanded by God and only to accomplish this relationship. The risk and incomprehensibility of the suspension of the ethical are the sources of the fear and trembling that characterize genuine religious faith.

Questions for Discussion

1. Kierkegaard offers several different versions of Abraham's ascent of Mount Moriah. Contrast the accounts in which he or Isaac lose faith with the accounts in which Abraham proves his faith.

2. Kierkegaard argues that if there were only nature, with its succession of generations and its endless cycles of growth and decay, we would be doomed to despair. Why?

3. How does the movement (leap) of faith differ from the movement of infinite resignation?

4. Is faith compatible with reason?

5. Why is the knight of faith indistinguishable from an ordinary citizen?

Chapter 12

Fyodor Dostoyevsky's "The Grand Inquisitor"

Introduction: Religious Doubt and Debate

Dostoyevsky's religious faith was not simple and unquestioning, but complex and sustained by perplexities and even gloomy reflections about the human capacity for virtue. The struggle of good versus evil was a common theme in his writings, and several of his works dared to unfold the moral consequences of atheism or the problem of God's relation to evil. His characters, whether pious or depraved, were memorable for their psychological depth. They did not fit obvious stereotypes of who is good and who is evil, but unsettled our facile appraisals of what kind of character would perform what kind of action. As they struggled with "eternal questions" about God and the world God created, these characters revealed how vulnerable saintly aspirations are, and how relentless malevolent forces are, within the human psyche.

Set within his lengthy last novel, *The Brothers Karamazov*, the legend of the Grand Inquisitor distills many of Dostoyevsky's most disturbing quandaries about religion. The scene is set when two brothers, for most of their lives distant from one another, meet to discuss their deepest motivations. The older brother, Ivan, represents an intellectual approach to religion; he seriously questions the dogmas of religion and presents the legend of the Grand Inquisitor as his indictment of religion for its failure to stop human beings from causing one another suffering. His brother, Alyosha, represents a devoted approach to religion; embodying the Christian values of meekness, humility, and hope, Alyosha willingly accepts the mysteries of religion over rational explanation of religious beliefs.

The legend of the Grand Inquisitor sets up a dialectic between, on the one hand, judgments about what is best for humanity which are based on human needs and desires, and, on the other hand, religious ideals which call for human freedom but which also seem to underwrite human failings and despair. The Grand Inquisitor is the highest judge on Earth who adapts religion to the needs and desires of humanity. He regards happiness as the aim of human life, and he criticizes God for challenging individuals instead of comforting them. His silent respondent is Jesus Christ, who returns to Earth and finds out what organized religion has done to his teachings. He offers no counterargument to the Grand Inquisitor's criticisms of religion, only the testimony of his presence on Earth.

Dostoyevsky's "The Grand Inquisitor" (Excerpts)[1]

". . . Do you know, Alyosha—don't laugh! I made a poem about a year ago. If you can waste another ten minutes on me, I'll tell it to you.

"You wrote a poem?"

"Oh, no, I didn't write it," laughed Ivan, "and I've never written two lines of poetry in my life. But I made up this poem in prose and I remembered it. I was carried away when I made it up. You will be my first reader—that is listener. Why should an author forego even one listener?" smiled Ivan. "Shall I tell it to you?"

"I am all attention," said Alyosha.

"My poem is called 'The Grand Inquisitor.' It's a ridiculous thing, but I want to tell it to you."

The Grand Inquisitor

"Even this must have a preface—that is, a literary preface," laughed Ivan, "and I am a poor hand at making one. You see, my action takes place in the sixteenth century, and at that time, as you probably learnt at school, it was customary in poetry to bring down heavenly powers on earth. Not to speak of Dante, in France, law clerks as well as the monks in the monasteries, used to give regular performances in which the Madonna, the saints, the angels, Christ, and God Himself were brought on the stage. In those days it was done in all simplicity. In Victor Hugo's *Notre Dame de Paris* an edifying and gratuitous spectacle was provided for the people in the Hôtel de Ville of Paris in the reign of Louis XI in honour of the birth of the dauphin. It was called *Le bon jugement de la très sainte et gracieuse Vierge Marie,* and she appears herself on the stage and pronounces her *bon jugement.* Similar plays, chiefly from the Old Testament, were occasionally performed in Moscow too, up to the times of Peter the Great. But besides plays there were all sorts of legends and ballads scattered about the world, in which the saints and angels and all the powers of Heaven took part when required. In our monasteries the monks busied themselves in translating, copying, and even composing such poems—and even under the Tatars. There is, for instance, one such poem (of course, from the Greek) 'The Wanderings of Our Lady through Hell,' with descriptions as bold as Dante's. Our Lady visits Hell, and the Archangel Michael leads her through the torments. She sees the sinners and their punishment. There she sees among others one noteworthy set of sinners in a burning lake; some of them sink to the bottom of the lake so that they can't swim out, and 'these God forgets'—an expression of extraordinary depth and force. And so Our Lady, shocked and weeping, falls before the throne of God and begs for mercy for all in Hell—for all she has seen there, indiscriminately. Her conversation with God is immensely interesting. She beseeches Him, she will not desist, and when God points to the hands and feet of her Son, nailed to the cross, and asks, 'How can I forgive His tormentors?' she bids all the saints, all the martyrs, all the angels and archangels to fall down with her and pray for mercy on all without distinction. It ends by her winning from God a respite of suffering every year from Good Friday till Trinity day, and the sinners at once raise a cry of thanksfulness from hell, chanting 'Thou are just, O Lord, in this judgment.' Well, my poem would have been of that kind if it had appeared at that time. He comes on the scene in my poem, but He says nothing, only appears and passes on. Fifteen centuries have passed since He promised to come in His glory, fifteen centuries since His prophet wrote, 'Behold, I come quickly.' 'Of that day and that hour knoweth no person, neither the Son, but the Father,' as He Himself predicted on earth. But humanity awaits Him with the same faith and with the same love. Oh, with greater faith, for it is

1 From Fyodor Dostoyevsky, *The Brothers Karamazov*, translated by Constance Garnett. New York: Macmillan, 1912. Revised by Linda E. Patrik.

fifteen centuries since humanity has ceased to see signs from Heaven.

No signs from heaven come today
To add to what the heart doth say.

"There was nothing left but faith in what the heart doth say! It is true there were many miracles in those days. There were saints who performed miraculous cures; some holy people, according to their biographies, were visited by the Queen of Heaven herself. But the devil did not slumber, and doubts were already arising among people about the truth of these miracles. And just then there appeared in the north of Germany a terrible new heresy. 'A huge star like to a torch' (that is, to a church) 'fell on the sources of the waters and they became bitter.' These heretics began blasphemously denying miracles. But those who remained faithful were all the more ardent in their faith. The tears of humanity rose up to Him as before, awaited His coming, loved Him, hoped for Him, yearned to suffer and die for Him as before. And so many ages humankind had prayed with faith and fervor, 'O Lord our God, hasten Thy coming'; so many ages called upon Him, that in His infinite mercy He deigned to come down to His servants. Before that day He had come down, He had visited some holy men, martyrs, and hermits, as is written in their lives. Among us, Tyutchev, with absolute faith in the truth of His words, bore witness that

Bearing the cross, in slavish dress,
Weary and worn, the Heavenly King
Our Mother, Russia, came to bless,
And through our land went wandering.

And that certainly was so. I assure you.

"And behold, He deigned to appear for a moment to the people, to the tortured, suffering people, sunk in iniquity, but loving Him like children. My story is laid in Spain, in Seville, in the most terrible time of the Inquisition, when fires were lighted every day to the glory of God, and 'in the splendid *auto da fé* the wicked heretics were burnt.' Oh, of course, this was not the coming in which He will appear according to His promise, at the end of time in all His heavenly glory, and which will be sudden 'as lightning flashing from east to west.' No. He visited His children only for a moment and there where the flames were crackling round the heretics. In His infinite mercy He came once more among us in that human shape in which He walked among us for thirty-three years fifteen centuries ago. He came down to the 'hot pavements' of the southern town in which on the day before almost a hundred heretics had, *ad majorem gloriam Dei,* been burnt by the cardinal, the Grand Inquisitor, in a magnificent *auto da fé,* in the presence of the king, the court, the knights, the cardinals, the most charming ladies of the court, and the whole population of Seville.

He came softly, unobserved, and yet, strange to say, everyone recognised Him. That might be one of the best passages in the poem. I mean, why they recognised Him. The people are irresistibly drawn to Him, they surround Him, they flock about Him, follow Him. He moves silently in their midst with a gentle smile of infinite compassion. The sun of love burns in His heart, light and power shine from His eyes, and their radiance, shed on the people, stirs their hearts with responsive love. He holds out His hands to them, blesses them, and a healing virtue comes from contact with Him, even with His garments. An old man in the crowd, blind from childhood, cries out, 'O Lord, heal me and I shall see Thee!' and, as it were, scales fall from his eyes and the blind man sees Him. The crowd weeps and kisses the earth under His feet. Children throw flowers before Him, sing, and cry hosannah. 'It is He!—it is He!' all repeat. 'It must be He, it can be no one but Him!' He stops at the steps of the Seville cathedral at the moment when the weeping mourners are bringing in a little open white coffin. In it lies a child of seven, the only daughter of a prominent citizen. The dead child lies hidden in flowers. 'He will raise your child,' the crowd shouts to the weeping mother. The priest, coming to meet the coffin, looks perplexed, and frowns, but the mother of the dead child throws herself at His feet with a wail. 'If it is Thou, raise my child!' she cries, holding out her hands to Him. The procession halts, the coffin is laid on the steps at His feet. He looks with compassion, and His lips once more softly pronounce, 'Maiden, arise!' and the maiden arises. The little girl sits up in the coffin and looks round, smiling with wide-open, wondering eyes, holding a bunch of white roses they had put in her hand.

There are cries, sobs, confusion among the people, and at that moment the cardinal himself, the Grand Inquisitor, passes by the cathedral. He is an old man, almost ninety, tall and erect, with a withered face and sunken eyes, in which there is still a gleam of light. He is not dressed in his gorgeous cardinal's robes, as he was the day before, when he was burning the enemies of the Roman Church—at this moment he is wearing his coarse, old, monk's cassock. At a distance behind him come his gloomy assistants and slaves and the 'holy guard.' He stops at the sight of the crowd and watches it from a distance. He sees everything; he sees them set the coffin down at His feet, sees the child rise up, and his face darkens. He knits his thick grey brows and his eyes gleam with a sinister fire. He holds out his finger and bids the guards take Him. And such is his power, so completely are the people cowed into submission and trembling obedience to him, that the crowd immediately makes way for the guards, and in the midst of deathlike silence they lay hands on Him and lead Him away. The crowd instantly bows down to the earth, like one man, before the old Inquisitor. He blesses the people in silence and passes on. The guards lead their prisoner to the close, gloomy vaulted prison in the ancient palace of the Holy Inquisition and shut Him in it. The day passes and is followed by the dark, burning 'breathless' night of Seville. The air is 'fragrant with laurel and lemon.' In the pitch darkness the iron door of the prison is suddenly opened and the Grand Inquisitor himself comes in with a light in his hand. He is alone; the door is closed at once behind him. He stands in the doorway and for a minute or two gazes into His face. At last he goes up slowly, sets the light on the table and speaks.

"'Is it Thou? Thou?' but receiving no answer, he adds at once, 'Don't answer, be silent. What canst Thou say? I know too well what Thou wouldst say. And Thou hast no right to add anything to what Thou hadst said of old. Why, then, art Thou come to hinder us? For Thou hast come to hinder us, and Thou knowest that. But dost Thou know what will be tomorrow? I know not who Thou art and care not to know whether it is Thou or only a semblance of Him, but tomorrow I shall condemn Thee and burn Thee at the stake as the worst of heretics. And the very people who have today kissed Thy feet, tomorrow at the faintest sign from me will rush to heap up the embers of Thy fire. Knowest Thou that? Yes, maybe Thou knowest it,' he added with thoughtful penetration, never for a moment taking his eyes off the Prisoner."

"I don't quite understand, Ivan. What does it mean?" Alyosha, who had been listening in silence, said with a smile. "Is it simply a wild fantasy, or a mistake on the part of the old man—some impossible *quid pro quo*?"

"Take it as the last," said Ivan, laughing, "if you are so corrupted by modern realism and can't stand anything fantastic. If you like it to be a case of mistaken identity, let it be so. It is true," he went on, laughing, "the old man was ninety, and he might well be crazy over his set idea. He might have been struck by the appearance of the prisoner. It might, in fact, be simply his ravings, the delusion of an old man of ninety, over-excited by the *auto da fé* of a hundred heretics the day before. But does it matter to us after all whether it was a mistake of identity or a wild fantasy? All that matters is that the old man should speak out, that he should speak openly of what he has thought in silence for ninety years."

"And the Prisoner too is silent? Does He look at him and not say a word?"

"That's inevitable in any case." Ivan laughed again. "The old man has told Him He hasn't the right to add anything to what He has said of old. One may say it is the most fundamental feature of Roman Catholicism, in my opinion at least. 'All has been given by Thee to the Pope,' they say, 'and all, therefore, is still in the Pope's hands, and there is no need for Thee to come now at all. Thou must not meddle, for the time at least.' That's how they speak and write, too—the Jesuits at any rate. I have read it myself in the works of their theologians. 'Hast Thou the right to reveal to us one of the mysteries of that world from which Thou hast come?' my old man asks Him, and answers the question for Him. 'No, Thou hast not; that Thou mayest not add to what has been said of old, and mayest not take from us the freedom which Thou didst exalt when Thou wast on earth. Whatsoever Thou revealest anew will encroach on our freedom of faith; for it will be manifest as a miracle, and the freedom of their faith was dearer to Thee than anything in those days fifteen hundred years ago. Didst Thou not often say then, "I will make you free"? But now Thou hast seen these "free" people,' the old man adds suddenly, with a pensive smile. 'Yes, we've paid dearly for it,' he goes on, looking sternly at Him, 'but at last we have completed that work in Thy name. For fifteen centuries we have been wrestling with Thy freedom, but now it is ended and over for good. Dost Thou not believe that it's over for good? Thou lookest meekly at me and deignest not even to be wroth with me. But let me tell Thee that now, today, people are more persuaded than ever that they have perfect freedom, yet they have brought their freedom to us and laid it humbly at our feet. But that has been our doing. Was this what Thou didst? Was this Thy freedom?'"

"I don't understand again," Alyosha broke in. "Is he ironical, is he jesting?"

"Not a bit of it! He claims it as a merit for himself and his church that at last they have vanquished freedom and have done so to make people happy. 'For now' (he is speaking of the Inquisition of course) 'for the first time it has become possible to think of the happiness of humanity. We were created rebels; and how can rebels be happy? 'Thou wast warned,' he says to Him. 'Thou hast had no lack of admonitions and warnings, but Thou didst not listen to those warnings; Thou didst reject the only way by which people might be made happy. But fortunately, departing, Thou didst hand on the work to us. Thou hast promised, Thou hast established by Thy word, Thou hast given to us the right to bind and to unbind, and now, of course, Thou canst not even think of taking it away. Why, then, hast Thou come to hinder us?'"

"And what's the meaning of 'no lack of admonitions and warnings'?" asked Alyosha.

"Why, that's the chief part of what the old man must say."

"'The wise and dread spirit, the spirit of self-destruction and non-existence,' the old man goes on, 'the great spirit talked with Thee in the wilderness, and we are told in the books that he "tempted" Thee. Is that so? And could anything truer be said than what he revealed to Thee in three questions and what Thou didst reject, and what in the books is called "the temptations"? And yet if there has ever been on earth a real stupendous miracle, it took place on that day, on the day of the three temptations. The statement of those three questions was itself the miracle. If it were possible to imagine, simply for the sake of argument, that those three questions of the dread spirit had perished utterly from the books, and that we had to restore them and to invent them anew, and to do so had gathered together all the wise ones of the earth—rulers, chief priests, intellectuals, philosophers, poets—and had set them the task to invent three questions, such as would not only fit the occasion, but express in three words, three human phrases, the whole future history of the world and of humanity—dost Thou believe that all the wisdom of the earth united could have invented anything in depth and force equal to the three questions which were actually put to Thee then by the wise and mighty spirit in the wilderness? From those questions alone, from the miracle of their statement, we can see that we have here to do not with the fleeting human intelligence, but with the absolute and eternal. For in those three questions the whole subsequent history of humanity is, as it were, brought together into one whole, and foretold, and in them are united all the unsolved historical contradictions of human nature. At the time it could be so clear since the future was unknown; but now that fifteen hundred years have passed, we see that everything in those three questions was so justly divined and foretold, and has been so truly fulfilled, that nothing can be added to them or taken from them.

"'Judge Thyself who was right—Thou or he who questioned Thee then? Remember the first question; its meaning, in other words, was this: "Thou wouldst go into the world, and art going with empty hands, with some promise of freedom which people in their simplicity and their natural unruliness cannot even understand, which they fear and dread—for nothing has ever been more insupportable for an individual and a human society than freedom. But seest Thou these stones in this parched and barren wilderness? Turn them into bread, and people will run after Thee like a flock of sheep, grateful and obedient, though forever trembling, lest Thou withdraw Thy hand and deny them Thy bread." But Thou wouldst not deprive people of freedom and didst reject the offer, thinking, what is that freedom worth, if obedience is bought with bread? Thou didst reply that man lives not by bread alone. But dost Thou know that for the sake of that earthly bread the spirit of the earth will rise up against Thee and will strive with Thee and overcome Thee, and all will follow him, crying, "Who can compare with this beast? He has given us fire from heaven!" Dost Thou know that the ages will pass, and humanity will proclaim by the lips of their sages that there is no crime, and therefore no sin, there is only hunger? "Feed people, and then ask of them virtue!" That's what they'll write on the banner, which they will raise against Thee, and with which they will destroy Thy temple. Where Thy temple stood will rise a new building; the terrible tower of Babel will be built again, and though, like the one of old, it will not be finished, yet Thou mightest have prevented that new tower and have cut short the sufferings of people for a thousand years; for they will come back to us after a thousand years of agony with their tower. They will seek us again, hidden underground in the catacombs, for we shall again be persecuted and tortured. They will find us and cry to us, "Feed us, for those who have promised us fire from heaven haven't given it!" And then we shall finish building their tower, for the one finishes the building who feeds them. And we alone shall feed them in Thy name, declaring falsely that it is in Thy name. Oh, never, never can they feed themselves without us! No science will give them bread so long as they remain free. In the end they will lay their freedom at our feet, and say to us, "Make us your slaves, but feed us." They will understand themselves, at last, that freedom and bread enough for all are inconceivable together, for never, never will they be able to share between them! They will be convinced, too, that they can never be free, for they are weak, vicious, worthless and rebellious. Thou didst promise them the bread of Heaven, but, I repeat again, can it compare with earthly bread in the eyes of the weak, ever sinful and ignoble race of humanity? And if for the sake of the bread of Heaven thousands shall follow Thee, what is to become of the millions and tens of thousands of millions of creatures who will not have the strength to forego the earthly bread for the sake of the heavenly? Or dost Thou care only for the tens of thousands of the great and strong, while the millions, numerous as the sands of the sea, who are weak but love Thee, must exist only for the sake of the great and strong? No, we care for the weak, too. They are sinful and rebellious, but in the end they too will become obedient. They will marvel at us and look on us as gods, because we are ready to endure the freedom which they have found so dreadful and to rule over them—so awful it will seem to them to be free. But we shall tell them that we are Thy servants and rule them in Thy name. We shall deceive them again, for we will not let Thee come to us again. That deception will be our suffering, for we shall be forced to lie.

"This is the significance of the first question in the wilderness, and this is what Thou hast rejected for the sake of that freedom which Thou hast exalted above everything. Yet in this question lies hid the great secret of this world. Choosing "bread," Thou wouldst have satisfied the universal and everlasting craving of humanity—to find someone to worship. So long as people remain free they strive for nothing so incessantly and so painfully as to find someone to worship. But humanity seeks to worship what is established beyond dispute, so that all people would agree at once to worship it. For these pitiful creatures are concerned not only to find what one or the other can worship, but to find something that all would believe in and worship; what is essential is that all may be *together* in it. This craving for *community* of worship is the chief misery of everyone individually and of all humanity from the beginning of time. For the sake of common worship they've slain each other with the sword. They have set up gods and challenged one another: 'Put away your gods and come and worship ours, or we will kill you and your gods!' And so it will be to the end of the world, even when gods disappear from the earth; they will fall down before idols just the same. Thou didst know, Thou couldst not but have known, this fundamental secret of human nature, but Thou didst reject the one infallible banner which was offered Thee, to make all people bow down to Thee alone—the banner of earthly bread; and Thou hast rejected it for the sake of freedom and the bread of Heaven. Behold what Thou didst further. And all again in the name of freedom! I tell Thee that people are tormented by no greater anxiety than to find someone to whom they can hand over that gift of freedom with which the ill-fated creature is born. But only one who can appease their conscience can take over their freedom. In bread there was offered Thee an invincible banner; give bread, and people will worship Thee, for nothing is more certain than bread. But if someone else gains possession of their conscience—oh! then they will cast away Thy bread and follow after him who has ensnared their conscience. In that Thou wast right. For the secret of our being is not only to live but to have something to live for. Without a stable conception of the object of life, we would not consent to go on living, and would rather destroy ourselves than remain on earth, though we had bread in abundance. That is true. But what happened? Instead of taking people's freedom from them, Thou didst make it greater than ever! Didst Thou forget that people prefer peace, and even death, to freedom of choice in the knowledge of good and evil? Nothing is more seductive for people than their freedom of conscience, but nothing is a greater cause of suffering. And behold, instead of giving a firm foundation for setting the conscience of people at rest forever, Thou didst choose all that is exceptional, vague and enigmatic; Thou didst choose what was utterly beyond the strength of people, acting as though Thou didst not love them at all—Thou who didst come to give Thy life for them! Instead of taking possession of people's freedom, Thou didst increase it, and burdened the spiritual kingdom of humanity with its sufferings forever. Thou didst desire our free love, that we should follow Thee freely, enticed and taken captive by Thee. In place of the rigid ancient law, people must hereafter with free heart decide for themselves what is good and what is evil, having only Thy image before them as their guide. But didst Thou not know that they would at last reject even Thy image and Thy truth, if they are weighed down with the fearful burden of free choice? They will cry aloud at last that the truth is not in Thee, for they could not have been left in greater confusion and suffering than Thou hast caused, laying upon them so many cares and unanswerable problems.

"So that, in truth, Thou didst Thyself lay the foundation for the destruction of Thy kingdom, and no one is more to blame for it. Yet what was offered Thee? There are three powers, three powers alone, able to conquer and to hold captive forever the conscience of these impotent rebels for their happiness—those forces are miracle, mystery and authority. Thou hast rejected all three and hast set the example for doing so. When the wise and dread spirit set Thee on the pinnacle of the temple and said to Thee, 'If thou wouldst know whether Thou art the Son of God then cast thyself down, for it is written: The angels shall hold him up lest he fall and bruise himself, and Thou shalt know then whether Thou art the Son of God and shalt prove then how great is Thy faith in Thy Father.' But Thou didst refuse and wouldst not cast Thyself down. Oh! of course, Thou didst proudly and well, like God; but the weak, unruly race of people, are they gods? Oh, Thou didst know then that in taking one step, in making one movement to cast Thyself down, Thou wouldst be tempting God and have lost all Thy faith in Him, and wouldst have been dashed to pieces against that earth which Thou didst come to save. And the wise spirit that tempted Thee would have rejoiced. But I ask again, are there many like Thee? And couldst Thou believe for one moment that people, too, could face such a temptation? Is the nature of people such that they can reject miracle, and at the great moments of their life, the moments of their deepest, most agonising spiritual difficulties, cling only to the free verdict of the heart? Oh, Thou didst know that Thy deed would be recorded in books, would be handed down to remote times and the utmost ends of the earth, and Thou didst hope that people, following Thee, would cling to God and not ask for a miracle. But Thou didst not know that when people reject miracle, they reject God too; for people seek not so much God as the miraculous. And as people cannot bear to be without the miraculous, they will create new miracles of their own for themselves, and will worship deeds of sorcery and witchcraft, though they might be a hundred times over rebels, heretics, and infidels. Thou didst not come down from the Cross when they shouted to Thee, mocking and reviling Thee, 'Come down from the cross and we will believe that Thou art He.' Thou didst not descend, for again Thou wouldst not enslave people by a miracle, and didst crave faith given freely, not based on a miracle. Thou didst crave for free love and not the base raptures of the slave before the might that has overawed him forever. But Thou didst think too highly of people, for they are slaves, of course, though rebellious by nature. Look round and judge; fifteen centuries have passed, look upon them. Whom hast Thou raised up to Thyself? I swear, people are weaker and baser by nature than Thou hast believed them to be. Can they, can they do what Thou didst? By showing them so much respect, Thou didst, as it were, cease to feel for them, for Thou didst ask far too much from them—Thou who hast loved them more than Thyself! Respecting them less, Thou wouldst have asked less of them. That would have been more like love, for their burden would have been lighter. They are weak and vile. What though they are everywhere now rebelling against our power, and proud of their rebellion? It is the pride of a child and a schoolboy. They are little children rioting and barring out the teacher at school. But their childish delight will end; it will cost them dear. They will cast down temples and drench the earth with blood. But they will see at last, the foolish children, that, though they are rebels, they are impotent rebels, unable to keep up their own rebellion. Bathed in their foolish tears, they will recognize at last that He who created them rebels must have meant to mock at them. They will say this in despair, and their utterance will be a blasphemy which will make them more unhappy still, for human nature cannot bear blasphemy, and in the end always avenges it on itself. And so unrest, confusion and unhappiness—that is the present lot of humanity after Thou didst bear so much for their freedom! The great prophet tells in vision and in image that he saw all those who took part in the first resurrection and that there were of each tribe twelve thousand. But if there were so many of them, they must have been not people but gods. They had borne Thy cross, they had endured scores of years in the barren, hungry wilderness, living upon locusts and roots—and Thou mayest indeed point with pride at those children of freedom, of free love, of free and splendid sacrifice for Thy name. But remember that they were only some thousands; and what of the rest? And how are the other weak ones to blame, because they could not endure what the strong have endured? How is the weak soul to blame that it is unable to receive such terrible gifts? Canst Thou have simply come to the elect and for the elect? But if so, it is a mystery, and we cannot understand it. And if it is a mystery, we too have a right to preach a mystery, and to teach them that it's not the free judgment of their hearts, not love that matters, but a mystery which they must follow blindly, even against their conscience. So we have done. We have corrected Thy work and have founded it upon *miracle, mystery* and *authority.* And people rejoiced that they were again led like sheep, and that the terrible gift that had brought them such suffering was, at last, lifted from their hearts. Were we right teaching them this? Speak! Did we not love humanity, so meekly acknowledging their feebleness, lovingly lightening their burden, and permitting their weak nature even sin with our sanction? Why hast Thou come now to hinder us? And why dost Thou look silently and searchingly at me with Thy mild eyes? Be angry. I do not want Thy love, for I love Thee not. And what use is it for me to hide anything from Thee? Don't I know to Whom I am speaking? All that I can say is known to Thee already. And is it for me to conceal from Thee our mystery? Perhaps it is Thy will to hear it from my lips. Listen, then. We are not working with Thee, but with *him*—that is our mystery. It's long—eight centuries—since we have been on *his* side and not on Thine. Just eight centuries ago, we took from him what Thou didst reject with scorn, that last gift he offered Thee, showing Thee all the kingdoms of the earth. We took from him Rome and the sword of Caesar, and proclaimed ourselves sole rulers of the earth, though hitherto we have not been able to complete our work. But whose fault is that? Oh, the work is only beginning, but it has begun. It has long to await completion and the earth has yet much to suffer, but we shall triumph and shall be Caesars, and then we shall plan the universal happiness of humanity. But Thou mightest have taken even then the sword of Caesar. Why didst Thou reject that last gift? Hadst Thou accepted that last counsel of the mighty spirit, Thou wouldst have accomplished all that people seek on earth—that is, someone to worship, someone to keep their conscience, and some means of uniting all in one unanimous and harmonious antheap, for the craving for universal unity is the third and last anguish of people. Humanity as a whole has always striven to organise a universal state. There have been many great nations with great histories, but the more highly they were developed the more unhappy they were, for they felt more acutely than other people the craving for worldwide union. The great conquerors, Timours and Genghis-Khans, whirled like hurricanes over the face of the earth striving to subdue its people, and they too were but the unconscious expression of the same craving for universal unity. Hadst Thou taken the world and Caesar's purple, Thou wouldst have founded the universal state and have given universal peace. For who can rule people if not he who holds their conscience and their bread in his hands? We have taken the sword of Caesar, and in taking it, of course, have rejected Thee and followed *him.* Oh, ages are yet to come of the confusion of free thought, of their science and cannibalism. For having begun to build their tower of Babel without us, they will end, of course, with cannibalism. But then the beast will crawl to us and lick our feet and spatter them with tears of blood. And we shall sit upon the beast and raise the cup, and on it will be written 'Mystery.' But then, and only then, the reign of peace and happiness will come for humanity. Thou art proud of Thine elect, but Thou hast only the elect, while we give rest to all. And besides, how many of those elect, those mighty ones who could become the elect, have grown weary of waiting for Thee, and have transferred and will transfer the powers of their spirit and the warmth of their heart to the other camp, and end by raising their *free* banner against Thee? Thou didst Thyself lift up that banner. But with us all will be happy and will no more rebel nor destroy one another as under Thy freedom. Oh, we shall persuade them that they will only become free when they renounce their freedom to us and submit to us. And shall we be right or shall we be lying? They will be convinced that we are right, because they will remember the horrors of slavery and confusion to which Thy freedom brought them. Freedom, free thought and science will lead them into such straits and will bring them face to face with such marvels and insoluble mysteries, that some of them, the fierce and rebellious, will destroy themselves; others, rebellious but weak, will destroy one another, while the rest, weak and unhappy, will crawl fawning to our feet and whine to us: 'Yes, you were right, you alone possess His mystery, and we come back to you, save us from ourselves!'

"Receiving bread from us, they will see clearly that we take the bread made by their hands from them, to give it to them, without any miracle. They will see that we do not change the stones to bread, but in truth they will be more thankful for taking it from our hands than for the bread itself! For they will remember only too well that in old days, without our help, even the bread they made turned to stones in their hands, while since they have come back to us, the very stones have turned to bread in their hands. Too, too well will they know the value of complete submission! And until people know that, they will be unhappy. Who is most to blame for their not knowing it? Speak! Who scattered the flock and sent it astray on unknown paths? But the flock will come together again and will submit once more, and then it will be once for all. Then we shall give them the quiet, humble happiness of weak creatures, such as they are by nature. Oh, we shall persuade them at last not to be proud, for Thou didst lift them up and thereby taught them to be proud. We shall show them that they are weak, that they are only pitiful children, but that childlike happiness is the sweetest of all. They will become timid and will look to us and huddle close to us in fear, as chicks to the hen. They will marvel at us and will be awe-stricken before us, and will be proud at our being so powerful and clever that we have been able to subdue such a turbulent flock of thousands of millions. They will tremble impotently before our wrath, their minds will grow fearful, they will be quick to shed tears like women and children, but they will be just as ready at a sign from us to pass to laughter and rejoicing, to happy mirth and childish song. Yes, we shall set them to work, but in their leisure hours we shall make their life like a child's game, with children's songs and innocent dance. Oh, we shall allow them even sin, they are weak and helpless, and they will love us like children because we allow them to sin. We shall tell them that every sin will be expiated, if it is done with our permission, that we allow them to sin because we love them, and the punishment for these sins we take upon ourselves. And we shall take it upon ourselves, and they will adore us as their saviours who have taken on themselves their sins before God. And they will have no secrets from us. We shall allow or forbid them to live with their wives and mistresses, to have or not to have children—according to whether they have been obedient or disobedient—and they will submit to us gladly and cheerfully. The most painful secrets of their conscience, all, all they will bring to us, and we shall have an answer for all. And they will be glad to believe our answer, for it will save them from the great anxiety and terrible agony they endure at present in making a free decision for themselves. And all will be happy, all the millions of creatures except the hundred thousand who rule over them. For only we, we who guard the mystery, shall be unhappy. There will be thousands of millions of happy babes, and a hundred thousand sufferers who have taken upon themselves the curse of the knowledge of good and evil. Peacefully they will die, peacefully they will expire in Thy name, and beyond the grave they will find nothing but death. But we shall keep the secret, and for their happiness we shall allure them with the reward of heaven and eternity. Though if there were anything in the other world, it certainly would not be for such as they. It is prophesied that Thou wilt come again in victory, Thou wilt come with Thy chosen, the proud and strong, but we will say that they have only saved themselves, but we have saved all. We are told that the harlot who sits upon the beast, and holds in her hands the *mystery* shall be put to shame, that the weak shall rise up again, and will rend her royal purple and will strip naked her loathsome body. But then I will stand up and point out to Thee the thousand millions of happy children who have known no sin. And we who have taken their sins upon us for their happiness will stand up before Thee and say: 'Judge us if Thou canst and darest.' Know that I fear Thee not. Know that I too have been in the wilderness, I too have lived on roots and locusts, I too prized the freedom with which Thou hast blessed people, and I too was striving to stand among Thy elect, among the strong and powerful, thirsting 'to make up the number.' But I awakened and would not serve madness. I turned back and joined the ranks of those *who have corrected Thy work.* I left the proud and went back to the humble, for the happiness of the humble. What I say to Thee will come to pass, and our dominion will be built up. I repeat, tomorrow Thou shalt see that obedient flock who at a sign from me will hasten to heap up the hot cinders about the pile on which I shall burn Thee for coming to hinder us. For if anyone has ever deserved our fires, it is Thou. Tomorrow I shall burn Thee. *Dixi.*'"

Ivan stopped. He was carried away as he talked, and spoke with excitement; when he had finished, he suddenly smiled.

Alyosha had listened in silence; towards the end he was greatly moved and seemed several times on the point of interrupting, but restrained himself. Now his words came with a rush.

"But . . . that's absurd!" he cried, flushing. "Your poem is in praise of Jesus, not in blame of Him—as you meant it to be. And who will believe you about freedom? Is that the way to understand it? That's not the idea of it in the Orthodox Church. That's Rome, and not even the whole of Rome, it's false—those are the worst of the Catholics, the Inquisitors, the Jesuits! . . . And there could not be such a fantastic creature as your Inquisitor. What are these sins of humanity they take on themselves? Who are these keepers of the mystery who have taken some curse upon themselves for the happiness of humanity? When have they been seen? We know the Jesuits, they are spoken ill of, but surely they are not what you describe? They are not that at all, not at all. . . . They are simply the Romish army for the earthly sovereignty of the world in the future, with the Pontiff of Rome for Emperor . . . that's their ideal, but there's no sort of mystery or lofty melancholy about it. . . . It's simple lust of power, of filthy earthly gain, of domination—something like a universal serfdom with them as masters—that's all they stand for. They don't even believe in God perhaps. Your suffering Inquisitor is a mere fantasy."

"Stay, stay," laughed Ivan, "how hot you are! A fantasy you say, let it be so! Of course it's a fantasy. But allow me to say: do you really think that the Roman Catholic movement of the last centuries is actually nothing but the lust of power, of filthy earthly gain? Is that Father Paissy's teaching?"

"No, no, on the contrary, Father Paissy did once say something rather the same as you—but of course it's not the same, not a bit the same," Alyosha hastily corrected himself.

"A precious admission in spite of your 'not a bit the same.' I ask you why your Jesuits and Inquisitors have united simply for vile material gain? Why can there not be among them one martyr oppressed by great sorrow and loving humanity? You see, only suppose that there was one such person among all those who desire nothing but filthy material gain—if there's only one like my old Inquisitor, who had himself eaten roots in the desert and made frenzied efforts to subdue his flesh to make himself free and perfect. But yet all his life he loved humanity, and suddenly his eyes were opened, and he saw that it is no great moral blessedness to attain perfection and freedom, if at the same time one gains the conviction that millions of God's creatures have been created as a mockery, that they will never be capable of using their freedom, that these poor rebels can never turn into giants to complete the tower, that it was not for such geese that the great idealist dreamt his dream of harmony. Seeing all that he turned back and joined—the clever people. Surely that could have happened?"

"Joined whom, what clever people?" cried Alyosha, completely carried away. "They have no such great cleverness and no mysteries and secrets. . . . Perhaps nothing but atheism, that's all their secret. Your Inquisitor does not believe in God, that's his secret!"

"What if it is so! At last you have guessed it. It's perfectly true, it's true that that's the whole secret, but isn't that suffering, at least for a person like that, who has wasted their whole life in the desert and yet could not shake off their incurable love of humanity? In his old age he reached the clear conviction that nothing but the advice of the great dread spirit could build up any tolerable sort of life for the feeble, unruly, 'incomplete, empirical creatures created in jest.' And so, convinced of this, he sees that he must follow the counsel of the wise spirit, the dread spirit of death and destruction, and therefore accept lying and deception, and lead people consciously to death and destruction, and yet deceive them all the way so that they may not notice where they are being led, that the poor blind creatures may at least on the way think themselves happy. And note, the deception is in the name of Him in Whose ideal the old man had so fervently believed all his life long. Is that not tragic? And if only one such stood at the head of the whole army 'filled with the lust of power only for the sake of filthy gain'—would not one such be enough to make a tragedy? More than that, one such standing at the head is enough to create the actual leading idea of the Roman Church with all its armies and Jesuits, its highest idea. I tell you frankly that I firmly believe that there has always been such a person among those who stood at the head of the movement. Who knows, there may have been some such even among the Roman popes. Who knows, perhaps the spirit of that accursed old man who loves humanity so obstinately in his own way is to be found even now in a whole multitude of such old men, existing not by chance but by agreement, as a secret league formed long ago for the guarding of the mystery, to guard it from the weak and the unhappy, so as to make them happy. No doubt it is so, and so it must be indeed. I fancy that even among the Masons there's something of the same mystery at bottom, and that that's why the Catholics so detest the Masons as their rivals breaking up the unity of the idea, while it is so essential that there should be one flock and one shepherd. . . . But from the way I defend my idea I might be an author impatient of your criticism. Enough of it."

"You are perhaps a Mason yourself!" broke suddenly from Alyosha. "You don't believe in God," he added, speaking this time very sorrowfully. He fancied besides that his brother was looking at him ironically. "How does your poem end?" he asked, suddenly looking down. "Or was that the end?"

"I meant it to end like this. When the Inquisitor ceased speaking, he waited some time for his prisoner to answer him. His silence weighed down upon him. He saw that the prisoner had listened intently all the time, looking gently in his face and evidently not wishing to reply. The old man longed for Him to say something, however bitter and terrible. But He suddenly approached the old man in silence and softly kissed him on his bloodless aged lips. That was all His answer. The old man shuddered. His lips moved. He went to the door, opened it, and said to Him: 'Go, and come no more . . . Come not at all, never, never!' And he let Him out into the dark alleys of the town. The Prisoner went away."

"And the old man?"

"The kiss glows in his heart, but the old man adheres to his idea."

"And you with him, you too?" cried Alyosha, mournfully.

Ivan laughed.

"Why, it's all nonsense, Alyosha. It's only a senseless poem of a senseless student, who could never write two lines of verse. Why do you take it so seriously? Surely you don't suppose I am going straight off to the Jesuits to join the men who are correcting His work? Good Lord, it's no business of mine. I told you, all I want is to live on to thirty, and then—dash the cup to the ground!"

"But the little sticky leaves, and the precious tombs, and the blue sky, and the woman you love! How will you live, how will you love them?" Alyosha cried sorrowfully 'With such a hell in your heart and your head, how can you? No, that's just what you are going away for, to join them . . . if not, you will kill yourself, you can't endure it!"

"There is a strength to endure everything," Ivan said with a cold smile.

"What strength?"

"The strength of the Karamazovs—the strength of the Karamazov baseness."

"To sink into debauchery, to stifle your soul with corruption, yes?"

"Possibly, even that . . . only perhaps till I am thirty I shall escape it, and then . . ."

"How will you escape it? By what will you escape it? That's impossible with your ideas."

"In the Karamazov way, again."

"'Everything is lawful,' you mean? Everything is lawful, is that it?"

Ivan scowled, and all at once turned strangely pale.

"Ah, you've caught up yesterday's phrase, which so offended Miüsov—and which Dmitri pounced upon so naïvely and paraphrased!" He smiled queerly. "Yes, if you like, 'everything is lawful' since the word has been said, I won't deny it. And Mitya's version isn't bad."

Alyosha looked at him in silence.

"I thought that going away from here I have you at least," Ivan said suddenly, with unexpected feeling; "but now I see that there is no place for me even in your heart, my dear hermit. The formula, 'all is lawful.' I won't renounce. Will you renounce me for that, yes?"

Alyosha got up, went to him and softly kissed him on the lips.

"That's plagiarism," cried Ivan, highly delighted. "You stole that from my poem. Thank you though. Get up, Alyosha, it's time we were going, both of us."

They went out, but stopped when they reached the entrance of the restaurant.

"Listen, Alyosha," Ivan began in a resolute voice, "if I am really able to care for the sticky little leaves I shall only love them, remembering you. It's enough for me that you are somewhere here, and I shan't lose my desire for life yet. Is that enough for you? Take it as a declaration of love if you like. And now you go to the right and I to the left. And it's enough, do you hear, enough. I mean, even if I don't go away tomorrow (I think I certainly shall go) and we meet again, don't say word more on these subjects. I beg that particularly. And about Dmitri too, I ask you specially, never speak to me again," he added, with sudden irritation; "it's all exhausted, it has all been said over and over again, hasn't it? And I'll make you one promise in return for it. When, at thirty, I want to 'dash the cup to the ground,' wherever I may be, I'll come to have one more talk with you, even though it were from America, you may be sure of that. I'll come on purpose. It will be very interesting to have a look at you, to see what you'll be by that time. It's rather a solemn promise, you see. And we really may be parting for seven years or ten. Come, go now to your Pater Seraphicus, he is dying. If he dies without you, you will be angry with me for having kept you. Good-by, kiss me once more; that's right, now go."

Basic Existentialist Concepts

Burden of Freedom In later existentialist theory, the concept of the *burden of freedom* became the claim that individuals are condemned to be free. Whether or not we acknowledge our freedom, we *are* free; we are not free to choose not to be free.

For Dostoyevsky, freedom is not only inescapable but precious. As the underground man argues, many individuals use their freedom for their own disadvantage just to prove to themselves that they are actually free because their own freedom is their most advantageous advantage.

The Grand Inquisitor, however, describes freedom as a burden because it exceeds the capacity of individuals to make good use of it. Even though it is a gift from God, freedom demands too much of us: the ability to decide for ourselves what is good and evil, the readiness to follow God or to abjure, and the power to resist or succumb to the temptations of materialism, religious servility, and political solutions. The Grand Inquisitor insists that freedom has cost too much and has led to a sharp divide between God's elect, who can handle their freedom, and the masses, who cannot, because they use their freedom to sin. Dostoyevsky allows both the positive and negative features of freedom to be seen, challenging religious theories on the compatibility of God's will and free will.

Questions for Discussion

1. Which is more essential for human life: bread or freedom? Is it necessary to ensure the basic survival of people before allowing them political and personal freedom?

2. Does individual freedom inevitably lead to unrest, perplexity, and unhappiness?

3. Why do the miracles, mystery, and authority of religion enslave people and undercut their freedom?

4. The Grand Inquisitor argues that he truly loves all people because his version of religion accommodates all people's weaknesses and satisfies all their deepest needs. Is he a benefactor to humanity?

5. Why does the Grand Inquisitor first say that he will burn the Prisoner at the stake? Why does he eventually release the Prisoner?

Chapter 13

Franz Kafka's "Before the Law"

Introduction: Inscrutability of God's Law

Franz Kafka (1883–1924) wrote novels and short stories about characters who struggle to make sense of their lives but never do. Many of his characters suddenly find themselves in absurd situations: One wakes up in the body of a beetle; another is continually frustrated by a bureaucracy that imposes impossible demands. In their search for solutions to their dilemmas, the characters stumble along without direction and without finding answers.

Although he was not strictly an existentialist, Kafka ventured into existential territory to uncover the uneasiness and defenselessness that trouble many people in the modern world, particularly those who cannot accept traditional religious answers. Neither an atheist nor a pietist, Kafka searched for answers in the twisting, turning paths of the human predicament, where there may be only lukewarm desire to understand oneself and one's God, and where many humans live out their lives as the godforsaken.

"Before the Law" is an allegorical story about religion, which is contained in Kafka's novel *The Trial.* In the novel, Kafka ruminates about the incomprehensibility of the Divine Law that supposedly rules human life. The novel's main character, K., believes he is innocent, but he is arrested and prosecuted as guilty according to this Law. He never knows what his crime is, and he never meets anyone who can explain the Law or why he is guilty.

Kafka entangles his main character and his readers in a futile search for the Divine Law. Presumably, the Law dictates what is good and what is evil. But no clear directions about good and evil are given to humankind, only disputable standards that differ from religion to religion. For Kafka, the divine origin of this Law does not make it any easier to understand; it actually makes the Law more mysterious because neither the Lawmaker nor the Judge appear on Earth to justify their Law. The story "Before the Law" implicates both the creator and the guardians of the Law for their seeming indifference to individuals who desperately seek answers to questions about religion, sin, and guilt.

Kafka's "Before the Law"[1]

. . . "Don't be deluded," said the priest. "How am I being deluded?" asked K. "You are deluding yourself about the Court," said the priest. "In writings which preface the Law that particular delusion is described thus: before the law stands a doorkeeper. To this doorkeeper there comes a man from the country who begs for admittance to the Law. But the doorkeeper says that he cannot admit the man at the moment. The man, on reflection, asks if he will be allowed, then, to enter later. 'It is possible,' answers the doorkeeper, 'but not at this moment.' Since the door leading into the Law stands open as usual and the doorkeeper steps to one side, the man bends down to peer through the entrance. When the doorkeeper sees that, he laughs and says: 'If you are so strongly tempted, try to get in without my permission. But note that I am powerful. And I am only the lowest doorkeeper. From hall to hall, keepers stand at every door, one more powerful than the other. And the sight of the third man is already more than even I can stand.' These are difficulties which the man from the country has not expected to meet. The Law, he thinks, should be accessible to every man and at all times, but when he looks more closely at the doorkeeper in his furred robe, with his huge, pointed nose and long, thin, Tartar beard, he decides that he had better wait until he gets permission to enter. The doorkeeper gives him a stool and lets him sit down at the side of the door. There he sits waiting for days and years. He makes many attempts to be allowed in and wearies the doorkeeper with his importunity. The doorkeeper often engages him in brief conversation, asking him about his home and about other matters, but the questions are put quite impersonally, as great men put questions, and always conclude with the statement that the man cannot be allowed to enter yet. The man, who has equipped himself with many things for his journey, parts with all he has, however valuable, in the hope of bribing the doorkeeper. The doorkeeper accepts it all, saying, however, as he takes each gift: 'I take this only to keep you from feeling that you have left something undone.' During all these long years the man watches the doorkeeper almost incessantly. He forgets about the other doorkeepers, and this one seems to him the only barrier between himself and the Law. In the first years he curses his evil fate aloud; later, as he grows old, he only mutters to himself. He grows childish, and since in his prolonged study of the doorkeeper he has learned to know even the fleas in his fur collar, he begs the very fleas to help him and to persuade the doorkeeper to change his mind. Finally his eyes grow dim and he does not know whether the world is really darkening around him or whether his eyes are only deceiving him. But in the darkness he can now perceive a radiance that streams inextinguishably from the door of the Law. Now his life is drawing to a close. Before he dies, all that he has experienced during the whole time of his sojourn condenses in his mind into one question, which he has never yet put to the doorkeeper. He beckons the doorkeeper, since he can no longer raise his stiffening body. The doorkeeper has to bend far down to hear him, for the difference in size between them has increased very much to the man's disadvantage. 'What do you want to know now?' asks the doorkeeper, 'you are insatiable.' 'Everyone strives to attain the Law,' answers the man, 'how does it come about, then, that in all these years no one has come seeking admittance but me?' The doorkeeper perceives that the man is nearing his end and his hearing is failing, so he bellows in his ear: 'No one but you could gain admittance through this door, since this door was intended for you. I am now going to shut it.'"

"So the doorkeeper deceived the man," said

1 From *The Trial*, by Franz Kafka. Translated by Willa and Edwin Muir. Copyright 1937, © 1956 and renewed 1965, 1984 by Alfred A. Knopf, Inc. Reprinted by permission of Alfred A. Knopf, a Division of Random House, Inc.

K. immediately, strongly attracted by the story. "Don't be too hasty," said the priest, "don't take over someone else's opinion without testing it. I have told you the story in the very words of the scriptures. There's no mention of deception in it." "But it's clear enough," said K., "and your first interpretation of it was quite right. The doorkeeper gave the message of salvation to the man only when it could no longer help him." "He was not asked the question any earlier," said the priest, "and you must consider, too, that he was only a doorkeeper, and as such fulfilled his duty." "What makes you think he fulfilled his duty?" asked K. "He didn't fulfill it. His duty might have been to keep all strangers away, but this man, for whom the door was intended, should have been let in." "You have not enough respect for the written word and you are altering the story," said the priest. "The story contains two important statements made by the doorkeeper about admission to the Law, one at the beginning, and the other at the end. The first statement is: that he cannot admit the man at the moment, and the other is: that this door was intended only for the man. If there were a contradiction between the two, you would be right and the doorkeeper would have deceived the man. But there is no contradiction. The first statement, on the contrary, even implies the second. One could almost say that in suggesting to the man the possibility of future admittance the doorkeeper is exceeding his duty. At that time his apparent duty is only to refuse admittance and indeed many commentators are surprised that the suggestion should be made at all, since the doorkeeper appears to be a precisian with a stern regard for duty. He does not once leave his post during these many years, and he does not shut the door until the very last minute; he is conscious of the importance of his office, for he says: 'I am powerful'; he is respectful to his superiors, for he says: 'I am only the lowest doorkeeper'; he is not garrulous, for during all these years he puts only what are called 'impersonal questions'; he is not to be bribed, for he says in accepting a gift: 'I take this only to keep you from feeling that you have left something undone'; where his duty is concerned he is to be moved by neither pity nor rage, for we are told that the man 'wearied the doorkeeper with his importunity'; and finally even his external appearance hints at a pedantic character, the large, pointed nose and the long, thin, black Tartar beard. Could one imagine a more faithful doorkeeper? Yet the doorkeeper has other elements in his character which are likely to advantage anyone seeking admittance and which make it comprehensible enough that he should somewhat exceed his duty in suggesting the possibility of future admittance. For it cannot be denied that he is a little simple-minded and consequently a little conceited. Take the statements he makes about his power and the power of the other doorkeepers and their dreadful aspect which even he cannot bear to see—I hold that these statements may be true enough, but that the way in which he brings them out shows that his perceptions are confused by simpleness of mind and conceit. The commentators note in this connection: 'The right perception of any matter and a misunderstanding of the same matter do not wholly exclude each other.' One must at any rate assume that such simpleness and conceit, however sparingly manifest, are likely to weaken his defense of the door; they are breaches in the character of the doorkeeper. To this must be added the fact that the doorkeeper seems to be a friendly creature by nature, he is by no means always on his official dignity. In the very first moments he allows himself the jest of inviting the man to enter in spite of the strictly maintained veto against entry; then he does not, for instance, send the man away, but gives him, as we are told, a stool and lets him sit down beside the door. The patience with which he endures the man's appeals during so many years, the brief conversations, the acceptance of the gifts, the politeness with which he allows the man to curse loudly in his presence the fate for which he himself is responsible—all this lets us deduce certain feelings of pity. Not every doorkeeper would have acted thus. And finally, in answer to a gesture of the man's he bends down to give him the chance of putting a last question. Nothing but mild impatience—the doorkeeper knows that this is the end of it all—is discernible in the words: 'You are insatiable.' Some push this mode of interpretation even further and hold that these words express a kind of friendly admiration, though not without a hint of condescension. At any rate the figure of the doorkeeper can be said to come out very differently from what you fancied." "You have studied the story more exactly and for a longer time than I have," said K. They were both silent for a little while. Then K. said: "So you think the man was not deceived?" "Don't misunderstand me," said the priest, "I am only showing you the various opinions concerning that point. You must not pay too much attention to them. The scriptures are unalterable and the comments often enough merely express the commentators' despair. In this case there even exists an interpretation which claims that the deluded person is really the doorkeeper." "That's a far-fetched interpretation," said K. "On what is it based?" "It is based," answered the priest, "on the simple-mindedness of the doorkeeper. The argument is that he does not know the Law from inside, he knows only the way that leads to it, where he patrols up and down. His ideas of the interior are assumed to be childish, and it is supposed that he himself is afraid of the other guardians whom he holds up as bogies before the man. Indeed, he fears them more than the man does, since the man is determined to enter after hearing about the dreadful guardians of the interior, while the doorkeeper has no desire to enter, at least not so far as we are told. Others again say that he must have been in the interior already, since he is after all engaged in the service of the Law and can only have been appointed from inside. This is countered by arguing that he may have been appointed by a voice calling from the interior, and that anyhow he cannot have been far inside, since the aspect of the third doorkeeper is more than he can endure. Moreover, no indication is given that during all these years he ever made any remarks showing a knowledge of the interior, except for the one remark about the doorkeepers. He may have been forbidden to do so, but there is no mention of that either. On these grounds the conclusion is reached that he knows nothing about the aspect and significance of the interior, so that he is in a state of delusion. But he is deceived also about his relation to the man from the country, for he is inferior to the man and does not know it. He treats the man instead as his own subordinate, as can be recognized from many details that must be still fresh in your mind. But, according to this view of the story, it is just as clearly indicated that he is really subordinated to the man. In the first place, a bondman is always subject to a free man. Now the man from the country is really free, he can go where he likes, it is only the Law that is closed to him, and access to the Law is forbidden him only by one individual, the doorkeeper. When he sits down on the stool by the side of the door and stays there for the rest of his life, he does it of his own free will; in the story there is no mention of any compulsion. But the doorkeeper is bound to his post by his very office, he does not dare go out into the country, nor apparently may he go into the interior of the Law, even should he wish to. Besides, although he is in the service of the Law, his service is confined to this one entrance; that is to say, he serves only this man for whom alone the entrance is intended. On that ground too he is inferior to the man. One must assume that for many years, for as long as it takes a man to grow up to the prime of life, his service was in a sense an empty formality, since he had to wait for a man to come, that is to say someone in the prime of life, and so he had to wait a long time before the purpose of his service could be fulfilled, and, moreover, had to wait on the man's pleasure, for the man came of his own free will. But the termination of his service also depends on the man's term of life, so that to the very end he is subject to the man. And it is emphasized throughout that the doorkeeper apparently realizes nothing of all this. That is not in itself remarkable, since according to this interpretation the doorkeeper is deceived in a much more important issue, affecting his very office. At the end, for example, he says regarding the entrance to the Law: 'I am now going to shut it,' but at the beginning of the story we are told that the door leading into the Law always stands open, and if it always stands open, that is to say at all times, without reference to the life or death of the man, then the doorkeeper cannot close it. There is some difference of opinion about the motive behind the doorkeeper's statement, whether he said he was going to close the door merely for the sake of giving an answer, or to emphasize his devotion to duty, or to bring the man into a state of grief and regret in his last moments. But there is no lack of agreement that the doorkeeper will not be able to shut the door. Many indeed profess to find that he is subordinate to the man even in knowledge, toward the end, at least, for the man sees the radiance that issues from the door of the Law while the doorkeeper in his official position must stand with his back to the door, nor does he say anything to show that he has perceived the change." "That is well argued," said K., after repeating to himself in a low voice several passages from the priest's exposition. "It is well argued, and I am inclined to agree that the doorkeeper is deceived. But that has not made me abandon my former opinion, since both conclusions are to some extent compatible. Whether the doorkeeper is clear-sighted or deceived does not dispose of the matter. I said the man is deceived. If the doorkeeper is clear-sighted, one might have doubts about that, but if the doorkeeper himself is deceived, then his deception must of necessity be communicated to the man. That makes the doorkeeper not, indeed, a deceiver, but a creature so simple-minded that he ought to be dismissed at once from his office. You mustn't forget that the doorkeeper's deceptions do himself no harm but do infinite harm to the man." "There are objections to that," said the priest. "Many aver that the story confers no right on anyone to pass judgment on the doorkeeper. Whatever he may seem to us, he is yet a servant of the Law; that is, he belongs to the Law and as such is beyond human judgment. In that case one must not believe that the doorkeeper is subordinate to the man. Bound as he is by his service, even only at the door of the Law, he is incomparably greater than anyone at large in the world. The man is only seeking the Law, the doorkeeper is already attached to it. It is the Law that has placed him at his post; to doubt his dignity is to doubt the Law itself." "I don't agree with that point of view," said K., shaking his head, "for if one accepts it, one must accept as true everything the doorkeeper says. But you yourself have sufficiently proved how impossible it is to do that." "No," said the priest, "it is not necessary to accept everything as true, one must only accept it as necessary." "A melancholy conclusion," said K. "It turns lying into a universal principle."

K. said that with finality, but it was not his final judgment. He was too tired to survey all the conclusions arising from the story, and the trains of thought into which it was leading him were unfamiliar, dealing with impalpabilities better suited to a theme for discussion among Court officials than for him. The simple story had lost its clear outline, he wanted to put it out of his mind, and the priest, who now showed great delicacy of feeling, suffered him to do so and accepted his comment in silence, although undoubtedly he did not agree with it. . . .

Basic Existentialist Concepts

Insecurity Bridges are apparent between Kafka's work and existentialist philosophy, for what Kafka shares with the existentialists is an interest in those facets of human experience that are not clear and rational and yet are defining for the human condition. Insecurity is one of these facets of human experience.

In *The Trial,* religious seekers are continually thwarted, left to die in a state of insecurity about their relationship to God and God's Law. This insecurity worms its way into their thoughts, despite their efforts to find God. Instead of expelling insecurity, Kafka leaves us with no resolution to the problem of uncertainty about God's Law. Insecurity is a troubling state of mind that calls into question the meaning and value of one's own life. Unlike the acceptance of absurdity that creates Camus' absurd hero or the leap of faith that creates Kierkegaard's knight of faith, the admission of insecurity does not create heroes: The old man from the country does not become a hero at the end of "Before the Law" but passes away quietly.

Questions for Discussion

1. Does the story "Before the Law" apply to all religions or only to Judaism and Christianity?

2. Why is the door meant only for one person? What does this imply about individuals who undertake a religious search?

3. How are interpretations of holy scriptures similar to the priest's interpretation of various elements in the story?

4. Does the story "Before the Law" provide more information or more confusion about religion?

5. Is insecurity a religious state of mind?

Suggestions for Further Reading

Most of the selections in this anthology were excerpted from novels or short stories. It would be best to read these works in their entirety, starting with Camus' *The Stranger* and then following with Sartre's *Nausea*, Beauvoir's *A Very Easy Death*, Dostoyevsky's "Notes from Underground," Kierkegaard's *Fear and Trembling*, Nietzsche's *Thus Spoke Zarathustra*, and Kafka's *The Trial*.

The next step would be reading works by the French existentialists that elaborate on the existentialist concepts defined at the end of the chapters in this anthology. Most highly recommended for this purpose are:

Jean-Paul Sartre, "Existentialism is a Humanism" (Philosophical Library, 1949).
Albert Camus, *The Myth of Sisyphus* (Penguin, 1986).
Simone de Beauvoir, *The Blood of Others* (Penguin, 1984).

Many commentaries on existentialism are available. Among the commentators who focus on the literary works of existentialists, on basic existentialist concepts, or on existentialist ethics are:

Terry Keefe, *French Existentialist Fiction: Changing Moral Perspectives* (Totowa, NJ: Barnes & Noble Books, 1986).
David E. Cooper, *Existentialism: A Reconstruction* (Oxford: Basil Blackwell Ltd., 1990).
Hugh Silverman and Frederick Ellison (editors), *Jean-Paul Sartre: Contemporary Approaches to His Philosophy* (Pittsburgh, PA: Duquesne University Press, 1980).
Frederick Olafson, *Principles and Persons* (Baltimore, MD: Johns Hopkins University Press, 1967).

For those readers who wish to study the technical, philosophical theories of existentialism, the classic texts are:

Martin Heidegger, *Being and Time*.
Jean-Paul Sartre, *Being and Nothingness*.
Simone de Beauvoir, *The Ethics of Ambiguity*.